In Praise of Gardens in the Midst of War
Saigon 1973 – 1975

This memoir is not just about a bloody war. Karen animates the scenes as she describes how people navigated life under the constant threat of violence. It is a rare depiction of a young Western woman's experiences at the apex of the Vietnam War and the resources she finds under the direst circumstances to survive and thrive.

Besides the occasional bombs exploding on the outskirts of Saigon, the war seemed far away for Karen and her husband enjoying their ex-pat lifestyle, traveling to exotic destinations, attending parties, and forming bonds with the locals and other expats.

But in the spring of 1975, everything changed. The communists began their campaign of conquest, bringing the war steadily closer to Saigon and causing confusion among expats. Should they go or stay? Could South Vietnam survive? The couple must make decisions without clear answers from those in authority. Karen describes their desperate attempts to escape the advancing communist forces.

The couple's experiences leave an indelible image in readers' minds of the strength of the human spirit, the resilience of the Vietnamese people enduring the violence of war, and these two young Americans who must come to terms with potentially life-threatening circumstances.

–Anna Drailios, MFA, University of Michigan

Have you ever dreamt of living in a far-off and exotic land? In a place where you can recreate your life as if from scratch, perhaps with household help, new and exciting cuisine, and seemingly endless opportunities for exploration?

What if you did find such a place—as this young American did in mid-1973 when she joined her husband in Saigon, Vietnam—only to find that the shimmering promise of an exciting adventure was limned by a political situation that was much more unstable than it had been portrayed?

Karen Kaiser's memoir takes readers into the often fun if disconcerting, experiences of setting up such a life. Challenges such as finding housing, coming to terms with the expectation to employ house servants, and navigating the harrowing city traffic could feel invigorating and worth surmounting if it weren't for the nagging sense that something was wrong, terribly wrong.

Her travels, which occurred after the official end of the Vietnam War, are dogged by living in a land where war refuses to end. But worse than the threat of an advancing enemy was the ever-sharpening anxiety caused by the U.S. Embassy's refusal to impart information and clear direction. What is one to do when the people who should be protecting you look the other way?

As you read this multifaceted tale, you'll take joy in the author's small victories even as you sense, as she does, that there are hidden vipers of dissolution threatening the garden she is so earnestly trying to cultivate.

–Kat Fitzpatrick, MFA, Author of
For the Love of Vietnam: a war, a family, a CIA official, and the best evacuation story never heard

"[Gardens in the Midst of War] was wonderful. Karen, I can't thank you enough for what you have done. This book has brought my Saigon experience back to full life for me, the good, the bad, the missed opportunities, and what could have been."

–Don Burgess, who shared the Saigon experience and appears in the narrative.

Gardens in the Midst of War

Gardens in the Midst of War

Saigon 1973 – 1975

Karen Kaiser

2023

Published by LightWriter Studios

For more information or to contact the author k1kaiser@hotmail.com

ISBN (paperback): 979-8-9885811-3-0
ISBN (eBook): 979-8-9885811-2-3

Cover art and photograph by Karen Kaiser
Book design by M.V. McLaughlin

Printed in the United States

Contents

"Small pleasures must correct great tragedies,
therefore of gardens in the midst of war I bold tell."

—VITA SACKVILLE-WEST
THE GARDEN

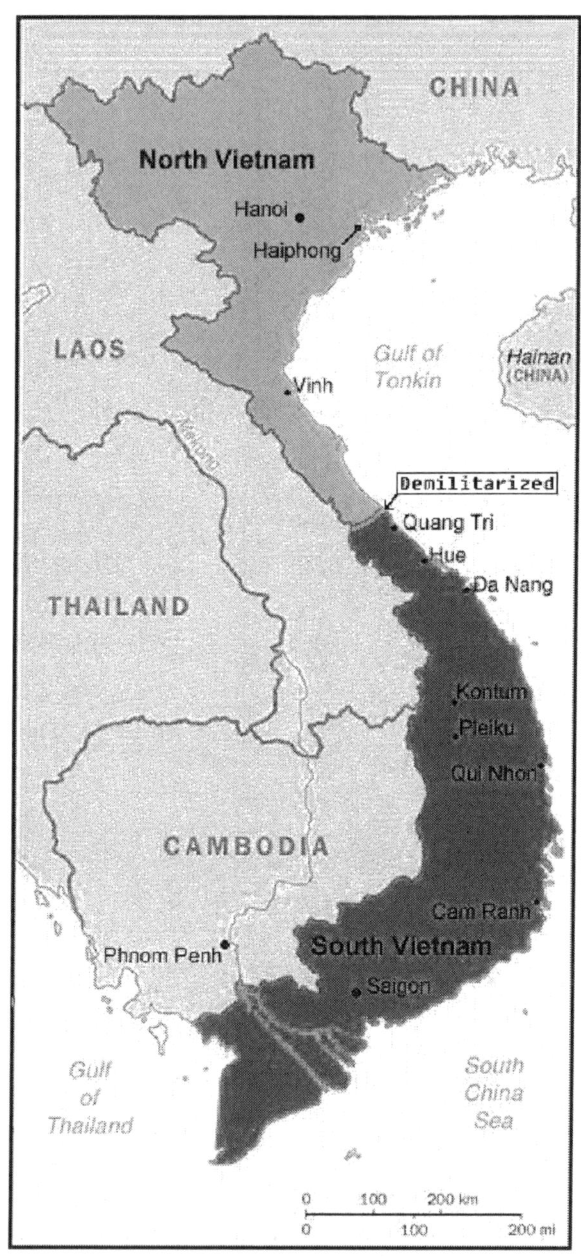

Map of Vietnam, 1975

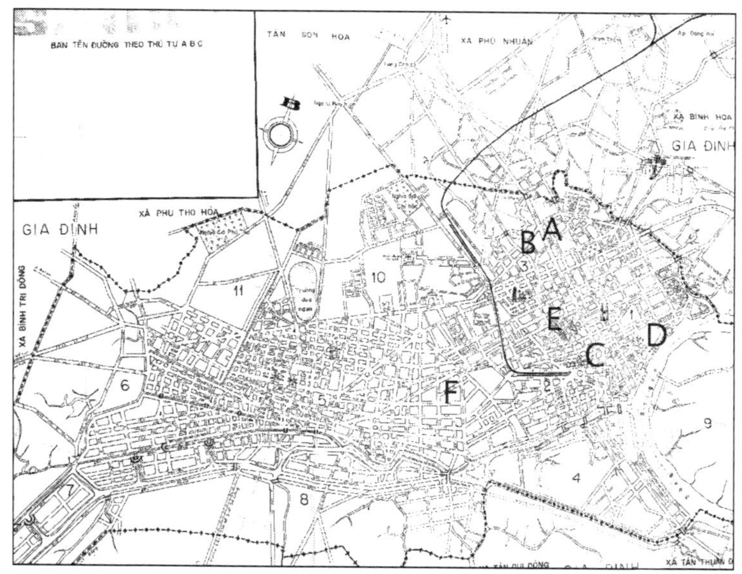

Street Map of Saigon, Vietnam, 1975

Key

- A Villa on Nguyen Dình Chieu Street
- B Apartment on Ky Dong Street
- C Ben Thanh Market
- D Institut Français
- E Cercle Sportif Saigonais
- F Church of Jesus Christ of Latter-Day Saints Chapel

Author's Note

In 1950, American advisors arrived in Vietnam to assist the French in their struggle against Ho Chi Minh's guerillas, the Viet Minh. The United States of America would continue to involve itself in Indochina for the next twenty-five years.

Much of the writing about that involvement has been from the military and/or political point of view. Missing from the body of work is an account of what life was like for the families of ordinary American expats living in the country, especially during the "decent interval" from the signing of the Paris Peace Accords in January 1973 to the fall of Saigon in April 1975.

This diary/memoir is just one account meant to help fill the gap. The events are real. The dialogue is necessarily reimagined except for unforgettable lines such as "I would die for you," words spoken to me by my husband at a crucial moment that time has no power to diminish.

Saigon, faded and shabby on the surface, presented an exotic and fascinating place of discovery and wonder. Living there felt like existing inside a bubble. Distant explosions may have rocked the night, but nothing bad ever happened in Saigon. That is, until it did. Meanwhile, like gardeners tending our crops, we expats cultivated connections that blossomed into a full life while unbeknownst to us, the country disintegrated from the inside out.

Dedicated to Gardeners everywhere.

Prologue

Moments Like These

September 2008

Tan Son Nhut International Airport looks nothing like I remember. I step out of the plane onto the jetway of a modern, streamlined terminal and am caught up in the orderly flow of other arriving passengers, following the well-placed signage to customs and baggage claim. The airport has the efficient look of many I've walked through in recent years, and the industrial smell of cleaning solutions and plastic greets me. Air conditioning cancels the humidity I know awaits with a vengeance outside the building. Customs officials operate with the efficiency and personality of robots.

"What is the purpose of your trip?"

"Pleasure."

The *thunk* of official stamps in my passport and the wave of a hand send me on my way. A conveyor belt delivers my suitcase, and I spot the driver I hired to meet me holding a sign with my name on it. I follow him to a late model, blessedly air-conditioned van. I hold on for dear life as he pulls the vehicle into a terrifying swarm of traffic and careens his way to the Hotel Metropole, the sound of the van's horn leading the way. The traffic hasn't changed in thirty-three years. If anything, it's worse.

The city unfolds before me as the van whizzes along the once-familiar streets. I sense my thirty-year-old self still here, like a specter, present but not quite visible. If I turn a corner, might I meet her going to French class at the *Institut Français*? Or catch her on her way to a tennis lesson at the *Cercle Sportif Saigonais*? No, that heady, uncertain time in the aftermath of the Paris Peace Accords is long gone.

The last American ground troops left Vietnam thirty-five years ago. I was naïve about the war back then and believed the ongoing hostilities between communist North Vietnam and democratic South Vietnam to be minor skirmishes that would soon wind down. Boarding the plane that July day in 1973, I didn't know my destination was a doomed country.

Since Vietnam opened to travelers again, I'd thought about returning but couldn't decide whether to make the long journey. There was more of the world I wanted to see. But Vietnam kept calling me.

After more than three decades, am I not free of her pull? Won't fog-blurry memories subside, eventually, into irrelevance?

Apparently not. Instead, the sound of children's voices, reciting lessons in the Buddhist school across the lane, comes to me at odd times, as clear as the day I first heard them. I miss the pungent flavor of authentic *nước mam* with spring rolls that my cook made. I cannot forget riding, like a human bumper, in a man-powered cyclo snaking along a dusty street, nor the nightly explosions that constantly reminded me I lived in a place surrounded by war.

Now I want to see as much of Vietnam as possible, starting with the places I'd lived that had been my sanctuaries, tiny restaurants where I dined on unexpectedly superb food, teeming markets selling all things imaginable, and grand, old French hotels with tiled verandas and menus offering cool *citron presse* on a hot afternoon.

I want to know how people live now and what life is like under Communism. This sentimental journey has been my destiny. So, I've returned to find out what remains of the place I once knew as Saigon, and the past tumbles over me like waves, polishing my memories until they are as bright as sea glass.

Chapter 1

Not Kansas

July 1973, Part 1

I came to Vietnam to join my husband, Steve, who had arrived in Saigon two months before. He met me in Hong Kong to continue the journey together. We had agreed that he would go ahead to check out the political situation and ascertain housing possibilities. He would tell me when he thought the time was right for me to follow. But I didn't wait for his go-ahead and booked a flight for early July.

As the Air China plane approached Tan Son Nhut Airport, more or less on schedule, I stared at the landscape: a tangle of brown roads, a village, and beyond, a flat green wetland stretching to a river.

The plane landed and rolled to a stop. The flight attendant opened the exit door, and a rush of intense heat assaulted my body. I shielded my eyes against the searing sunlight. It was noon. A strong, pungent odor that I would come to know as *nước mam* (fermented fish sauce) filled the air and stung my nostrils.

The airport, constructed by the French colonial government in the 1930s, began as a small airfield with unpaved runways. During the Vietnam War, it was one of the busiest military airbases in the world. Steve and I descended the stairs positioned by the airport's ground service crew and walked across the scorching tarmac to the terminal, the humidity dragging at our heels.

A cacophony of sharp, atonal voices greeted us as we entered the building, and a gaggle of people clamored for attention from ticket agents. Others talked in groups on the fringes. Drivers of an odd assortment of vehicles sat on their haunches on the concrete floor, chattering to each other as they waited for a fare.

We joined the ragged line of other arriving passengers and waited an hour to reach the customs officer. Trickles of sweat saturated my thin cotton blouse, which clung to my back and arms. *Can we please find some air conditioning?* Once officially stamped and processed to enter the country, we proceeded to what passed for the baggage claim area.

I had no idea how we would find our luggage in the chaos. Somehow, Steve managed to rescue our suitcases from the growing pile. He spotted the driver sent from his office to take us to our lodgings, and we followed him out of the terminal to an older but spotlessly clean sedan.

The driver opened the vehicle's back door, and we climbed aboard. I prayed it was air-conditioned. It wasn't. He maneuvered the car onto a wide, dusty boulevard swarming with motorbikes, buses, trucks, jeeps, and other vehicles.

As the car veered onto the road, the hot breeze wafting through the open windows provided no relief. Crowds of pedestrians in conical hats ambled along the fringes, weaving in and out of traffic to cross the road. Vendors shuffled along, each bent under the weight of a heavy wooden pole balanced across one shoulder. Baskets loaded with their wares swung on ropes from each end. Others trudged by pushing handcarts. A gang of ragged children ran after us, grubby hands extended. Exhaust and dust filled the air, washing everything in sepia. This was Cach Mang, the main road into the city.

The traffic was terrifying, rules of the road be damned. Vehicles in need of bodywork swarmed around the car. Everything overwhelmed my senses: noise, odors, chaos, dirt, heat, humidity, and crowds of people. Thus began my introduction to Saigon, a city that grew from a sparsely populated settlement on a marshy strip of land near the ancient Chinese trading port of Cholon. Ceded to the French in 1862 by the last Nguyen dynasty, it became the central market for all of Indochina. "The Pearl of the Orient."

U.S. military involvement in Vietnam ceased after the signing of the Paris Peace Accords on January 28, 1973. But the United States continued to involve itself in the country's affairs by, among other things, awarding contracts to private firms for work in support of the government of The Republic of [South] Vietnam. One such firm was Roy Jorgensen Associates, Inc. (RJA), Steve's employer. The company had won a contract with the U.S. Agency for International Development (USAID) to manage Vietnam's infrastructure, formerly handled by the U.S. Army Corps of Engineers.

In the year and a half of our marriage, we'd relocated three times with Steve's work—Oklahoma, West Virginia, Nebraska—always within the continental United States. Wherever we went, I focused on making our rented accommodations homey and finding work in local libraries.

Because of our temporary resident status, I took unexciting but necessary jobs that didn't involve much long-term responsibility:

staffing the circulation desk, filing date-due slips, shelving books, and registering people for library cards. Sometimes, depending on the library, I'd be assigned my favorite job, reading to youngsters during story hour. With a degree in Library Science, I might have landed a nice job in a school library somewhere, but I enjoyed our transient lifestyle, full of adventure and discovery.

Steve's phone call telling me the news of our next assignment found me cataloging master's and doctoral theses at Love Library, University of Nebraska, Lincoln. When that became too boring, I checked the main card catalog for errors until my mind went numb.

"How'd you like to go to Vietnam?" he'd asked.

It didn't take me any time at all to decide. To live in a country that had been in the news for more than two decades was a unique opportunity. The very boldness of it gave me a rush of adrenaline. I loved the serendipity of never knowing where Steve's job would take us, but this was beyond exciting.

We were ready for an international assignment and had applied to the Peace Corps a few months earlier. But the Peace Corps hadn't gotten back to us yet, and Steve accepted the Vietnam job. We were young and adaptable, and we had few possessions. Moving had always been easy.

Vietnam, however, was another story. We would be joining the 6,000 American families already living and working in Saigon between 1973 and 1975 and a group of ex-pats from all over the world. The makings of a fascinating life lay before us. Naïve as we were, navigating among them would present something of a challenge.

The announcement that we'd be moving to Vietnam for at least two years received mixed reactions from our families. My parents and Steve's mother questioned the safety of such a move, but neither asked us not to go. To them, it was just another reassignment. My father, a veteran of World War II, didn't have much to say about the Vietnam War. I don't think he considered it a "real" war like the one he was in, which he also didn't talk about.

My brother-in-law, however, took a different tack. "You know there's a war going on over there. You wanna get yourself killed?"

We'd heard about some skirmishes, but they hadn't affected Saigon. "I don't think the government would send civilians there if it weren't safe." I countered. "Besides, the U.S. Ambassador, Graham Martin, says Saigon is safe for families."

What wasn't clear to us then was the extent of the damage inflicted upon the Vietnamese way of life by America's involvement. Vietnam could no longer feed its people and depended on American aid. It was a country not only of refugees but also one that desired peace after decades of war. American GIs were gone, and the citizens of Saigon weren't quite sure what would come next.

No one in the realm of high government in the United States believed South Vietnam could survive without American support. A sea change was coming, and when the tidal wave threatened Saigon, we had little warning. The news, at first incomprehensible, became terrifying.

Hanoi's communist leaders were deeply committed to achieving a unified Vietnam no matter how long it took or how much it cost. They pushed for escalation of military action in South Vietnam even after the cease-fire. But that information was unknown to us civilians. Looking back with 20/20 hindsight, we should have been more afraid than we were.

Steve spent his first week in Saigon at the Majestic Hotel. He described it as something out of a classic film like Casablanca. The hotel, built in 1925 by a wealthy Chinese-Vietnamese businessman named Mr. Hui Bon Hoa, or Uncle Hoa, as he came to be known, sat on the corner of Tu Do Street overlooking the Saigon River.

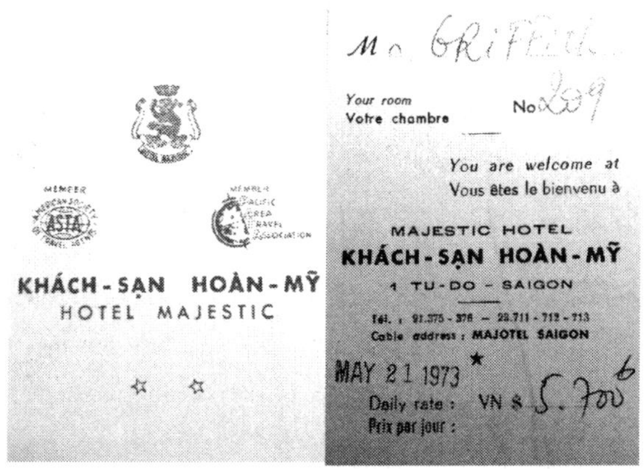

MEMBER ASTA

MEMBER PACIFIC AREA TRAVEL ASSOCIATION

KHÁCH-SẠN HOÀN-MỸ
HOTEL MAJESTIC

Your room
Votre chambre
No 209

You are welcome at
Vous êtes le bienvenu à

MAJESTIC HOTEL
KHÁCH-SẠN HOÀN-MỸ
1 TU-DO - SAIGON

Tél.: 91.375-376 — 22.711-712-713
Cable address: MAJOTEL SAIGON

MAY 21 1973

Daily rate:
Prix par jour:
VN $ 5.700

Majestic Hotel registration card (front and back)

By the time Steve met me in Hong Kong, he was no longer at the Majestic but renting a room in the villa of co-worker Don Smail and his wife, Alice, where we stayed until we found a place of our own. I had no idea what to expect, but the word "villa" conjured romantic visions of a charming stucco dwelling with a couple of balconies, a large veranda shaded by a vine-covered pergola, a barrel tile roof, and maybe a fountain with goldfish in the middle of a courtyard.

When the car pulled into a dusty street and stopped before a sizable metal gate the color of dried algae, my romantic vision dissipated like steam. The gate was set into a tall security wall topped by concertina wire. A blast of the car's horn announced our arrival and a housemaid pulled back the squeaky gate to reveal a plain box of a house made of concrete and cement with neither balcony nor fountain in sight.

A motherly, practical-looking woman, about five feet five, waited for us on the front steps. She wore a brown skirt and orange checked blouse that looked smart with her short, pixie-styled red hair. Her amber-colored eyes smiled a welcome. I noticed three small black dots tattooed above her left eye that looked like those used to guide radiation treatments. *What's her story?*

"Hello, I'm Alice. You must be overwhelmed by all this," she said, gesturing toward the city.

That's an understatement if there ever was one. I tried not to show it, but Alice saw the truth. The city overwhelmed and confused me. My ability to live in the relentless heat and humidity came into question. Beyond that, I didn't know how to cope with everyday life. I didn't know what to think.

Inside the villa, functional furniture occupied a cavernous living room. The tile floor was faded like everything else about the place but had been scrubbed to gleaming. Décor consisted of a few examples of local craftsmanship placed here and there—a pair of colorful ceramic lamps, vases featuring lithe female figures in flowing dresses, and, hanging on one wall, the same style of conical hat I'd seen people wearing.

"How was your trip?" she asked me.

"Great. I did some sightseeing on the way: a weekend in San Francisco, two days in Tokyo, then three days in Hong Kong after Steve met me, and now here. My head's spinning. I hardly know what day it is or what country I'm in."

"Your first time in Asia?"

"Yes, and I feel like I'm still moving."

A slightly balding, middle-aged man, just shy of 6 feet tall, walked into the room.

"Don," said Alice, "Steve and Karen are here."

Dressed in khaki trousers, a short-sleeved plaid shirt, and a gleeful smile, Don seemed like a pleasant everyman having the time of his life. The couple hailed from Montana and had been in Saigon for about five months when I arrived.

"Welcome to the former 'Pearl of the Orient,'" said Don. "What's left of it." Indeed, nothing on the route from the airport looked at all refined. Where were the grand villas I had read about or the fabled tree-lined boulevards? The only things I'd seen were dusty streets, dismal storefronts, and deteriorating buildings with masses of electrical wire hanging from the eaves.

"How did Hong Kong work out?" Don wanted to know.

"Fine," said Steve, "but it was busy, crowded, and hot! Just like here. Good bargains, though. Great shopping. Great food. The Peninsula Hotel has a fantastic brunch."

"Speaking of which, I bet you're hungry," said Alice. "Let's not stand around here. Come into the dining room. We've waited lunch for you, and Wong has made fresh lemonade!"

During the meal, I met the household staff: a cook, Wong, and a maid, who scurried busily from room to room but whose name I could never remember. Wong, a quiet ethnic Chinese man, went diligently about his business like the White Rabbit as if he were going to be late for something and had many things to do first. His English was good, and his repertoire in the kitchen was excellent.

After lunch, Steve and Don headed back to work for the afternoon while Alice showed me to a comfortable bed/bath on the second floor, where Steve had already installed himself. I kicked off my sandals; the floor tiles felt surprisingly cool. It was comforting to see my husband's familiar paraphernalia sitting around.

A window looked out on a narrow walkway, below which sat a small garden. I was happy to see an air conditioner protruding through the wall under the window. It felt so good to stop traveling.

"Tired?" Alice asked.

"I am exhausted. The trip was great, but I've been running on adrenaline since I left the States."

"Why don't you take some time to get settled? The locals take naps this time of day, and so do I. One of the luxuries of this place. It's too hot to do anything else. We'll see you downstairs later."

Alice showed me how to work the air conditioner, started the ceiling fan, and left me to rest. The room at the back of the house, away from the constant street noise, was a godsend. I unpacked and turned on the shower, got out of my sweat-damp clothes, and stepped into the deliciously steamy water, washing away the travel grime. Feeling clean relieved some of the stress, but I couldn't relax. My mind reeled, for, unlike other moves, this one would take some getting used to.

"You're still napping!" Steve said when he came in that evening. "Still wiped out?" I heard the worry in his voice.

"Yeah, a little shaky. I feel like I can't stop moving . . . can't seem to relax."

"I know that feeling," he said. "It'll pass. This place makes your head spin at first."

"How long did it take you to feel normal after you got here?"

"Well, after the initial shock, it was about two weeks before I calmed down and noticed some interesting things. I'll take you on a tour this weekend."

"That would be fun! Right now, I'm overwhelmed . . . and hungry!"

We joined Don and Alice in the dining room, and Wong revealed his culinary skill once more with a Chinese dish consisting of chicken and vegetables cooked in a tasty sauce and served with aromatic rice.

For dessert, he served us cool slices of a fresh pineapple cut in a way that created ruffle-like grooves around the outside of each slice. The pineapple's sharp sweetness flooded my tongue, a revelation. I'd only ever eaten canned pineapple.

"Feeling better?" Alice asked me when we'd finished eating.

"A little better, but is there always so much traffic noise? I can't seem to block it out."

"That's pretty much it," said Don. "The only time traffic slows down is after midnight when curfew starts."

"I wonder about the crowds of people. There seems to be a lot of poverty."

"That's a sad thing," explained Alice, "most of these people are here because they were driven out of their villages during the war when their homes were destroyed along with their agriculture. They could not make a living and came to the city to survive."

"I've heard there's a plan to relocate them back to the country," Steve said.

"Do some of them find jobs as household help?" I asked.

"Most of the maids are Chinese from Cholon. Anyway, the best ones are," said Don.

"Alice, what do you do all day since you don't have to take care of the villa?" I wanted to know.

What will I do with my free time every day? What sort of "little jobs" will be available to me here with a war going on? Saigon's shaping up to be the most challenging of all. I'm going to have to figure something out.

"Don and I like to visit the shops sometimes. There's a lot to do, but I usually stay in the villa and read as much as possible if my vision isn't too blurry. I don't like to go on about it, but I had brain surgery for cancer a few months before we came here."

"She's getting her strength back," said Don.

That explains the tattoos.

"Coming here must have been stressful after going through something like that," I said. "Was it hard to adjust?"

"I didn't want to come at first, but Don was persuasive. He tries to get me out doing things, and I like to go when I feel up to it. That helps."

"How has the war affected you?"

"I try not to think about it, but it's hard with armed soldiers on every street corner."

"There hasn't been any action in Saigon," said Don.

"But I heard gunfire the other night," Steve said, "sounded close."

"Yeah, ARVN target practice," added Don, using the acronym for the Army of the Republic of Vietnam.

Before leaving Lincoln, we had sought information from others who had spent time in Vietnam, particularly in Saigon, about what to expect.

"If you want to understand Vietnam," said our friend Rick, who had been there with the Navy, "you should read Frances Fitzgerald's *Fire in the Lake*. It's well worth it. Beyond that, the climate is oppressive . . . hot and humid, unlike anything you've experienced in the States. You won't be able to function like you did before. You'll need household help."

"Really? I'm not so sure how that would work," I said. "The thought of having strangers in the house whose language I don't speak or understand makes me uncomfortable . . . and vulnerable. Can we trust them?"

"You really can't trust anybody. Desperate people are unpredictable. The way around that is to leave anything valuable at home with your family or in storage."

I planned to function in Saigon as I had in the States, create an attractive, comfortable living environment, and find a job. However, my only experience with international living, a one-year stint in not-so-foreign England five years ago, had not prepared me for the absolute culture shock of Vietnam. I wondered if I was equal to the challenge.

Chapter 2

It's No Use Going Back to Yesterday

July, Part 2

My first week in Saigon passed in a haze. I felt lightheaded and sluggish. Alice insisted I needed to leave the villa for a while and invited me to go with her to a meeting of the American Women's Association of Saigon (AWAS) at the group's headquarters at 2 Lam Son Square. Perhaps the arrival of a Saigon novice like me motivated her to venture out. The fact that such a group existed sounded promising. I wanted to know more.

On the meeting day, Don sent his car and driver to spare us the stress of dealing with a local taxi. We arrived early to take advantage of the coffee hour before the meeting. A surprising number of women dressed in snappy casual attire occupied the large room and chatted animatedly in groups. One of them had been assigned greeter duties.

"Alice!" she said, hurrying over to us. "How nice to see you again."

"Hello, Dorothy. Nice to see you, too. I'd like you to meet a new arrival," Alice said, introducing us.

"Welcome," Dorothy said, offering me her hand. "When did you arrive?"

"Thanks, I've been here a week."

"Well, you won't be bored. We have a lot going on, as you will see." Alice and I took seats as the president called the meeting to order.

"Most everybody here is attached to the embassy or USAID," Alice explained. "You'll meet some contractors, too. One gal is an engineer working for a Jorgensen competitor."

A touch of shyness, left over from childhood, usually hampered me in new situations, but the anonymity of this large group kept it at bay. AWAS was a community of women dedicated to providing a place to socialize and meaningful ways to become involved in the city's life through volunteer opportunities, monthly programs, and other group events. Although I didn't know it at the time, in one way or another, AWAS would influence my life for the next two years.

I looked forward to getting involved with this group and its many activities. The first was a tour of the Vimytex Textile Mill. Alice and I both signed up. Whatever I was expecting to find in Saigon, it wasn't industry.

On the day of the tour, Don's driver dropped us off at AWAS early in the morning. The assembled group climbed aboard a bus hired to take us to the mill.

The tour nudged a memory of my mother. An accomplished seamstress and amateur clothing designer who made professional-quality clothing for my sister and me, Mom taught us to create everything from our prom dresses to tailored suits. Those teaching sessions were the best times because we had her full attention. It was lovely when she took us to fabric stores, but acrid fumes made our eyes water and our noses run.

Mom would have enjoyed seeing the commercial weaving process, but we could share this or any experience only in words. Thus, I began the challenge of describing my Vietnamese life in weekly letters. She would keep every one.

I encountered the same unpleasant, penetrating smell at the mill when I'd gone fabric shopping with Mom. A young woman guided us down narrow aisles to the rhythmic whoosh-clank of enormous Japanese looms. She described how the mill spun U.S.-grown cotton into yarn and then wove it into finished cloth that could be either printed or dyed.

As the tour finished, she escorted us to a showroom and invited us each to choose a six-yard bolt of fabric as a gift. The cotton fabric felt unpleasantly coarse in my hands. Alice told me about a seamstress who could turn the fabric into any garment I wanted. The concept of having custom-made clothes was intriguing. What other surprises were in store?

The day had gone from hot to hotter by the time the bus returned us to AWAS. I was drenched in sweat. My clothes clung to my skin as if I were encased in plastic wrap.

"I'm ready for some AC and a nap," I told Alice. "How about you?"

"Me, too," she replied. "And here's the driver, right on time."

But no cool bedroom awaited me that afternoon. Nothing happened when I pressed the button to turn on the air conditioner. I frantically twisted dials and pushed buttons—still nothing. Frustrated, hot, and tired, and with no other option, I started the ceiling fan over the bed, lay down, and closed my eyes. It felt good to be still, and I soon dozed.

—

"How long do you think it'll take to get the AC fixed?" Steve asked Don at dinner.

"Good question. I'll ask Bei first thing tomorrow. He probably knows someone."

As the Jorgensen project's fixer, Mr. Bei could get anything done, from finding someone to repair a malfunctioning appliance to shepherding exit/entry visas through the bureaucracy. He spoke excellent English and was vital to our lives in Saigon.

Two days later, Wong's knock on the bedroom door woke me from a nap on another hot afternoon. With him were a couple of reedy young men hauling a replacement air conditioner that looked like it had cooled someone else's life at one time. New appliances were hard to come by.

I let them in. Having seen my Dad tackle similar projects gave me an idea of what should happen. I expected them to carefully remove the molding that framed the non-functioning unit. Then, they'd gingerly wiggle it out of its opening so as not to tear up the plastered wall. When the job was done, they'd reinstall the molding as a finishing touch. Curious, I hung around to watch their progress.

The two men took in the situation from all angles while chattering to each other in that harsh, mysterious Vietnamese tongue. A decision was made. One of them went out onto the narrow walkway and sat down opposite the business end of the air conditioner. He leaned back, pulled up one knee, raised one sandal-clad foot, took careful aim, and began kicking the air conditioner with a stunning show of force from such a small person.

"Wait, aren't you going to . . ." I stammered, in a panic, thinking of the molding. Of course, they didn't understand a word I said and paid no attention to me, as if I were merely an accessory in the room—a plant, or a vase, maybe.

Before I could say anything else, Thud! Screech! Crash! With shoves and kicks, that sandal-clad foot forced the old air conditioner, centimeter by centimeter, through the opening while the man inside pulled. With every thump of a foot, the unit advanced slowly into the bedroom, scraping the plastered wall and creating a powdery, white dust that settled on everything.

I watched, speechless, as the molding cracked and splintered and the air conditioner scuffed its way through the opening onto the bedroom floor. The men slid the second-hand replacement into position and plugged it in. There wasn't going to be any neat finishing trim after this installation. But after two days of sticky Saigon heat, I didn't care. I just prayed the thing worked. One of the men pushed the power button. *Voila!* The unit roared to life, sending cool air in my direction. It was not a tidy job, but the means mattered less to me than the ends. It was the beginning of acceptance.

Chapter 3

Getting to Know You

July 1973, Part 3

Not long after my arrival, Lew Chittim, chief of party for RJA's project, and his wife, Vi, hosted a dinner party at their villa for the project staff.

"This should be an interesting evening," Steve said as we dressed for the party. "Everybody's anxious to meet you. But are you ready to meet them?"

"That sounds like a warning. What do you mean?"

I enjoyed meeting new people but was nervous at first. This group would make up the core of our new social circle, and I wanted to start on the right foot.

"Well . . . everyone is quite a bit older than we are. Most of the guys are retired from state highway departments and will want to talk about their careers."

"I'll remember that. What about the women?"

"Um, . . . they're a mixed bag. There's Betty Ainsley, an opinionated woman if there ever was one, and Ingrid McGuire, a fading beauty in her forties trying to look young. She'll probably be jealous of you. You are young."

"Can't wait for that," I said.

"Then there's Lew. He's dedicated to the project, but he and I have very different ideas about how it should go. I've seen ways to make the work run smoother, but he will not take my word for anything. He has thirty years of experience on me and is in charge. I don't want any problems."

"What kind of problems?"

"He believes he can do things the way he did in Montana. 'If it's good enough for Montana, it's good enough for Vietnam,' is his favorite line. But that approach won't necessarily work. He doesn't understand the Vietnamese."

"And you do? You're pretty new here yourself. How are you going to handle him?"

"I'll try to be diplomatic. But I will have to push back if he jeopardizes the project."

"OK, but avoid a confrontation if you can," I said, knowing how excessively my husband cared about his work. "Now, you've filled me in on the villains. Who are the heroes?"

"You already know the Smails, of course, and you'll also like the Kleins and Alonzos. The Alonzos are from Baton Rouge, by the way."

I flashed on a memory. Baton Rouge, "Red Stick," the Louisiana city on the banks of the Mississippi where Steve and I first met one June evening three years before. I was on a date with Steve's neighbor in the apartment complex, Sherill Allen.

We stood outside Sherrill's apartment admiring the Porsche he'd just had painted the color of a bright, blue Florida sky. Across the parking lot, I noticed a tall, slim man walking purposefully toward us. He had a slight limp, but it didn't detract from his rugged good looks. A breeze ruffled his crop of thick auburn hair and tugged at the open jacket of his sports coat. When he stopped to chat, I saw he was about my age, twenty-six.

"Uh . . . Karen, this is Steve," Sherrill said. "Another Aggie."

"Hi, Steve. What's an Aggie?" I asked.

"Texas A&M," Steve said.

"Ahh, yes. I've heard of it. Would you like some Screaming Yellow Zonkers?" I offered him my box of flavored popcorn, the latest fad in junk food.

"Mmm . . . no, thanks."

"Well then, would you like to buy a necktie?" I asked.

I had a side gig in addition to my job at the Baton Rouge Parish Public Library. I made men's neckties using the craziest prints I could find. I lined each tie with an utterly off-the-wall fabric that clashed, an iridescent green snakeskin print lined with hot pink and yellow stripes, for instance. It cost about fifty cents to make one tie that I sold for four dollars. It was 1970. I thought it was a cool thing to do.

"I'd be interested in your neckties," said Steve. "We can talk about that sometime."

"Now, just wait a minute," Sherrill said. "You're not moving in on my date!"

"You don't own her," Steve shot back. The two of them glared at each other for a beat. I stood there, wondering how far they were going to take this. Finally, Steve smiled, and I stopped holding my breath.

"It was nice to meet you," he said to me and sauntered away.

Steve disappeared into one of the units, and Sherrill led me to the complex's snack bar for happy hour. The next thing I knew,

Steve was sitting beside me at the bar, and Sherrill was off talking to someone else.

"I'd like to see your neckties sometime," Steve said, his electric blue eyes shooting sparks. I gave him my number. If someone had told me where we'd be three years later, I'd have thought them delusional.

Steve's prodding to hurry up and finish dressing snapped me back to the present. Saigon, half a world away, resembled Baton Rouge in climate only. How far we'd come.

Don and Alice met us in the courtyard when we came down to go to dinner. Don's driver delivered us to the Chittim's pretty white villa surrounded by flowering vines and tropical plants. It seemed small compared to the Smails' but looked more like my idea of what a villa should be.

A maid answered our knock and led us into the cozy living room, where Lew and Vi greeted us. Like Don, Lew had retired from the Montana Highway Department. A hulk of a man, well over six feet tall, he towered head and shoulders above his petite wife.

"You must be Karen! So happy you are here, at last. I know Steve is, too," Vi said with a wink.

"Come with me. I'll introduce you to everyone." We moved through the room, shaking hands. I felt lost in the forest of people.

Bill Ainsley carried his middle-aged physique comfortably. Betty, his wife, sported a cone of perfectly sculpted white hair atop her stocky frame. Their hobbies were acquiring Vietnamese and Chinese antiques and spoiling their household help. I got the impression that Betty would be full of advice on just about everything, just as Steve had predicted.

Dick and Sally Klein, a clean-cut, bespectacled couple from the Midwest, looked to be in their mid-thirties. They had two children,

Dean, 9, and Sondra, 11. Dean was the gregarious one, and Sondra was more of an introvert, like me. I wondered what educational options existed for them in Saigon. The Kleins also had a dog that they kept secured within their compound. Dogs could be a meal for a hungry, displaced villager.

White-haired and plump, Lawes Alonzo had retired from the Louisiana Highway Department. He loved to use his Cajun French with locals and always carried a French dictionary. His wife, Verna, and her mother, Maudie, accompanied him. They were a sweet trio of roly-poly people who embodied Southern charm.

Arriving fashionably late were the McGuires, who did so with a flourish. Ingrid, as advertised, was a forty-something, high-maintenance blonde who spoke German-accented English and carried off a flamboyant style. As a result, she managed to project an air of glamour. She talked and acted like a woman who knew exactly what she wanted and would trample anyone who got in her way. I made a mental note to steer clear, but at the same time, I admired her style. Jim, a trim, good-looking, fifty-ish gentleman in aviator glasses and a safari suit, smiled as he followed in his wife's wake like he'd just won a prize at the fair.

The Chittim's small villa became stuffy, the air conditioner no match for the humidity. I wondered aloud to Vi if I was the only one who felt uncomfortably sticky.

"Don't worry," said Vi. "You'll eventually appreciate the difference between dirty-sticky after a busy day and clean-sticky after a shower. You get used to it."

During the cocktail hour, guests mingled, drifting from room to room and chatting cheerfully. One by one, the ladies found me and, with what seemed to be an excessive concern for my well-being, took turns making me wiser about life in this city. Steve hovered nearby as if he thought I might need protection.

"You must be careful if you walk around the city alone. And never wear jewelry. Young cowboys on motorbikes will whiz by and grab it right off you," warned Betty.

"I never walk anywhere alone," said Vi. "It's just too dangerous. I heard about a woman whose purse was snatched off her arm. Her arm almost went with it!"

"And if you decide to walk somewhere, look out for the dog poop all over the sidewalk," said Sally.

"You need to visit one of *zuh* beauty salons," observed Ingrid, giving me a critical look. "*Zuh* girls *vill* do *vonders*." Steve was right. She was a piece of work.

The cocktail hour stretched on and on until everyone was so hungry they could have eaten their cocktail glasses with the napkins for a chaser. Our hosts finally ushered us into the dining room three hours after our arrival.

Just as the cook brought out the first course, the room went dark, and the struggling air conditioner groaned to a stop. No electricity! I sensed an emergency that would delay the remedy for my growling stomach. How wrong I was! No one batted an eyelash.

"Not again!" Vi sighed. "This happens every other day lately. Not to worry, though. We're prepared."

She placed candles on the table and touched a match to their wicks. Flickering candlelight danced around us. The cook resumed serving the delicious meal. We relaxed into the sultry night, focusing on the food and ignoring the climate.

As the clatter of cutlery slowed, dinner conversation turned serious as it veered toward talk of the war, the effects of the war, and predictions of the future.

"The Viet Cong were blowing off steam again last night," Bill said, referring to members of the National Liberation Front of South Vietnam. "The same old 'boom-booms' we hear almost every night," he joked.

"More likely, it was the ARVN," said Jim.

"I heard the explosions, too," said Lawes. "Seemed close. Just after ten p.m., I think. Wasn't the Paris Peace Agreement supposed to end all this?"

"The problem with that agreement," said Jim, "is that it allows Hanoi to keep its troops below the DMZ. The South wants them outta here."

"Unless the fighting stops in the provinces, it'll be tricky setting up the new organizational structure for the Vietnamese Highway Administration out there," said Lew. "You don't know if the district engineer you're talking to is friend or foe."

"The ARVN needs to step it up and take back their country," Jim declared.

"The greatest tragedy of this war," said Alice, "is that it destroyed an entire way of life along with the villages. The people crowded into the city with nowhere else to go, no way to support their families."

"And you should see the condition of the children in the orphanages, their poor little bodies covered with sores and scabies," Betty added. "Not to mention the beggars everywhere. You can hardly step outside your villa without being accosted by one of them."

"I know what you mean," Sally said. "Some of them are so pathetic it breaks your heart. The other day one poor little fellow with crippled legs hobbled after Dick and me. He was so dirty, his grubby little hands held out for a few piasters. I wanted to scoop him up, take him home, and give him a bath and some food."

"I've even heard of children being intentionally maimed so they'll look more pitiful," Dick added.

"I never give *zem anyzing*," said Ingrid. "After you've been here for a few months, you *vill* learn to ignore *zem. Zen zey vill* leave you alone."

"Have I told you what happened to me?" Jim asked. "Last week, I was parking the car downtown when this charming street urchin kid materialized and offered to guard the car for 200 *piasters*! Outrageous! But, of course, I accepted. I told him he'd get a nice tip if the air was still in the tires and the windshield wipers were in place when I returned. It worked."

Saigon was a city of many things, including street gangs and beggars that were so common that they were considered part of the fabric of the city. Bored, uncivilized children who joined gangs were the offspring of peasants whose anchor to the land and traditional way of life had been destroyed by Agent Orange and napalm. They roamed the streets, taunting foreigners and pestering shopkeepers with crafty ploys.

While one cute little boy beguiled you with his broken English patter, his buddy helped himself to the contents of your pocket or purse and disappeared into the back alleys and slums as quickly as he had come. Begging provided a means of survival.

Some, however, occupied a regular place in our life, like the cute little girl who hung around outside the gates of the building that housed U.S. Agency for International Development offices and an American-style restaurant where we went for breakfast on Sundays.

Steve always dropped a few *piasters* into the cap she held out to us. I wanted to photograph her, but she always ran away before I could. Then, one day, when we arrived for breakfast, I grabbed a shot from inside the taxi before she could run for cover. In the photograph, she has an expression that makes me think she'd been playing hide and seek with me all along, the little minx!

Girl outside USAID II, Saigon, Vietnam, 1973

Chapter 4

Never Let Them See You Cry

July 1973, Part 4

The weeks living at Don and Alice Smail's villa offered a glimpse of what my life would be like, and reality set in big time. Long days filled only with sleeping late, reading, occasional AWAS outings, and dinner parties didn't seem very fulfilling. I enjoyed those things but wanted more.

How can I create a life in a place so strange that I question my ability to function?

Various options constantly tumbled around in my brain, making sleep impossible and leaving me exhausted in the morning. I needed to think. To think, I needed to write. Grabbing pen and paper, I listed my priorities:

1. *A place to live*
2. *Household help*
3. *Communication*

4. Local culture
5. Job
6. Travel

When Steve announced that Mr. Bei had found a villa for us to rent, I mentally checked off the first item on my list. The news hadn't come a moment too soon.

"It's a large, brand-new villa," Steve said. "Sounds perfect—three stories, modern bathrooms, and *three* air conditioners—but the rent is five hundred US dollars monthly, $360 more than our housing allowance."

"Can we afford that?" I asked. "Didn't we want 'cheap but comfortable'?"

"I know, but it looks like comfort doesn't come cheap. I don't think $200 will get us anything we'd want to live in. Maybe I can make a bargain."

A few days later, we had a deal, almost. The person Steve had to negotiate with turned out to be the wife of an officer in the Army of the Republic of Vietnam (ARVN), who agreed to rent us the villa for $460US per month, but she wanted an up-front cash payment equal to one year's rent in U.S. dollars before she'd sign a lease. Our cash on hand didn't extend that far. Besides, Steve questioned the legitimacy of the deal. We needed opinions from people who'd been in Saigon longer, Don and Alice.

"The owner insists on a full year's rent upfront," Steve said. "Is that normal?"

"It's not uncommon in this part of the world," said Don. "She wants the rent in case the country collapses, we all leave, and the money dries up."

"That sounds ominous. If the country collapses, we're out a hunk of cash."

"Yes, but what other option is there? You need a place."

"So, it's legitimate, you think? Is she not going to take the money and bail? Keep the keys?"

"You said the husband's an Army officer. I think you're safe there."

"Then I guess we've got ourselves a house. It'll take a few days to transfer the funds from the States. Mind if we bunk with you a little longer?"

"You're welcome to stay here as long as you like," Alice said.

While we waited for the rent money to arrive, I turned my attention to the next item on my list of priorities, household help, a concept as foreign to me as Vietnam itself. Everyone I'd met so far had a least one maid, if not two, plus a cook, all at unbelievably low wages. Such a privileged lifestyle didn't mesh with the poverty around us. I needed clarity to understand the situation. For that, I turned to Alice for level-headed advice.

"It's simple," she said. "As ex-pats, we're expected to hire people. We provide them with jobs, and they help us survive. Living here is hard, not to mention exhausting, what with the oppressive climate and all."

"I don't know. It feels like we're taking advantage of them," I said.

"Look at it this way. We ought to give something back to these people to make up for what we've done to them. Providing a livelihood is one way to do it. We can't help them all, but we can help a few."

"Okay . . . I see your point. Now where do I start?"

"Word of mouth is the best way. I'll mention it to Wong. Maybe he knows someone."

—

Word spread that we were looking for help, and, as if he were a conjurer, Wong soon brought us Patty. She was a slight wisp of a woman who arrived at the Smail's villa on a motorbike to meet us. She wore traditional work clothes with a fitted *chinois* top over loose, pajama-style pants and had pulled her long black hair into a low ponytail. An ethnic Chinese like Wong, she appeared to be in her early thirties. Her demure posture suggested shyness.

Steve preceded me into the courtyard to meet her, and Wong introduced them. Patty's frown when she laid eyes on Steve puzzled me. She cupped a small hand over her mouth and whispered something to Wong.

But when Wong introduced me, Patty relaxed, replacing the frown with a shy smile. Later, she told me that working for Steve worried her because of his brooding, ruggedly handsome features.

"I no want work it," she said. "*Monsieur* look mean, but you look nice. I can work it."

Patty spoke functional English and had worked for Americans before. According to Wong, her cooking rivaled his. We hired her on the spot. Now we needed the money for the rent and a move-in date. And just like that, the search ended, taking care of item number two on my list. What fantastic luck! What could possibly go wrong?

I didn't see the villa until the day we moved in. A brand-new, sharp-angled structure made of concrete and tile asserted itself beside its humbler neighbors at number 84D Nguyen Dinh Chieu Street.

An eight-foot-high concrete security wall topped with iron spikes framed the property. Two entrances in the street-facing portion of the wall allowed access to pedestrians and vehicles through appropriately sized, pine-colored gates, which were kept padlocked. A button in the concrete pillar beside the pedestrian gate sounded a bell inside the villa to announce someone's arrival. There was a paved driveway next to a small grassy patch with two trees, a *bánh mai* (peach), and a coconut palm.

Although it lacked a fountain and a vine-covered veranda, the villa exceeded my expectations. Anxious to explore every inch of the tall, narrow building, I threw open the French doors and found myself walking right into . . . Christmas.

Red and green dominated the space. Pistachio-colored walls soared to a ceiling twelve feet above, encasing us like a shell. Darker green curtains hung at windows protected by decorative ironwork. New, modern furniture, fitted with slipcovered cushions the color of cherries, occupied the living room. A teak wall unit separated the living room from the dining room, which sported a large table of dark wood and six chairs with cherry-red vinyl seat covers.

The festive color scheme reminded me of my mother's penchant for unusual color combinations. The kitchen in the house my parents built in 1949 on a hill overlooking the Onondaga Reservation south of Syracuse, New York, included brown cabinetry and an elderly refrigerator. My mother painted the refrigerator chartreuse and stenciled dark green leaves cascading over the front. I wished she could see this place.

At the far end of the living room, a tile walkway stretched beside a small, open-air courtyard/garden/atrium to the large kitchen. Upstairs, two bedrooms, an office, and a large sitting room completed the floor plan. The villa boasted five modern, tiled bathrooms and three air conditioners, one in each bedroom and one in the sitting room. A game room occupied the third floor, and a clothesline extended across an open-air patio.

Numbered teak doors, seventeen in all, secured each room. Tiny blue enamel tiles attached below the keyhole displayed numbers engraved in white. Numbered keys hung from corresponding numbered hooks in the living room.

"Look at this," I said to Steve. "All the keys are numbered to match the doors."

From the second-floor office overlooking the street, I had a view of the refuse dump at the corner of Nguyen Dinh Chieu and rue Pasteur. Rubbish and other detritus accumulated throughout the day. Workers came in the morning and shoveled the garbage and trash into dumpsters that they carted away, leaving the area clear. The sharp smell of *nuoc mam* from neighborhood kitchens masked any odors that emanated from the dump. In the afternoon, women and children scavenged through the junk in search of anything that might improve their lot—tin cans and cardboard boxes to sell or, sometimes, even food.

The U.S. Department of Defense operated a commissary and PX for the Military Assistance Command Vietnam (MACV) during the years of military involvement. When that ended, MACV became what we knew as the Defense Attaché Office (DAO). In addition to the PX and commissary, the facility included a swimming pool, bowling alley, tennis courts, a movie theater, a library, and a restaurant, all available to us.

Because Steve worked on a government contract, he enjoyed the privilege of shopping at DAO's PX and commissary. There he bought pots and pans, glassware, dishes, tableware, groceries, and a few cleaning items.

Construction had left the villa's rooms dusty and in need of a good cleaning. Since Patty couldn't join us until her current job ended in two weeks, I decided to tackle the cleaning on my own. *How hard could it be?*

Digging in with a vengeance, I struggled to make our new home habitable. My efforts managed only a superficial job before sticky sweat slid uncomfortably under my clothes, and heat overcame me. I could see some progress but needed to cool down before doing more.

In the hottest part of the day, the refrigerator quit. Whom could I call? No one! Even though the villa had a telephone, I didn't speak a word of Vietnamese. There was no such thing as the Yellow Pages, but it didn't matter. I wouldn't have been able to read it anyway.

I grabbed the mop and worked fast to clean up the water pouring out of the refrigerator, flooding the kitchen floor. *Would the food inside spoil before a repairman could get here? How long would that take? Days? Weeks?*

Tears of frustration overcame me. I threw down the mop, collapsed onto the sofa, and admitted defeat. I would have help in two weeks, but those weeks seemed years away.

When Steve walked through the door that evening, I dissolved into tears once more.

"Karen, what happened? What's wrong?" He hugged me close, let me cry on his shoulder, and listened to my tale of woe.

"Jeez! That refrigerator is a piece of shit," he said.

"We're going to lose all that food," I whined, feeling that I'd somehow caused that disaster.

"Look, I know, it's bad. But we can't do anything about it tonight. I'll talk to Bei in the morning. C'mon, we'll go out for dinner."

"Out for dinner"— the most beautiful words in the English language. Steve was nothing if not pragmatic.

That night, he introduced me to the wonderful Viet My restaurant. A band played "Desperado," a waiter served tasty American-style food, and people spoke English.

For the moment, at least, I felt a connection to home and, for the first time, put a name to the painful longing roiling in my gut—homesickness—a new sensation. It seemed to have come from nowhere but had been building since the first heady days with the Smails when everything was new and mysterious. I'd face it again tomorrow, but right then, I felt saved. Next time, I'd know where to find comfort. The following day, Mr. Bei sent someone to repair the refrigerator.

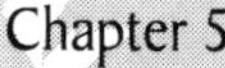

Chapter 5

Outside Your Comfort Zone

July 1973, Part 5

Patty caught me off guard on her first day. "Good morning, *Madame*."

I thought a woman earned that designation of respect after demonstrating that she deserved it. Managing household help was new to me. So far, I hadn't demonstrated anything. Patty and I had yet to find out what kind of employer I would be. Nevertheless, from that day on, I would be known as "*Madame*." In her gentle way, Patty let me know my duty as I aspired to live up to expectations, my own and hers.

Not long after she began work, Patty came to me with a request. Would we hire another person? The housekeeping, marketing, cooking, laundry, and ironing created too much work for her to handle alone. She knew a woman willing to work, and I agreed to meet with her.

The next day, Yao arrived. Also ethnic Chinese, she spoke no English, only Chinese and Vietnamese. Her lack of English didn't bother me, but domestic work posed a new experience for her. She would have to rely on Patty for guidance. Patty assured me Yao was a reliable, trustworthy choice and that helping Yao learn her duties would not be a problem. Because I trusted Patty, I hired Yao. They were a package deal for which we paid $76US a month.

Once a week, I gave Patty market money, which she kept track of in a small notebook. She shopped daily at Saigon's huge Ben Thanh market that supplied us with excellent fruits and vegetables from Da Lat. Located in the Central Highlands, Da Lat's cooler temperatures nurtured the best produce. We also dined on tender Cambodian beef, succulent seafood fresh from the South China Sea, and veal from G. Brandt, the butcher, his source unknown to me.

With seventeen years of experience in the kitchen, Patty never used a recipe and could cook anything I asked for, eagerly trying new dishes. When she allowed me into her kitchen, I taught her to make some favorites, like Russian dressing, using ingredients Steve brought from the commissary. One evening, she delighted us by serving hamburgers on buns she'd made from scratch. But her Chinese and Vietnamese dishes remained her *pièces d'résistance*.

Patty (L) and Yao (R) in the kitchen at
84D Nguyen Dình Chieu, Saigon, 1973

Before she left for the day, Patty turned down our bed, and in the morning, either Patty or Yao waited to open the gate for Mr. Pho, the company driver, who came to take Steve to his office.

Patty and Yao soon whipped the villa into shape, cleaning it daily, top to bottom. While Patty did the marketing first thing every morning, Yao collected the laundry and hand-washed everything. By evening, she had dried, folded, and pressed the lot. If she needed to communicate with me, Yao smiled and pointed to whatever required attention, and I never had to decide what to make for dinner. The two women became indispensable.

Our household goods finally arrived after a month en route. Several enormous cardboard boxes cluttered the living room. Patty and Yao watched the unpacking with delight as if they expected me to reveal an emperor's treasure.

The toaster and the hand mixer fascinated them. But when I unpacked the rolling pin and pastry cloth, Patty's eyes grew wide with wonder.

"*Madame*, what this?" she asked.

"You use this to roll dough for a pie crust or cookies." I spread the pastry cloth out on the kitchen counter. Grasping the rolling pin's handles, I pantomimed flattening the imaginary dough.

"I not see this before."

"Well, now they're yours. Have fun."

I unpacked sheets, towels, clothes, my sewing machine, and my hairdryer. The living room looked like a rummage sale when Steve walked in the door at the end of the day.

"What are those?" He scowled at the set of black towels with gold lions' heads embroidered on them.

"They're towels. We should have something exotic for our exotic new home. Don't you like them?"

"They're awful! I hope you didn't spend a lot of money." His taste leaned toward the sophisticated, while I was more playful.

"They were on sale."

"I can see why."

I didn't want to pick that fight and let the matter drop. When I bought the towels, I knew they would be a surprise, but his reaction seemed out of proportion. *Why does an unimportant set of towels irritate him so much? What button have I pushed?*

We were in the beginning stages of our marriage and just getting to know each other. Our courtship had been long-distance and short. I left Baton Rouge soon after we met and returned to Pennsylvania to attend graduate school while Steve finished the project in Louisiana. We'd see each other on holidays and occasional weekends during that year. The rest of the time, we kept the telephone lines busy.

Steve, the youngest of three, spent his early years in Kingwood, a small West Virginia town near the Pennsylvania border south of Pittsburgh. His father, an executive in the state's Department of Transportation, spent the week in Charleston, the capital, and commuted to Kingwood on weekends.

When Steve was in high school, his father became the executive director of the National Asphalt Pavement Association. He moved the family to Washington, D.C., where Steve lived a somewhat privileged life and developed a sophisticated taste for the finer things. The lion's head towels were not up to his standards. I hid my disappointment but wished he could occasionally allow some fun and playfulness into his life.

I hadn't thought to take Patty and Yao for physical checkups and blood tests, but the idea took hold when Alice Smail suggested it.

Checkups seemed like a good idea. But when I brought this up with her, Patty's cheerful expression changed to one of fear.

"Madame, blood go out make us sick," she said. She knew what I was talking about.

"Patty, nothing bad will happen, I promise. It's important to make sure you and Yao are both healthy. Steve and I have checkups all the time in America. It's how things should be done."

Eventually, Patty agreed and convinced Yao that it would be safe. On the day of their checkups, Patty hailed a taxi, and the three of us headed to the hospital. The Seventh-Day Adventist Church established a presence in Vietnam in 1929 and opened its first hospital in downtown Saigon in 1952. By the mid-1970s, the hospital needed more space and moved to a building near Tan Son Nhut airport, vacated by the U.S. Army's 3rd Field Hospital. Expats used the facility for all their medical needs.

The staff saw patients on a first-come, first-served basis. Patty and Yao sat as still as Madame Tussaud's wax figures, not even chattering with each other like they usually did. *If they change their minds while we wait, will I give in and take them back to the villa?*

Half an hour passed before a nurse beckoned us into the examination room. I watched the nurse check vital signs and prepare the girls for blood tests. They stared straight ahead as if mentally disconnected from their bodies while the nurse drew blood from each of them. *Do they understand why I brought them here? Do they think their jobs depended on it? Do they trust me?*

A few days later, when the test results came back indicating no health issues, I felt relieved. But something bothered me about the episode. *Why have I imposed standard Western medical procedures on them without considering their culture?* It had never occurred to me to ask about that. Did I think Patty and Yao would thank me?

In their culture, people doubted the accuracy of invasive laboratory tests and didn't trust the competence of doctors who couldn't diagnose symptoms quickly and accurately. Slowly, I realized that what's good for America isn't always good for Vietnam, no matter what Lew Chittim said. Neither Patty nor Yao ever mentioned the incident again. I was thankful that I didn't lose them because of it, and I wondered if I'd just made a grave error in the "*Madame*" department.

After I'd emptied all the crates of household goods and stowed everything away, empty days stretched before me. I pulled out my list of priorities. *This seems like a good time to work on number 4, getting acquainted with the "Local Culture."* I decided to explore my new neighborhood on foot before the day turned too hot and steamy.

Vi Chittim and Betty Ainsley warned me about walking anywhere alone, but I knew my way around my part of town and felt safe. I wore no jewelry and left my purse at home, but tucked 500 Vietnamese piasters, worth about $1.00US, safely into a hidden pocket for emergencies.

The instant I stepped through the pedestrian gate, my walk turned into an extreme sport. The chaotic traffic paralyzed me. Exhaust-spewing busses roared past, and motorbikes wove crazily toward me as if the drivers were taking aim. I froze. *Maybe a walk isn't such a great idea, after all. But if I don't learn to deal with this, I'll be stuck in the villa alone all day.*

Taking a deep breath, I turned left and made my way nervously along the edge of Nguyen Dinh Chieu Street to rue Pasteur, where the sidewalk began, and mature shade trees obscured the sun. Known for most of the colonial period as rue Pellerin, Pasteur grew from an ancient inner-city waterway into one of Saigon's most desirable streets. I headed to Nguyen Hue Street in Saigon's downtown, eight blocks away.

Soon, I encountered a two-man crew working on what looked like a sewer drain. They struggled with the various parts, like working a jigsaw puzzle. Spotting me, one of the men chuckled and nudged his partner, pointing in my direction.

"Look at that strange creature," he might be saying.

Not only did I stand head and shoulders above everyone else on the street, but everything about me was different, from clothing to coloring. For the first time, I understood what it felt like to be a minority. When I asked Patty about the incident later, she told me that laughing and pointing were signs of approval. I never got used to it, though.

Doing my best to ignore them, I left the men to their work and continued along Pasteur, admiring the once elegant French buildings in all their faded glory. Here was the "Pearl of the Orient" Don Smail talked about.

At number 161, a small brass plaque identified it as the residence of the President of the Republic of Vietnam, where the current president, Nguyen Van Thieu, lived. A guard held the gate open to allow a car through, and I glimpsed the white, three-story structure with its grand *porte cochère*. This building wasn't faded.

Further on, the aged French buildings gave way to narrow storefronts, their offerings spilling onto the sidewalk. Proprietors sat fanning themselves languidly in the increasing heat, waiting for customers.

I stood in front of a shop, deciding if I wanted to go inside. A wiry man wearing a battered, brown fedora approached me and began to play a plucky tune on an instrument resembling a crude mandolin. It appeared to be made from half of a coconut, a couple of sticks, and some string.

The vendor carried several more of these strange instruments in a sling on his back. Using hand signals, I indicated I wanted to buy one, thinking it would be a nice indigenous decoration for the villa's den. *Will 100 piasters be enough?* I showed him the money.

Out of nowhere, street kids appeared, crowding around us. *Did they want a handout?*

The vendor held up two fingers. *He wants 200 piasters.* I handed him another 100 piaster note and claimed my prize—a breakthrough. I had bargained for and bought something with local currency from a Vietnamese vendor on the streets of Saigon. A surge of power boosted my confidence. The kids didn't leave immediately, but I felt formidable and ignored them. They soon grew bored with me.

It was only 10 a.m., but the city had turned into a sauna, and I'd turned into a hot, sweaty, listless human being who no longer felt like shopping or walking back to the villa. That meant only one thing—a taxi ride. Although I'd never dealt with a Saigon taxi, I'd ridden in them a few times and had a sense of the protocol.

Feeling confident from the experience with the vendor, I hailed one of the blue and yellow taxis. At first, he didn't understand when I told him the street's name. But I pointed in the right direction and kept talking to him in English. He was polite, not impatient, as I'd expected him to be. Instead, he seemed like a kind person who just wanted to help. We arrived at my gate between the two of us pointing and talking in our own languages. I didn't know the fare, but I handed over the 300 piasters I had left. He seemed satisfied with that and drove off.

I pushed the call button on the pedestrian gate. Patty ran to open it.

"Madame, where you go?" She looked worried.

"It's all right, Patty. I just went for a little walk."

"Madame can play it?" Patty said, pointing to my musical acquisition.

"It's just for decoration."

"I no understand Americans," she said, shaking her head. "What *Madame* do tomorrow?"

Indeed, armed with my new-found confidence, what *would* I do tomorrow?

Chapter 6

Adventure Is Dangerous

July 1973, Part 6

Sunday night. Immersed in a book, Steve sprawled on the rattan loveseat in the upstairs den, as close to the air conditioner as he could get. I concentrated on answering letters. After an hour or so, I craved a snack. On any day but Sunday, I'd push the den's call button, and Patty or Yao would appear to find out what I wanted. But they had the day off. If I wanted something to eat, I would have to get it myself.

I made my way downstairs through the dark villa to the kitchen, running a hand along the walls to locate the light switches in the still unfamiliar space. I froze in shock when I opened the kitchen door and turned on the light, for there, having their way on the counter, were two of the biggest cockroaches I'd ever seen.

Some insect spray will make quick work of them. I doused the pair with the poison. For good measure, I sprayed along the bottom of the lower cabinets to discourage roach relatives from lurking there. Suddenly, hundreds of panicked insects streamed out in every direction to escape the toxin. They swarmed over the floor, onto the counter, up the walls, into the pantry, everywhere.

"Stop," I screamed, feeling the adrenalin rush. My heart hammered in my chest. Frantic, I couldn't think what to do. The scene resembled a movie—*Fantasia*—with cockroaches instead of marching brooms and water buckets.

Frantic, I grabbed the palm-frond broom and smashed the insects with it, releasing an awful odor. It was a wasted effort. There were too many. More spray under the cabinets didn't help. The nightmare seemed endless.

Exhausted, I finally surrendered and stopped spraying the invincible critters. After cleaning up the mess, I retreated to the den, red in the face, breathless, and sweating. I'd forgotten all about food.

"What happened to you?" Steve asked, alarmed.

"You don't want to know."

From then on, I left the kitchen in Patty's capable hands. Sometimes it's best not to know everything.

The long narrow room off the kitchen that served as a pantry needed shelves. I visualized neat rows of built-ins along the back wall filled with non-perishables and small appliances. Patty said she didn't need shelves and stacked everything on the floor. However, the cockroach adventure left me uncomfortable, so Steve asked Mr. Bei to send someone who could handle the job.

A few days later, the carpenter arrived with his tools and materials and set to work in the courtyard behind the kitchen. After the hammering and sawing stopped, I heard Patty and the carpenter having an agitated exchange. *Now what?*

I marched into the kitchen to have a look. To my astonishment, an exceedingly long, chunky structure resembling an enormous bookcase stood in the middle of the floor. Somehow, the man had managed to maneuver it into the kitchen, where it took up most of the space. But he'd neglected to consider how to fit it through the pantry door.

I fussed in words neither Patty nor the carpenter understood and tried to come up with a solution. They ignored me.

Stroking his chin, the carpenter studied the situation from all angles while muttering to himself under his breath. Finally, he picked up a hand saw and cut his masterpiece in half. Problem solved. I was, once again, left speechless. The shelves were nothing fancy, but they served the purpose. Patty and Yao never understood why I wanted them in the first place.

Although the embassy discouraged travel outside Saigon's city limits, an official would grant approval from time to time for short journeys to the coast. Steve arranged a trip to the beach at Long Hai, fifty-six miles to the east, with three other couples from his office.

The town, located in territory recently held by the Viet Cong, once housed thousands of Cambodian and Chinese Nung indigenous soldiers undergoing training with U.S. Special Forces personnel. The VC hadn't been active there lately, but traveling through the area after dark required an armed escort.

I stared out the window as we rattled along, imagining how easy it would be for soldiers to hide in the thick jungle. A person could completely disappear in there. The surrounding hills provided a perfect lookout point. No one would expect a thing until it was too late. Had someone told me this beach would become an evacuation site for masses of boat people in less than two years, I wouldn't have believed them.

The RJA project drivers hired for the trip made slow progress along bumpy roads to our destination. Finally, they pulled our small convoy into the welcome shade of the hotel's parking lot, just in time for lunch. The French-style building, constructed in the 1940s, looked exhausted from years of hosting pleasure seekers, but I found it quaint.

Overly concerned about sanitation, Betty Ainsley brought along a large box of cleaning supplies. It almost seemed an insult to the staff. *After all, hotels take care of housekeeping, don't they?*

But, when I saw the condition of our room—no hot water, no towels, plumbing lines in open trenches in the floor, and a shower in need of Betty's box of supplies—I understood. *Why did she want to come here*?

We couldn't return to Saigon that night even if we wanted to. The tired drivers lacked an escort to see us safely through dangerous territory. Besides, Steve and I were used to roughing it. We had camped in all kinds of places. We'd handle this. At least I remembered to bring rubber shower shoes, and the bed felt comfortable.

After lunch, everyone headed into the small town for sightseeing and shopping, to the beach, or back to their rooms for a siesta.

By late afternoon, we all needed a hot shower. The maids brought rough, petrified-looking towels. Donning my rubber shoes, I tried to avert my eyes from the shabby facilities and stepped under the water, which was blessedly warm—any *port in a storm.*

Feeling clean-sticky, as Vi Chittim would say, we met the others for dinner in the open-air dining room that looked quite exotic. Leafy vines climbed the wooden roof supports. *Is this the vine-covered veranda I've been expecting?* Large, dusty fans whirring overhead provided a warm breeze. Dim lighting created a cozy mood and hid the flaws of the building.

The bumpy drive and the day's heat left us all feeling groggy. Small talk filled the time until the server brought our meal. Just when we'd relaxed into this place, Sally Klein screamed and pointed to something behind me. I turned to see a huge rat scurry up a post into the rafters. My appetite disappeared along with the rat.

In the morning, we packed our bags and piled into the cars, anxious to return to Saigon and the sanctuary of the villa. But almost nothing was that straightforward.

Heavy rain had fallen during the night and continued throughout the morning. A muddy sludge ran down the hillside onto the road, creating a slippery mess. On the way out of town, we encountered a rain-soaked road crew trying to install a culvert. They'd progressed as far as digging a deep pit in the middle of the road that looked big enough to hold an armored combat vehicle.

Opposite the pit sat a large logging truck that had slipped on the slick surface and landed in the roadside ditch, its front half stuck in the road. An impossibly narrow space remained as the only way past the gaping pit on one side, and the truck stuck firmly in the ditch on the other.

Of the two available choices—keep going forward or turn back and try again the next day—the intrepid drivers chose to press on. I imagined us splattered at the bottom of the pit and silently asked for divine intervention as the cars fishtailed, centimeter by terrifying centimeter, between the two obstacles. Total silence encompassed us. After the drivers had maneuvered safely out of danger, everyone finally exhaled. The drive back to Saigon took only ninety minutes.

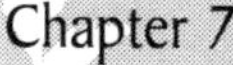

Chapter 7

Knowing You Know Nothing

July 1973, Part 7

As surprised as I was to find a Seventh-Day Adventist hospital in Saigon, finding a branch of The Church of Jesus Christ of Latter-Day Saints surprised me more. The organization occupied a tidy bungalow nestled into a quiet Cholon neighborhood and hosted six missionaries.

The building, almost entirely obscured by shrubbery, featured a screened porch that extended the length of the façade. It reminded me of the screened porch at the lake cottage my family rented every summer. Its screen door opened with a particular squeak, and I could almost smell the familiar scent of marine fuel and water whenever I went to church.

The primarily Vietnamese congregation numbered about 200, including a handful of Americans, and offered an opportunity to connect with the local people, a priority of mine. Familiar hymns sung in Vietnamese introduced us to the language. Although challenging to pronounce, the words formed a unique connection between our two cultures.

LDS Chapel, Saigon, South Vietnam, 1973

Church members organized regular social events like picnics in the countryside featuring tables piled high with food. The Vietnamese women wore their lovely *ao dai*, the traditional Vietnamese dress consisting of a fitted bodice, long sleeves, and flowing panels, front and back, worn over long pants. They looked like butterflies, floating from table to table, filling their plates.

The author, fifth from left; Pauline, third from left, at a church picnic, Thu Duc, Vietnam, 1973

Church Picnic, Thu Duc, Vietnam, 1973

The carefree mood in the beautiful country setting away from the noise and dust of the city lifted everyone's spirits, and for an hour or two in that peaceful environment, the sound of explosions couldn't reach our ears.

Because the church had no paid ministry or pastor to deliver a sermon, members gave talks at the meetings. The branch president, Nguyen Van The, called on me shortly after I arrived.

"Will you give a talk next Sunday?" he asked.

"I don't speak Vietnamese," I said. "Will people understand me?"

"Don't worry about that. We have Minh."

Nguyen Cao Minh spent time in the U.S. for military training and spoke excellent English. He became my interpreter. Although he had a near-perfect command of the language, he hesitated over a few English words, and I wondered if he had much experience translating in real time.

I found it difficult to speak through an interpreter because of the pauses between ideas and sentences. I'd say something and wait for Minh to translate before moving on. Public speaking always made me nervous, even in the most favorable circumstances. I was new to the culture and worried I would inadvertently say the wrong thing.

While Minh translated, I looked at the congregation during the pause, trying to judge their reaction. Blank expressions left me wondering, but everyone showed enthusiasm over the map of the U.S. and where we came from. And then, disaster. I made a grave social/cultural error.

I pointed out that although we looked different on the outside, on the inside, we were more alike than not. However, I offended the Vietnamese members by calling attention to our physical differences. They took my words to mean that Americans were superior, which was not my intention. I didn't learn about this until several weeks later when an American friend clued me in. The Vietnamese showed me only courtesy.

Every church member had a job, and mine was teacher training. My class consisted of seven English-speaking adults, the majority young, with a few older individuals mixed in. Like most teacher-training courses, this one included student teaching. I mistakenly assigned a young woman to student-teach in a class of church members older than she was. I would never have made that move had I been less naïve or known more about the culture. The Vietnamese do not accept a younger person trying to teach them anything. The same experienced American friend pointed out my error. *Will I ever get it right?*

Karen, second from right, back row, with teacher training class, Saigon, Vietnam, 1973

Steve (third from L) and Karen (fifth from L) standing in back, talking to a man in glasses, LDS chapel, Saigon, 1973

Steve (L) and Karen (R) seated in the back row, LDS chapel, Saigon, 1973

I disliked my lack of independence and occasionally ignored warnings about going out alone. Steve escorted me just about everywhere. We'd planned a shopping trip to Cholon on a Saturday, and I looked forward to it. But Steve seemed out-of-sorts when he arrived home that day after a long work week.

"I'm beat," he said. "The office was like a sauna, and it was so disorganized we couldn't get started on the project work. It's getting to me."

He collapsed onto the sofa, letting his briefcase slip to the floor. "I need a little peace," he said.

"I'm sorry," I said. "That sounds frustrating."

In truth, I had very little sense of the problems at Steve's office. It didn't occur to me that he might like an afternoon to himself. I persisted.

"Since you brought the car home, we could make a quick trip to the brass street and come right back. We don't have to hang around over there."

It took him several minutes to answer.

"Uh . . . all right . . . just give me a minute to cool down," he sighed, resigned.

Is he feeling put upon?

"You do know there's no such thing as a 'quick trip' in this city," he added.

He's irritated.

But we climbed into the car and headed to the Cholon market. As predicted, the drive was maddeningly slow. The market was a vast and mysterious place, full of shoppers, vendors, and vehicles of every description. It could be overwhelming if you didn't have a specific goal in mind.

On one street, a woman stacked hand-made baskets crafted from grasses and rice straw into functional shapes. Each basket served a purpose. One held a canteen made from a gourd.

Vendors hawked ceramic ware—bowls for rice and cups for tea—among other things. Clothing and shoes took up shelf after shelf. The pungent scent of fresh fish hung in the air, and huge baskets full of strange colorful fruits—durian, mango, papaya, and dragon fruit - beckoned. Cackling chickens and singing birds drew crowds of shoppers in conical hats.

In the brass street, I found a large tray with a pierced edge and a traditional dragon/phoenix design etched into its center. People said anything made of brass probably began life as a shell casing. They may well have been right. The Vietnamese were not wasteful, repurposing everything. Even Patty sifted through our trash for anything she could sell—cans, bottles, paper, cardboard.

The youths who ran the brass shop played the bargaining game with me. I won, or they let me think I did. Satisfied with the purchase, we headed home. I stared silently out the side window while Steve gripped the steering wheel and concentrated on the street ahead.

The very thing we had both wanted, this overseas assignment, caused an uncomfortable wrinkle in our relationship. My dependence on Steve added new demands to those he faced on the job. The situation entangled both of us in a strange world of miscommunication. I felt it was up to me to smooth out the wrinkle, but how?

Karen and Steve in Cholon, Vietnam, 1973

Street scene, Cholon, 1973

Chapter 8

New Again

August 1973

What is holding me back? Is it the English-speaking bubble I live in? Is it fear? Both contributed to a sense of isolation and dependence, and they caused problems in my marriage. I needed to figure out how to change things.

The time had come to burst the bubble and overcome my fear. To do that, I decided to learn Vietnamese, a complicated and intimidating language that few Westerners spoke well. Still, I believed it to be the key to the changes I sought. I had to try and began looking for a tutor.

It didn't take long to realize I might already know someone. Pauline, a young Vietnamese woman who spoke fluent English, sat in my teacher-training class at church. She enthusiastically agreed when I asked if she'd take me on as a student. I taught her. Now, she would teach me. We had high hopes for each other.

Two afternoons a week at the Nguyen Dinh Chieu villa, Pauline worked with me to learn pronunciation, which determined a word's meaning. Vietnamese has six tones—six different word pronunciations—indicated by diacritical marks. Using the wrong tone completely alters the meaning. To understand and be understood, I had to differentiate among the tones and reproduce them.

She introduced numbers and everyday greetings: *how are you? I'm fine, good morning, good night, my name is, do you speak English?* She grilled me for hours. But I struggled to hear the tones when she spoke and couldn't get them quite right.

Vietnamese use many words to express a simple thought. If that weren't enough to discourage me, I knew learning the vowel marks and the complicated rules about word usage according to gender and age would ultimately do me in. Pauline persisted.

It didn't happen overnight, but after several sessions of patient coaching, I began to see progress. I rejoiced when Pauline declared my tones good enough, though still imperfect. Patty and Yao thought it funny when I practiced with them and fell short.

"Patty, please put the plates on the *table*," I meant to say but used the wrong tone for "table."

"*Madame* want plates on *beach*?" A smile teased the corners of Patty's eyes as she spoke. She knew what I meant but enjoyed her joke.

To pronounce the word table, which is *bàn*, the tone drops from neutral to low. The word for beach is *bãn*. To Western eyes, the two words look almost the same. The difference is the tone, which, for *bãn,* starts low and undulates upward, like a question.

Mr. Pho, Steve's driver, chuckled when I greeted him in halting Vietnamese. His language must have sounded strange coming from a foreigner. But he understood me, at least, and responded.

I accepted that I wouldn't ever be fluent enough to carry on a conversation, so I settled for learning numbers, the correct pronunciation of street names, bargaining terms—*how much, too much*— and a couple of common expressions. I felt ready to face the city on my own in a new, more confident way.

As a bonus, Pauline taught me to bargain with taxi drivers. "A taxi ride, anywhere you want to go, only pay 250 piasters, not more," she explained. "You have to agree on the price before you get in the taxi."

"What about tips?"

"You can if you want. Up to you."

Taxis intimidated me, but they represented independence. Confident that I could now tell a taxi driver an address and a street he would understand, I tried my new-found language skills with a trip downtown to the monthly meeting of the American Women's Association of Saigon on Lam Son Square, not far from the Continental Palace Hotel. I figured a taxi driver would understand if I asked to go there. They all knew it. The famous landmark had occupied the same corner on Tu Do Street long before journalist Thomas Fowler had drinks on the veranda in Graham Greene's novel, "*The Quiet American*."

With a few hundred Vietnamese piasters for the fare tucked into a small elephant hide purse in my pocket, I hailed a taxi with a put-on air of confidence.

"*Bao nhieu*, Continental Palace?" I asked through the open passenger-side window. How much to the Continental Palace?

"*Nam tram*," the driver answered. Five hundred.

"*Toi tra hai tram*," I answered. I pay two hundred.

"*No, Madame, ba tram*," he countered. Three hundred.

"*Hai tram ruoi.*" Two hundred fifty.

With a stiff nod, he signaled okay, and I climbed into the little blue and yellow 4CV Renault. Hundreds just like it made up Saigon's taxi fleet. When the driver pulled up to the hotel, I cheered silently. My plan had worked.

From the hotel, I could see the Opera House on Lam Son Square. No longer offering performances, the building served as a meeting place for South Vietnam's legislature.

Across Tu Do Street from the hotel, the Eden Arcade beckoned. It occupied the ground floor of a six-story apartment building. Young boys sat at the entrance selling newspapers from the stand inside that displayed French, German, and Chinese periodicals. A shop crowded with luxury goods—perfume, gold jewelry, antiques—sat farther back. Decorative items sat in the window of another shop. I asked Pauline how to say "just looking" at our next session . . . *Chi can nhin.*

I left the arcade and turned down Le Loi, joining the other pedestrians on the busy shopping street. A gigantic, crudely made sculpture caught my eye. It depicted two helmeted soldiers caught forever in a desperate lunge toward something unseen. Was one soldier pushing the other forward? Or was the other soldier pulling his comrade forward? I couldn't tell. People called it the "Push Me/ Pull You" statue.

Marine Memorial Statue, Saigon, 1974
(Photo credit: Bill Mullin, Flickr Pro)

Two women sat on the sidewalk selling fruit and vegetables from a pair of pole baskets. I caught the pungent, ripe smell of the produce before I saw them. Their conical hats shielded their faces as they arranged and rearranged their wares. When I got closer, I saw the older woman had no teeth, and her lips were stained red. Someone told me later that people chewed Betel nut to soothe aching teeth and gums, and the juice stained their skin.

Crafty street kids dressed in ragged T-shirts and shorts ran after me, their skinny, bare legs streaked with grime, thin hands offering trinkets for sale, *"mua My ba,"* they shouted . . . American woman buy. Startled, I kept walking, ignoring the boys' chatter.

I had to cross a main street, but heavy traffic roared by in clouds of exhaust, blocking my way. Vehicles wove in and out, moving to the rhythm of a strange dance with mysterious choreography. When I thought I saw a break, I stepped off the curb.

A firm hand gripped my arm and tugged me back just in time for a speeding motorbike to miss me by centimeters. *What in the world?* Yanking my arm free, I whirled around and looked into the weathered face of an ancient Vietnamese woman, one of the fruit vendors.

She shook her head as if she pitied me, the foreigner, *"Tsk, tsk,"* she seemed to say. I felt embarrassed and frustrated. *I should be able to cross a street, for heaven's sake!*

Firmly holding my elbow, the good Samaritan escorted me expertly through the river of traffic flowing around us, never stopping. She urged me forward at a calm, steady pace as if crossing a room in her home. Delivering me safely to the other side, she turned and shuffled off without a backward glance.

I watched her go. She ignored the motorbikes and other vehicles swerving around her as she returned to her place on the sidewalk. *What motive could she possibly have had for helping me? Should I have tipped her?* She hadn't held out her hand as if she expected money. Whatever I hoped to find downtown, it wasn't a lesson in compassion from such an unexpected teacher.

The street-crossing incident demonstrated just how dangerous Saigon could be for pedestrians. The greatest threat, by far, came from motorbikes. They cost much less than cars, which only the wealthy could afford, and many more people owned them. Prestige went with that ownership.

Of the most popular motorbike brands—Mobylette, Vespa, and Honda—everyone preferred the Honda if they could afford one. If they couldn't, they referred to whatever they had as a Honda, anyway. Over time, all makes and models of the ubiquitous vehicles became known as "Hondas." In a city like Saigon, where all vehicles vied for street space, pedestrians had to be alert to the possibility of a motorbike sharing the sidewalk.

Vietnamese of all ages transported not only themselves but everything from livestock to furniture on their "Hondas." The sight of living room furniture traveling through town on the back of a motorbike looked comical. A family of six piled bumper to bumper brought a sense of wonder. *How do they even do that?*

Of all the ways a person could use a motorbike, the slick young hooligans, known as "Honda cowboys," used theirs to create fear. Mostly poor, uncivilized kids, the "cowboys" stole from unsuspecting pedestrians by zipping past on their bikes, slicing the straps of unprotected cameras, purses, or watches, then roaring away into the bowels of the city, completely disappearing. Their numbers remained a mystery. Luckily, I never encountered any of them.

The catalyst for my first Honda-riding experience, a fellow from Maryland named Bob Brink, had introduced himself to me on the flight from San Francisco to Tokyo en route to Saigon. As it happened, he was also among the passengers on the Tokyo city bus tour I took while waiting for my ongoing flight.

"Where are you headed?" he asked.

"Saigon, how about you?" I answered, feeling every bit the exotic traveler.

"Same. I'll be there in a couple of weeks." I gave him Steve's name and office phone number, and Bob said he'd call when he got to town.

True to his word, Bob called, and we invited him for dinner. He asked if he could bring his friend, Yan, a Vietnamese woman he'd met three years earlier when he'd worked in Saigon.

The dinner party was the first of many Steve and I hosted in the villa. Patty and Yao managed everything, allowing us to concentrate on socializing with our guests. I'd never experienced the luxury of having a cook and housekeeper before and wasn't entirely comfortable with our privileged life. Yet, it was expected in this part of the world.

"Have you been to Ben Thanh market?" Yan asked me at dinner in perfect English.

"Not yet, no."

"I am going there tomorrow. I will take you."

Yan arrived the following day on her Honda motorbike, which was to be our ride. "Sit sideways on this seat," she instructed, indicating the passenger seat behind her.

Sitting there, towering over Yan, I felt like a giant. She seemed too tiny to protect us if we had an accident. I recalled riding a motorbike once and how to relax into the bike's motion. But that ride terrified me as Yan zipped in and out of traffic in its dance of death. I held onto the edge of my seat with a white-knuckle grip and only started to breathe again when we reached the market.

Ben Thanh market covered 140,000 square feet, the size of four football fields. Four compass-oriented entrances offered shoppers access to designated areas for specific goods. A clock tower sat above the south entrance, which faced a bustling traffic circle. Everything was for sale there, from needles to live chickens that the vendor would slaughter for you on the spot.

The market's name was derived from the words *Bến* (harbor) and *Thành* (citadel). Initially, it occupied a wet market on the Saigon River where merchant ships docked to pick up and drop off goods. Street vendors congregated there, as well, until the French conquered the Citadel of Saigon and built a formal structure. Inside, the adventure began.

"There are four entrances," Yan pointed out. "Each leads to an area for different things.

The south side is for clothes, shoes, jewelry, and other personal things. The north side is where you can buy fresh fruit, live chickens, and fresh fish. Also, it is a place to have a meal, like an American food court. Dried foods like nuts, coffee, herbs, and spices are on the east side. And over there, on the west side, are things for the house—lamps, art, pottery. What do you want to buy today?"

"This is a lot to take in," I answered. I was not much of a shopper, and the sensory overload confused me. Still, it was fun to be there with Yan. We walked through the market, looking at everything. I turned up my nose at the smell and sight of squid and other strange sea creatures in the fresh fish section and tried to hide it from Yan, but she caught me.

"I don't think you like the fish," Yan said.

"You're right. Let's go to the west side. I want to look at things for the villa."

The home goods area turned out to be my favorite. I soon spotted a woven straw rug I wanted for our upstairs den.

"Should I bargain for this?" I asked Yan, indicating the rug.

"Oh yes, definitely. Just ask him how much he wants for it. Then offer him half."

"Really? That seems unfair."

"It's not. He'll first tell you a price that's too high."

I followed Yan's advice using the Vietnamese I learned, but the vendor shook his head "no," as if I'd insulted him, his family, and all his ancestors. He made a counteroffer.

"Now what?" I whispered to Yan.

"Offer him a little more, but not your top price." Once again, the vendor rejected my offer but came back with a new offer of his own.

"Now," said Yan, "you say "no" and walk away."

"What? I want this rug."

"Trust me. Just do it. He wants to make a sale."

I shook my head "No," turned, and walked away. I had taken only a few steps when I heard the vendor's voice.

"Madame. Okay." He motioned me back, nodding.

The success boosted my confidence to a new level. Not only had I survived a ride on the back of a Honda, but I'd also bargained for something I wanted and gotten it. Afterward, Yan returned me and the rug, unscathed, to the villa. That would not be my last ride on Yan's Honda.

When one of Steve's coworkers told me about the Goethe Institute, I wasted no time visiting the mustard-colored French colonial building. The dark green shutters framing the windows and louvered doors stood open in welcome. Inside, notices tacked to a small bulletin board in the entrance hall advertised concerts, art exhibits, and German language classes.

A young woman sitting behind a government-issue desk made of smoke-gray metal greeted me. Her name tag read 'Tuyet."

"Guten morgen," she said. Good morning. *People speak German here. Who would have guessed?*

"Guten morgen" was all I could manage in response. I had studied German literature in school, but that didn't equip me to hold everyday conversations. I signed up when Tuyet handed me a brochure listing a three-month conversation class for two dollars and eighty-eight cents US.

"Good morning, *Madame,*" Yao greeted me one morning in English.

"Patty, what's going on here?" I asked, happily surprised. "Yao's speaking English."

"I teach Yao one English word every day." *News to me.*

I wanted to meet Yao halfway and asked Patty to teach me one Chinese word every day. My Chinese vocabulary and Yao's English allowed us only brief exchanges—thank you, good morning, good night, pretty, and bye-bye—but they connected us in a new, delightful way.

By then, my brain tossed words together like a language salad. *How many languages can a person handle at once?* I followed every lead and every new opportunity. I began to lose focus. Learning languages became an end rather than the means to an end. *Why am I doing this?* Something had to give.

The Vietnamese American Association (VAA) promoted understanding and cooperation between the two nationalities by mounting art exhibits, producing music recitals, and offering English classes, among other things. Amid an ongoing war, the existence of organizations like this astounded me. Could it have been a front for something? I didn't know and, frankly, didn't care. I had an idea.

Doing a complete about-face, I inquired about the possibility of teaching English there. The pleasant receptionist directed me to the office of Mrs. Bui Thanh, the person in charge of hiring English teachers at the VAA.

"No, there are no openings at the moment," she told me, "but why don't you apply in case something opens up?"

"All right. What's the process?" I asked.

"You fill out this form," she said, handing me an application. "All applicants must observe two classes in session, then teach a trial class."

On a quiet Friday afternoon, I arrived at the VAA, along with several other applicants, to observe my first English class in session. I was the only American. The teaching method involved rote memorization and repetition, which seemed straightforward enough. I observed my second class the following week and prepared to take my turn teaching a trial class. *How hard can it be to teach my own language?* I was about to find out.

Mrs. Bui Thanh assigned me to a large class of young boys the following week. They intimidated me. Stage fright took hold. Being too close to a subject can be a negative thing. I tried to give them too much information all at once and completely lost them.

The boys tried hard to give me a chance, but I had no formal training as a language teacher, and it showed. The students giggled at my efforts. I agreed with Mrs. Bui Thanh that I should follow a different path. Something else awaited me in this city. I knew it. I just needed to keep looking.

"We need to join the *Cercle Sportif*," Steve announced one night at dinner.

"What's the *Cercle Sportif*?"

"A sort of sports club left over from the French. Jim McGuire and I had lunch there today. He gave me a tour. You'd love the enormous swimming pool. Henry Cabot Lodge used to hang out there in the '60s when he was the U.S. ambassador."

"I would love that for the exercise . . . not getting much these days. What else do they have?"

"There's tennis and a restaurant, of course. Jim showed me the billiards room and gymnasium. They have exercise classes. Jim said there are handball courts next to the tennis courts. There's a library and reading room, mostly books and newspapers in French."

"Sounds great. How do we join?"

"Two members have to sponsor us. Jim's a member, and I know another guy at work who'll be the second. Then the director general will interview us if they accept our application."

The *Cercle Sportif Saigonaise* (CSS) occupied a sprawling building on a 12-acre site. A once well-tended park surrounded the structure. Constructed in 1925, it still offered a sanctuary in the middle of the noisy city, although a bit ramshackle and faded around the edges. The membership had comprised the French elite and wealthy Vietnamese in the early days. As that population dwindled, the CSS admitted almost anyone who paid the membership fee, especially Americans.

A large veranda furnished with rattan furniture faced four tennis courts. Members and guests relaxed under whirring fans to the pop-pop of racquets against tennis balls while they watched a set or two. White-coated servers scurried to and fro, taking orders for *citron pressé* (lemonade) or perhaps something stronger.

Entrance to *Cercle Sportif Saigonais*, 1973

Cercle Sportif Saigonais tennis courts ca. 1973
(Doling,Tim.www.historicvietnam.com/cercle-sportif-saigonnais.)

Steve submitted our membership application, and we awaited the final step in the membership process, the official interview with CSS's director general, that would take place in two weeks.

During that time, the Viet Cong shelled Cay Lay schoolyard in Dinh Tuong Province, seventy miles south of Saigon, killing seven ARVN soldiers and wounding twenty others. Naturally, news of the attack circulated throughout the foreign community. Yet, nothing changed in Saigon.

"Just more boom-booms," everyone said. If anyone took these attacks seriously, we didn't know about it. Like other expats, Steve and I continued living as if we were rich in that forsaken country of the poor.

Pauline worked tirelessly with me to improve my Vietnamese, and I succeeded in picking up a few more words. But the tones still eluded me. I could function with what I had and gave up the idea of becoming more proficient.

When her college courses started again, Pauline's availability declined, and I understood she needed to concentrate on her own education. Our sessions grew infrequent until they finally stopped. Although we saw each other less often after that, she remained a treasured friend.

It didn't take many afternoons at the *Cercle Sportif* to realize French would be more useful to me than German, and I dropped out of the class at the Goethe Institute without a second thought. My mind began to regain its focus.

I had taken a one-semester French class as an elective in college, but needed more. Then, I overheard a group of ladies at the AWAS meeting talking about just that.

"Does anybody know where I can take French lessons?" One woman asked. "My maid only speaks French and Vietnamese."

"Have you heard about the *Institut Français*?" asked another.

"Do you know the address?" I inquired, butting in.

"It's on Don Dat, I think. Let's see, there should be some brochures around here someplace," she shuffled through a pile of papers lying on a counter.

"Yes, here you go. Don Dat number 31. This says registration starts next Monday."

On registration day, I used my new bargaining skills and my small Vietnamese vocabulary to arrange a ride in a taxi, thankful that the driver understood where I wanted to go. I prided myself on remembering to ensure that both the driver and I agreed on the fare before I climbed aboard.

The ride took only a few minutes. The driver stopped in front of the *institut,* and I stepped out onto the dusty street, pulled out bills for the fare, and reached through the passenger-side window to pay. The driver's wiry hand lashed out. Quick as a lizard grabbing a bug, he caught my wrist in a grip stronger than his slight frame suggested. He motioned that he wanted more money. I froze.

What do I do now? Fear and confusion disoriented me for a second. *Does he mean to harm me?* I looked around for help. We had an agreement, and I meant to hold him to it.

I knew how to release a grip by applying pressure against the thumb. With a quick twist of my wrist, I wrenched my hand away. These words came to me, thanks to Pauline:

"*Bạn nói hai trăm năm mươi, tôi trả hai trăm năm mươi.*" You say 250. I pay 250. I tried to sound as indignant as possible.

Turning my back on the driver, I hurried toward the *institut's* entrance trying to regain my composure. As the taxi pulled away, I heard him yelling angry, unintelligible words at me. I stood there shaking. The incident lasted no more than a minute or two, but I realized, to my horror, just how vulnerable I was.

The chaotic scene outside the *institut* did nothing to calm my nerves. Noisy students crowded together on the front steps, jostling toward the registration counter. I joined them and tried to ignore what had just happened, taking their example as the way to get things done. I wanted to appear as if I knew what I was doing. But when I faced the registrar, I couldn't think what to say. Still shaken from the altercation with the taxi driver, the commotion confused me. Then, I spotted a friendly face amidst the mob.

"Karen, hello!" I looked up to see Yan waving at me. "What are you doing here?" she asked.

"What are *you* doing here?"

"I work in the office. Are you trying to register?"

"Well, I was, but it seems impossible."

"Look, this is the first day of registration. It isn't very good today. Come, I'll show you around the school. You can register tomorrow. It won't be so busy then."

The *institut* occupied two nondescript buildings set at right angles around a small parking area. One building housed the administration offices, and the other several classrooms and the language lab. There was a library. After the tour, Yan offered me a ride home, and I hopped onto her motorbike side saddle, as before.

She expertly navigated the traffic, weaving us smoothly through pedestrians and vehicles. As we became part of the crazy traffic dance that had kept me on the curb a few days before, I realized how easy it would be to lose an arm or a leg on one of those things. *Am I pushing my luck in more ways than one?*

The next day, I returned to the *Institut Français,* where a good-looking Frenchman named Guy Nandillon helped me register for beginning French. The class, set to start in September, would meet Monday through Friday from 4 to 6 p.m. I was about to fall in love.

Chapter 9

In Teaching, You Will Learn

September 1973

"I think I'm in love," I told Steve.

"Should I be worried?" he teased.

"No, nothing like that . . . it's just that French class is an absolute joy."

"Whew, had me going there for a minute," he said. "You've been working on a couple of languages. What's different about this class?"

"Well, for one thing, Monsieur Prioux, the professor—pretty darn handsome, by the way—had us speaking French in the first session. I feel like a kid learning to talk. This is a language I can use."

Steve stared at me. "Handsome, you say? Now I *am* worried."

"Kid all you want. You'll appreciate my French the next time we're at *Cercle Sportif.*"

Three weeks before, a roomful of young Vietnamese students had stared openly at me when I entered the room for the first French class. Their reaction didn't surprise me. I smiled at them and said, "Hello." Then, I spotted a group of five adult women sitting together at the end of the long room. I joined them. We would eventually become an informal sorority.

Tini Wadjdi, the elegant wife of the director of the Indonesian Chamber of Commerce in Saigon, spoke perfect English. With her *café au lait* complexion and dark hair, she personified the exotic Southeast Asian woman. A late-model, chauffeur-driven *Renault* dropped her off for class and picked her up every day, yet she seemed very down-to-earth.

Sara Bilecky, her husband, Tony, and two young children had been in Saigon for several months by the time I met her. Tony worked for USAID. Everything about Sara, from her no-nonsense French twist to her utilitarian wardrobe, said "practical." It wasn't that she lacked style. She just approached Saigon life in a casual way.

Jean Mayfield, her husband, Steve, and teenage daughter were missionaries. Jean had a smile for everyone and a curly mass of strawberry blonde hair piled atop her head like a halo. I ran into Jean and her daughter a few times shopping in town and envied their command of Vietnamese. Working in communities where no one spoke English made them almost fluent.

A decade or so older than the rest of us, Helen Mitchell came to Saigon with her contractor husband, Roger. Helen struggled to adjust but dressed to the nines. Her southern drawl delighted us. How she pronounced *salle à manger* . . . dining room . . . became legendary—"*sawhl ah* mawwn-*jhaay.*"

Linette Gohmert, a cheerful woman with round, wire-rimmed glasses, was born in the United States to immigrant parents from the Philippines. Her husband flew helicopters for Air America, the airline that began life as a passenger and cargo operation in 1946. But, from 1950 to 1976, the Central Intelligence Agency (CIA) secretly owned the airline and used it to support covert operations in Southeast Asia.

I had never encountered language learning the way M. Prioux taught it. A system of film strips and cassette tapes presented everyday situations with dialog between characters in a story. After watching and listening, M. Prioux posed questions in French, never speaking English in class.

We worked in pairs, each of us taking on the role of one of the characters and recreating the conversation from memory. Neither textbook nor homework figured into the process. Inflection tones didn't matter, either.

Grammar came naturally through dialogue without having to memorize complicated rules. The filmstrip illustrated the meaning of the words. Most of us couldn't recognize French words on a page, but M. Prioux didn't care as long as we knew when and how to use them.

Five days a week, for two hours each day, we added more words. Pretty soon, our French became functional. It was thrilling to have one more means of communication. I began to relax, and my life took on a new independence.

One afternoon, I arrived at class to find a pretty, matronly woman of about forty instead of M. Prioux. She wore a fashionable summer dress made from expensive-looking fabric with a floral pattern and high heels. She had styled her dark hair into a perfect French twist.

Where is the handsome M. Prioux?

Madame Nuquet introduced herself as M. Prioux's replacement. He had returned to Paris, she told us. Gone without warning! I felt abandoned as much as disappointed. Our leader had gone back to civilization and left us behind. But *Madame* Nuquet took us expertly through the routine drills and proved to be as excellent a teacher as her predecessor.

I happened upon her and her two children one day as we were both waiting to cross a street downtown.

"*Bonjour, où allez-vous*?" she asked. Good morning. Where are you going?

I fumbled for words. "*Bonjour, je vais a. . . .*" Good morning, I'm going to. . . .

I couldn't find the words to tell her "I'm going to meet my husband for lunch and buy a tennis racket." However, I understood the question. A good start, but the words I needed didn't yet exist in my vocabulary. Besides, I always overcomplicated things.

She didn't press me. Instead, she changed the conversation and introduced me to the children. One of them, a little boy, extended his left hand to shake hands with me. His mother corrected him, "*À la mains droite.*" Ah-ha! I recognized the square dance call "with the right hand." My passive language seemed okay, but the active part needed work.

The speaker at the monthly AWAS meeting talked about local job opportunities. One happened to be at the Nguyen Noch Linh International English School, an elementary-level institution looking for teachers.

Even though I had failed as an English teacher at the Vietnamese American Association, I thought I could successfully work with younger children. My college curriculum had required one semester of student teaching in public schools, and I especially liked the elementary grades. I decided to follow up.

A no-nonsense administrator, Mrs. Nguyen Noch Linh ruled the International English School like a tiny kingdom. She received me in an office lined with jam-packed bookshelves. A teak desk stood at the far end, covered with neatly stacked paperwork. Matching teak chairs faced the desk. Immaculate in her prim traditional *áo dài,* severe hairdo, manicured hands, and perfect posture, she spoke fluent English. I envied her ability to switch easily between English, Vietnamese, and French. I wanted to know more about her.

"May I ask where you learned English, Mrs. Nguyen? You speak it perfectly," I said, remembering that in Vietnamese last names come first, middle names second, and first names last.

She stared at the ceiling for a beat. "That was long ago when I lived in New York City," she answered.

"What were you doing in New York?" I hoped she'd keep talking. With an impatient sigh, she said, "Getting an education. NYU. That's where I met my husband. We were married in New York. I know all about that city," she said with a dismissive wave of a hand, wanting to get on with questioning me.

"What brought you and your husband back to Vietnam?" I knew I was testing her tolerance now, but she continued.

"Linh and I returned to Saigon in 1955. The Geneva Convention split our country in two in 1954. The French were out, and President Diem called us home. He needed everyone to help rebuild Vietnam for Vietnamese. Linh started this school last year. Now, no more questions. Let's take a tour. I'll show you where you will meet your class if you decide to work here." She stood and ushered me out of her office and onto a dusty concrete walkway.

The school consisted of three one-story bungalows set at right angles. Shutters at the windows could be closed or opened to provide either shade or a breeze if there was one. The classroom doors opened onto a common area in the center used as the playground. Tufts of grass struggled to survive. A scraggly tree grew from the dry brown earth. One of the buildings had a large room with a narrow platform at one end, which I assumed was for assemblies.

I would work with post-kindergartners of mixed nationalities and languages to improve their English language skills before first grade. Mrs. Nguyen showed me to a small classroom and said the class size would be 20 to 25 students.

Desks and chairs for the children occupied most of the space. A teacher's desk sat near a blackboard where bits of chalk and an eraser rested in the tray. The hours were good, 8:30 to 10:10 in the morning, including a 30-minute recess. The pay might cover the cost of a taxi ride to the school. I agreed to start in one week. Mrs. Nguyen didn't care about my experience level. She just wanted teachers who were native English speakers.

On the first day of school, I arrived to find 34 children crowded into the small classroom. As expected, they were of mixed nationalities, as well as mixed-race American-Vietnamese. Raised primarily by their Vietnamese mothers and their extended families, the children of these unions spoke Vietnamese but little English.

Overwhelmed didn't come close to describing how I felt. The children's English language ability proved almost non-existent. Once again, I found myself in a situation where I struggled to communicate. As hope faded, Mrs. Nguyen appeared in the classroom with a young ethnic Chinese woman.

"This is Janet," Mrs. Linh announced. "She is in college studying to be a teacher. She will be your assistant."

The children and I might be saved.

On my second day, 42 children were crammed into the room, which now felt as tiny as a doll house. Two children shared desks designed for one. I felt so flustered that I could not cope. Fear grew in my mind, and nerves tied my stomach in knots. Neither Janet nor I could make ourselves heard over the noise in the room. The craziness of the situation bonded us in a strange way.

I wanted so much to help them, but college courses had trained me only to teach young, English-speaking children short lessons about libraries! I wasn't prepared to handle what faced me—forty-two adorable children with short attention spans, most of whom couldn't understand a word I said.

I enjoyed the children, one on one, but so many in such a tight space didn't work. I marched into the office of Mrs. Nguyen Noch Linh to resign.

"You will have to find someone else," I told her. "It's ridiculous to have so many students assigned to one teacher. I don't think teaching here is going to work for me."

"Now, Mrs. Karen," she said, unmoved by my despair. "Yes, it's a lot of children. But they have to go somewhere. I promise to find a way to reduce the size of your class. Then you will stay. Okay?"

I hung on for the rest of the week. When I arrived at school the next Monday, eighteen youngsters greeted me. Mrs. Nguyen had hired a second teacher and divided my class in two. Carolyn Moore, a trained, experienced teacher from Toronto, took on the second section.

This is more like it. I can figure out how to do this. Maybe Carolyn will help me.

Twenty young faces greeted me the following Monday morning, two more than last week. Mrs. Nguyen appeared at the classroom door before I could confront her.

"Mrs. Karen, how are you this morning?" she asked brightly.

"Fine. Why are there two more children in my class today?" I demanded, lowering my voice to hide the anger I felt. "I thought we agreed. No more."

"I am glad you are well." She ignored my protest. "I need to ask your help."

She has a lot of nerve. I'll give her that.

"With what?"

"I would not ask if it were not important. You will take just one more student in your class, yes?" She lifted an elegant index finger toward heaven as if issuing a royal edict.

I sensed her testing me. "No. Absolutely not! Out of the question. I will not take one more. How can you even suggest that? You already added two more without telling me. My patience is wearing thin."

"All right . . . all right. Do not be upset. I will assign no more children to you." With that, she turned and walked back to her office.

An easy win for me? Impossible. What else does she have up her sleeve?

"Mrs. Karen, I am hosting tea at my home on Thursday at 3:30 for all the new teachers," said Mrs. Nguyen. "I do this each year. I would like you to come."

"Thank you," I said. "I will be there."

"Good. We need to get to know each other better."

The afternoon of the tea, we gathered in a formal sitting room furnished with black lacquer furniture inlaid with a floral design in mother-of-pearl, typical in Vietnam. Four of us made up the guest list, but I was the only American among the teachers from Canada, Australia, and New Zealand. The usual light conversation took place, everyone sharing their origins and a bit about themselves. Then Mrs. Nguyen turned to me and asked, "What about your President Nixon?"

I expected her to make a sneaky move like that. President Nixon faced a major political scandal known as Watergate. She put me on the spot and knew it, but I bore a responsibility as an American not to throw my president under the bus and deflect the question.

"He's having a difficult time at the moment," I answered, leaving it at that. An understatement, to be sure, but no one pressed the issue.

—

Carolyn Moore suggested I observe one of her classes when I asked for teaching help. Watching her lead the children logically from one concept to the next, I began to understand. What is the child's point of view? To teach them, I first needed to think like them.

On Confucius Day, a school holiday, Carolyn and I created lesson plans for the coming month. Everything made sense the way she explained it. I finally got it, and the children made progress.

After the first week, they could read and write their names. When I asked, "What is your name?" in English, they answered correctly.

We moved on to pronouns, "What is his/her name?" I took a lesson from French class and used pictures to introduce new words. Janet and I took turns reading to them from the small collection of children's books in the school library. The children responded. Even the quiet ones found their voices. I was no longer overwhelmed. "Thrilled" better describes how I felt.

Steve's Work Diary

> ***17 September 1973:*** *We had our regular staff meeting this morning. See meeting notes for items reported upon. Points of discussion—Accounting system. Lawes [Alonzo] is still not progressing too well. I was supposed to review the forms, but Laws gave them directly to Jim McGuire. I can't help out when I'm left out. Bill Ainsley and I will try to get Lawes started on the budget.*

The word "chatterbox" never described Steve in those days, but as we enjoyed Patty's delicious food at dinner, he seemed unusually quiet, distant, and lost in thought.

"How did your day go?" I ventured.

"Sorry," he said, returning his attention to the room, ". . . frustrating day."

"Want to talk about it?"

"It's just meetings, meetings, meetings, but nothing gets done."

"What do you mean?"

"For instance, the new budget procedures. Our counterpart from the Vietnamese Highway Administration, Mr. Hue, said he'd give us the data we need, and I suggested Lawes draft a budget outline. Mr. Hue went out to the provinces without giving us any data, and Lawes is having trouble with the outline. I asked to review what he has so far, but he bypassed me and sent his drafts directly up the line. Now, there'll be *another* meeting to reconcile *that*. I'm afraid the monthly progress report will be another bomb."

Steve at work, Saigon, 1973

"What does your chief of party say about all this?"

"Lew? Lew's holed up in his office with the district engineers all day. We were supposed to get together to talk about forms for the roads and bridges inventory in the provinces, but that didn't happen."

Once he started, he couldn't seem to stop. "Oh, and get this, Lew asked Dick Klein and me to find out about having a party for the whole office, including the Vietnamese Director General of Highways staff! Lew means well, but I don't think the man is in touch with reality."

"I can help with that. Do you want to delegate the party to me? I think Sally Klein and I can handle it.

"You sure? That'd be great. You're good at parties."

"It's the least I can do for the cause."

Vung Tau . . . anchorage . . . a small, picturesque fishing village formerly known as Cap St. Jacques during the French colonial period, lay at the tip of a peninsula sixty-one miles east of Saigon. Trading ships frequented the town during the fourteenth and fifteenth centuries. Malay pirates used it as their home port in the eighteenth century. During the war, Australian, U.S., and New Zealand armies stationed troops near Vung Tau.

Abandoned military buildings lined the beach road, rusted remains of ships-run-aground dotted the beaches, Buddhist temples sat tucked into hillsides, and horse-drawn taxis waited to transport passengers to the village center. Short of leaving the country, Vung Tau was the best place to go for relief from the pollution and congestion of Saigon.

Steve, exhausted by struggles at work, needed a break. We got together with Don and Alice Smail, our hosts when we had first arrived, Dick and Sally Klein, their two children, and Lew and Vi Chittim for a weekend at the Palace Hotel on Vung Tau's main street. The hotel offered good food, a nice bar, live music in the evenings, and a dance floor. We arrived just in time for lunch. The pizza turned out to be surprisingly good. Some of us made for the beach while the others went into town.

With towels spread out on the soft, white sand in the shade of a pile of huge boulders and a couple of wonky umbrellas that Dick and Steve rented from a vendor, we settled in for a quiet afternoon. Until the shrill screech of a sports whistle splintered the air.

A group of men dressed in dazzling white shirts and shorts marched over the dunes in two straight lines. They followed the whistleblower in perfect step and marched past us up the beach to who-knew-where as if they were part of some ghost army.

Beach at Vung Tau, 1973

The next day, Don and Alice invited us to visit one of the nearby Buddhist pagodas with them. Don told his driver to take the day off and drove us, himself, along the winding road by the South China Sea. We soon arrived at a small parking lot. Leaving the car at the bottom of a rise, we approached the temple up a wide curving stairway bordered by a waist-high wall, its top surface decorated with a concrete serpent.

L-R: Vi Chittim, driver, Karen, Lou Chittim, *Vung Tau*, 1973

At the top of the stairway, I caught the acrid/earthy smell of incense. Smoke clouded the interior of the pagoda. I stepped inside but couldn't immediately make out what lay before me. As my eyes adjusted, I saw the snakes. Lots of them. They undulated lazily atop the altar in an incense-induced stupor and coiled themselves around slim branches that protruded from ornate ceramic vases.

"Are they poisonous?" Steve asked.

"These are pythons," said Don. "They squeeze their victims to death."

"What do snakes have to do with Buddhism?" I wanted to know.

"These snakes symbolize rebirth, transformation, immortality, healing, something to do with the fact that they shed their skin," Don explained. "They're also regarded as fierce guardians of sacred places because they don't back down from a fight. It's illegal to harm them."

No one ventured very far into the temple. Leaving the snakes, we drove to the hotel and checked out the vendors set up outside before heading back to Saigon.

—

On the twenty-first day of September, the North Vietnamese army, supported by artillery and tanks, captured Plei Djereng Camp, a former U.S. Army Special Forces facility in the Central Highlands northwest of Pleiku and twelve and a half miles east of the Cambodian border along the Ho Chi Minh Trail. Saigon lay 265 miles southeast. During the battle, 200 of the 293 ARVN rangers operating the camp were either killed or captured.

Our family and friends wrote worried letters about TV reports of fierce fighting in and around Saigon. We assumed they must have heard about Plei Djereng. Skirmishes between the armies of North and South Vietnam frequently flared north of us in the Central Highlands and south in the Mekong Delta.

We didn't worry about the news. Saigon remained untouched by the war. Even so, we could hear mortar fire in the distance at night. Long-time expats insisted none of it threatened Saigon. And so, our days unfolded as usual, with Steve going to work five and a half days a week and me pursuing language classes and my part-time job at the International School.

Chapter 10

Where Ignorance Is Bliss

October 1973

Fifty-one miles southwest of Saigon, ARVN troops attacked North Vietnam's 207th Regiment at Ap Da Bien in Long An Province, killing more than 200 soldiers. In Saigon, nothing changed. The unmistakable, pungent odor of *nuoc mam* still clung to the stifling afternoon air. The muffled sound of traffic on Nguyen Dinh Chieu Street still reached me in the cool comfort of the air-conditioned den, where I wrestled with lesson plans, as oblivious to the war as a chrysalis in a cocoon.

Life at the villa settled into a comfortable rhythm measured by the familiar sounds of Patty and Yao moving about the house—the rustle of a palm-frond broom sweeping tile floors, the thud of a knife chopping vegetables, the soft slap of bare feet carrying laundry to the clothesline on the roof.

Steve's Work Diary

> ***31 October 1973:*** *Bill said Tuoi was upset because Tang was afraid that there were some internal problems between Lew [Chittim] and the rest of us, the advisors. They realize there is a lack of communication. We discussed among ourselves what could be done. Dick wanted to talk to Roy [Jorgensen] and lay everything out so he can understand what is going on. We didn't agree on what to do except that we would argue with Chittim and document our recommendations.*

"You're quiet tonight," I said to Steve as we sat down to dinner. "The project going okay?"

"Honestly, reorganizing the Vietnamese Highway Administration is like herding cats. We make recommendations to Tuoi, our client contact, who runs them by his boss at VHA, Tang. Then Chittim contradicts us. And the clients keep changing their minds about what they want. It's frustrating."

"Have you talked to him about it?"

"We've tried, but he's either in meetings or out of town."

At the Jorgensen office, life was anything but comfortable.

A window in the main second-floor bedroom overlooked the open kitchen door and the atrium on the first floor, letting in the morning sounds. I heard Patty activating her favorite gadget, the toaster. Eggs would be bubbling their way to soft-boiled. Sweet slices of fresh papaya and pineapple would be waiting on the dining room table by the time we got there.

I finished dressing and headed downstairs. The owners had done an excellent job furnishing the place with streamlined pieces that echoed the modern architecture. The living room accent rug and a few decorative items I'd added looked good.

I was anxious to eat and get going, but Patty hurried in from the kitchen before I reached the bottom step. I'd never seen her so agitated. "*Madame*," she said. "Cat in courtyard."

"Oh, for heaven's sake. Show me," I followed her outside where a small, white and orange creature, a few weeks old, sat trembling.

The kitten looked in bad shape, its fur matted and grimy. I checked its ears and found them black with dirt. Its thin little body looked "no bigger than a minute," as my mother used to say, referring to the thin lines on the face of a clock that marked the minutes. I couldn't tell the sex but declared it female until proven otherwise.

My scant knowledge of felines had come from the litters of kittens that turned up regularly among the hay bales in my father's barn, the offspring of our two female barn cats. They earned their keep by suppressing the mouse population. My mother never allowed animals, particularly barn cats, into the house.

I had no idea how to take care of this animal, but I knew she needed nourishment, fast. I carried her into the kitchen, set her on the floor, and grabbed a saucer from the cupboard.

"Patty, pour some milk into this," I said, handing her the saucer.

Patty looked skeptical but did as I asked without comment. The kitten lapped hungrily at the milk. Patty and Yao looked upset.

"Is something wrong?" I asked Patty.

"*Madame*, kitty bad luck."

"Why? She's cute."

"No, *Madame*! Chinese say, 'Dog in house bring good luck; cat in house bring bad luck.' We afraid for bad luck."

"Cats aren't bad luck. That's just a superstition," I scoffed.

Patty shook her head, resigned. *Does she understand what "superstition" means?* I asked her to look after our feline guest until I got home from school later that morning. The kitten needed a bath before Steve saw her, and I needed Patty and Yao to help me.

"*Madame*, water make kitty sick," Patty said when I told her my plan.

"Nonsense, she'll be fine, Patty," I said. "Please get my shampoo and a bath towel, and ask Yao to fill the bucket with warm water, not too hot . . . and bring my hair dryer, too."

They didn't look at all happy about it, but loyal women that they were, they went along. With the tools close at hand, I took the kitten into the small washroom off the kitchen and set her down in the sink. Patty held the bottle of shampoo. Yao brought the bucket of water. I knew I had to work fast. Holding the kitten firmly, I splashed a little water over her body. Patty handed me the shampoo, and I dropped a minuscule amount onto the soft kitten fur.

She let out a few soft meows, and I felt her tremble, but she didn't try to get away. I kept a firm hold on her in case she changed her mind and gently scrubbed her ears, eyes, and body until I could see pink skin showing. Patty and Yao watched intently as if I were performing surgery.

I motioned for Yao to set the bucket of warm water on the floor next to me and hold on tight. Picking kitty up by her front legs, I gave her a quick up-and-down dunk to rinse off the suds. The girls gasped in shock, but they weren't as shocked as the kitten that let out a screech of terror.

With kitty firmly on my lap, Patty handed me the bath towel. I worked fast to wrap the animal in a snug cocoon, then held her for a few minutes hoping she would calm down and feel safe.

The kitten trembled and cowered but didn't try to escape. Still shaking but calm, she stayed put while I removed the towel and flipped the hair dryer switch to the lowest setting. The appliance hummed to life. Warm air blew gently over her fur. She didn't move.

Bath time over, Patty and Yao relaxed and took all the tools away. The kitten sat calmly on my lap, letting me scratch her ears and stroke her fur. Then, with her yellow eyes focused on me, kitty began to lick my hand as if to say "thank you." I'd never been so charmed by anything.

When Steve met her that evening, she charmed him, too. He wanted to keep her, so she stayed and became known simply as Kitty. We would all adjust.

Steve picked up a supply of cat food from the PX and a few cat toys. She got used to us, and over the next few days, we got used to her rambunctious, affectionate personality. Kitty kept us company in the evenings, chasing her toys, nipping at our heels, and learning her way around.

But during the day, our pet annoyed Patty and Yao. They complained that she interrupted their work. She liked to chase Yao's broom and hang around underfoot in the kitchen. I understood but thought they'd learn to accept the kitten in time.

A week went by, and the complaints stopped. Everything seemed fine until I found Patty waiting at the bottom of the stairs one morning, looking nervous.

"*Madame,*" she said, her voice wavering, "Kitty die. Maybe bath make kitty die."

"What? No! Show me where she is." *How could this have happened?*

Sure enough, our vivacious little companion lay cold and still in the courtyard behind the kitchen where she spent the night.

"What's going on?" Steve wanted to know when he came for breakfast and saw us all outside.

"Kitty's dead. We don't know why," I said. "Why didn't we keep her inside at night?"

"Well, we didn't . . . can't go back."

Natural causes? Some feline diseases? Or, a dreadful thought, foul play? The girls didn't like Kitty, but I couldn't believe either would end her life.

Steve investigated. He thought another cat had probably come over the wall and attacked our pet in the night. Strange, though, no one heard a thing. There would have been a noisy fight. Sleeping above the carport next to the courtyard, Yao would surely have heard it. Maybe Kitty was still too weak to defend herself. We'd never know for sure, but one thing I did know for sure was that she hadn't died because I bathed her.

We now faced the problem of a dead animal in the courtyard and how to dispose of the remains. The idea of digging up the landlord's front yard to bury her didn't feel right. Finally, Steve carried Kitty across the street in a shovel and deposited her in the refuse bin. A tiny life that couldn't be saved among too many others of every species in that country. The villa seemed emptier in the evenings. Neither of us considered a kitty replacement.

I didn't feel heartbroken, exactly. Kitty hadn't been with us all that long. Still, I'd devoted a piece of myself to the care of another life and failed. Should I have kept her inside? It didn't seem natural to keep a cat in the house. Our barn cats had always done well outdoors. Common sense told me to let it go, yet the loss was palpable even though my upbringing didn't allow for that kind of sentimentality.

What would I do without Patty? I hoped I'd never find out. Besides helping me bathe a cat, Patty had taught me how to function. I wanted potted plants to fill the empty corners of the living room. Patty said she knew a place that would give me a reasonable price, and I took her plant shopping with me.

I bought more than the small blue and yellow taxi could hold, so Patty flagged down a motorized cyclo. The contraption looked like a three-wheeled motorcycle with an open cab on the back and a convertible top over the passenger seat. I'd never ridden in one.

We loaded all the greenery into the cargo space in the back, then squeezed ourselves onto the narrow bench seat behind the driver. Roaring off toward home, we passed a group of workmen who laughed and pointed, calling out to us in Vietnamese words I didn't know.

"Do they think it's funny we have all these plants?" I asked Patty.

"No," she laughed, "they say you *dep lam*."

"Is that bad? What does it mean?"

"It mean pretty," Patty said.

That's the thing about international living. You never stop learning.

My teaching became more structured and results-driven at school with Carolyn's help. She offered a lifeline, and I followed her lead, emulating whatever she did. I also found helpful reference books in the library at the Defense Attaché Office.

Instead of flagging down a cyclo one morning. I hitched a ride to school with Mr. Pho when he came to drive Steve to his office. I wedged a large packing box left over from our move into the back seat beside me. At school, I hauled the box to my classroom and set it up. Janet assembled art supplies and the colored construction paper my mother sent from the States.

. "Class, this is a box," I began, indicating the cardboard structure. "Today, we are going to make a house." Janet translated. I wrote "house" on the blackboard and drew a simple house shape. The excited children cheered.

Cyclos in downtown Saigon, 1973

I drew a window on the side of the box.

"Window," I said. The class repeated the word.

I cut out a door.

"Door," repeated the children.

I used a couple of end flaps to form the roof.

"Roof," they repeated.

Everyone helped paint the house learning new words all the time. Some drew more windows and decorated the house with construction paper flowers. The class had fun, and, to my amazement, so did I.

Parents' Week approached, and the anticipation brought on all kinds of anxiety. I had no idea what to expect. Parents could drop in anytime, and I wanted to impress them. I couldn't control events, but I could control the classroom's appearance and, to some extent, the children's behavior. Janet and I organized our supplies and generally tidied up, and I planned lessons to keep the children extra busy.

First, they made their own English readers using simple sentences. I taped labeled animal pictures on the blackboard. To get them started, I pointed to Janet, then to a cat, and said, "Janet is a cat." Taking turns, each child had a chance to write their sentence. The final book read, "Vu is a dog, Minh is a duck, Terry is a bear, Bobby is a tiger." Some children added drawings.

Janet and students at the Nguyen Noch Linh International English School, Saigon, 1973

The class made paper chains and compared them for the longest, shortest, and most rings. They cut out circles, squares, triangles, and unique shapes of their own design to make mobiles, which Janet and I assembled with bent-open paper clips. We hung the mobiles around the room. Young eyes lit up in delight when the colorful shapes twisted and turned in the breeze from the ceiling fans.

I took a lumpy, brown Vietnamese pumpkin to school and cut out a jack-o'-lantern. The children made masks using brown paper bags and construction paper and, then paraded through Carolyn's classroom to show off their work.

Few parents showed up. Those who did, however, observed a neat classroom and twenty youngsters either in the middle of a lesson or busy at their desks . . . or on the floor . . . a habit I could never break so I gave up trying. The parents never stayed long and didn't ask many questions.

When I thought no more visitors would come by, Terry's father, an American, stopped in a second time. From the beginning, Terry stood out for being extremely shy and rarely speaking.

Uh-oh. What have I done now?

"I just want you to know," her father said, "I've seen a marked improvement in Terry."

It was the highest praise. I became more sure of myself and my ability to make a difference. Struggles with Mrs. Nguyen didn't matter as much, and the hours spent with Carolyn had paid off. Had I found my niche at last?

The cyclo driver leaned into his task, pedaling faster and faster toward the glowing sphere in the distance. We sped through the night. The wind on my face felt cool and clean as it carried the cyclo upward on shimmering golden threads into the heavens. Jasmine's sweet perfume surrounded us. The sphere grew more prominent as we neared. Around us, thousands of red stars twinkled and spun in the darkness.

Suddenly, the cyclo jolted to a stop, spilling me out. Like a bird, I floated on a gentle current of air, wrapped in the warm glow of the moon, feeling completely happy, secure, and joyful.

Steve coaxed me awake . . . still dark outside. The air conditioner hummed. "What's the matter?" I groaned as I blinked myself to consciousness.

"You were talking in your sleep," he said.

"Hmm . . . what did I say?"

"I don't know . . . couldn't understand you."

"I was having the most blissful dream . . . didn't want it to end," I told Steve about my dream.

"The Moon Day legends Janet told the kids at school must have triggered it."

"What legends?"

"There are a couple. One was about an emperor whose wizard took him to the moon on the back of a golden carp, where he watched fairies dancing in the moonlight. The second is more popular. It's about a man named Uncle Cuoi who discovered the healing powers of the banyan tree when he spotted a mother tiger using its leaves to cure her sick cub. Uncle Cuoi wanted the tree for himself, so he pulled it out of the ground and planted it in his garden. He told his wife that the tree was unique and to water its roots daily and only use pure water from the well.

One day, when Uncle Cuoi was away working in the rice fields, his wife forgot the instructions and poured dirty water on the tree's roots. The banyan tree became angry and began to uproot itself. When Uncle Cuoi came home and saw what was happening, he grabbed the tree's roots to keep it from flying away. But the tree was strong and carried Uncle Cuoi all the way to the moon. People say if you look at the full moon, you can still see two black shadows that look like a man sitting under a tree."

"So, a man in the moon story."

"Yeah, guess so."

Dozens of shiny, red lanterns shaped like stars and animals appeared at the entrance to Kim Phuong's shop near the villa. I asked Patty what they meant.

"They for Moon Day," she said.

The ancient Vietnamese holiday Tet Trung Thu, the Harvest Moon Festival, second in importance only to the Lunar New Year, meant time off from work. Busy parents could be with their children, who looked forward to toys and stomachs full of moon cake.

During the celebration, families played games, sang songs, and told stories about their ancestors. Neighborhood lantern parades and dragon dances entertained children lucky enough to live in a safe part of town. I brought twenty lanterns to school. Janet helped me hang them around the classroom as gifts for the students. One parent brought moon cakes, adding a touch of magic to the week.

Like so much of Vietnamese cuisine, mooncakes derive from a Chinese tradition. Their flavor reminded me of fruit cake mixed with dried meat wrapped in a sticky rice crust. The yolk of a hardboiled duck egg, placed in the center, represented the moon. Round cakes dominated the market, but I loved the fanciful shapes—stars, rabbits, butterflies—decorated with sticky rice flowers.

To me, it was a reward. I had worked at a dull but familiar library job before coming to Vietnam. Not much stress, nothing that pushed me very far or asked much of me. I didn't care about any of it. A mistake on that job carried few repercussions. The classroom full of children, however, required every bit of ingenuity I had, and twenty young faces delivered immediate feedback. I cared very much about handling this job well.

Back in the States, I had often made my clothes using those tricky, trendy Vogue patterns that took lots of time, energy, and workspace, none of which I had in Saigon.

There existed one place in the city to buy ready-made clothes and shoes in American sizes, the PX at the Defense Attaché Complex. We could also order clothes from Sears or Penney's catalogs, but the chance they would be spirited away to the black market on arrival at the port always loomed. Besides, those choices offered nothing special.

The well-dressed, stylish ladies I met at the American Women's Association, dinner parties, and the *Cercle Sportief* stirred my curiosity.

Where do they find chic outfits like that? Bangkok? Hong Kong? Singapore? I have to know.

My world changed when I discovered their garments were custom-made by a local seamstress, Alice Fabré. Alice led a crew who could create anything from a picture. With all sorts of French, German, and American magazines to choose from at the newsstand in Eden Arcade, pictures abounded.

French-trained Alice Fabré enjoyed the reputation of being the best dressmaker in Saigon. Her inviting atelier, a lovely French colonial villa painted the color of heavy cream, sat two blocks from our villa in a shady side street off rue Pasteur. Large pots of tropical plants graced the front steps. French doors opened wide to let any hint of a breeze circulate over the black-and-white tile floor. Inside, the rat-ta-tat-tat of sewing machines echoed off high ceilings. A buzz of activity filled the room as busy assistants and seamstresses went about their work.

Karen and Alice Fabré on the porch of her atelier, Saigon, 1973

I arrived at Alice's atelier one afternoon excited about the first fitting of a raw silk safari suit I'd ordered two weeks earlier. Alice, an exotic mix of French and Vietnamese lineage, greeted me with a smile and excellent English, then asked me to wait while she checked my order.

I took a seat on one of the black lacquer side chairs arranged around a square coffee table in the neat, well-appointed lounge. A servant brought tea. Ceiling fans hummed. Still, I tugged at the neck of my shirt, trying to dry the sweat creeping over my skin.

"I'm sorry," Alice said after I'd waited longer than usual, "your order is not ready."

"You said to come back today. Why isn't it ready?"

"The wife of our Minister of Education has just arrived. I did not expect her, but she is here now, and I must take care of her. You understand."

Politics again!

An angry monster took hold of me, yet I said nothing. It took every bit of self-control I had not to walk out in a huff and go elsewhere. Besides, no "elsewhere" existed that could compare with Alice's.

I hated the unfairness of preferential treatment. Alice had specifically scheduled me for that day. I felt wronged, yet realized I had little choice. If I wanted quality work, I had to play the game.

Alice apologized again in words verging on contrition. I understood the importance of her well-connected customers to her livelihood. So, agreeing to return the following Saturday, I set out to walk the two blocks back to the villa.

The idea of custom-made shoes seemed extravagant, but other than the limited offerings at the PX, it represented our only choice for new footwear. Steve and I chose a shoemaker's shop from among many on Ly Chinh Tang Street because the owner, Mr. Trinh Ngoc, had once been a royal shoemaker to Cambodia's King Norodom Sihanouk.

In 1970, after a coup sent King Sihanouk into exile in China, Mr. Trinh returned to his native country and continued making shoes, the best in Saigon.

The narrow shop Mr. Trin inhabited looked like it had been built a century ago. Sunlight streaming through the front door revealed an interior of wood and leather. Rows of rough, wooden shelves spanned two walls. Smooth wooden cobbler's lasts, labeled by customer, crowded the shelves. A sturdy wooden workbench bore scars from years of service. Cobbler's tools lay lined up next to a well-used style catalog. Rolls of leather tied with colored string stood four rows deep, like sentries, against another wall. The scent of leather permeated everything.

Mr. Trinh traced our feet on a piece of brown paper. We showed him pictures of the styles we wanted, and he told us to come back in one week. There was something surreal about buying shoes that way in the twentieth century, as if we'd traveled a hundred years back in time.

Would our new shoes look like the pictures? Would they fit? Would they be comfortable? Would they last longer than a month or two? Anticipation built throughout the week.

The day we arrived to pick up our shoes, we found the shop closed, the shoemaker nowhere about. The neighboring shopkeeper told us Mr. Trinh had gone home to his family in the countryside because his father died. He would be away for two weeks, leaving no one to run the shop. *How can he maintain a business that way? Surely, he will lose customers.*

I was naïve. To understand the Vietnamese, one had to know something about the Confucian system of ethical and moral behavior that informed Vietnam's ancient social structure. A man's first loyalty belonged to his family, second to his village, and third to his country or to the emperor, in earlier times.

Mr. Trinh, like his fellow citizens, believed that if he followed this ritual perfectly—did the right thing—Providence would reward him and provide for his needs. Therefore, leaving his business unattended to go to his father's funeral did not worry him; by doing so, he fulfilled his first duty and felt secure in the belief that Providence would take care of everything else.

In due time, we got our shoes and a lesson in patience, setting priorities, and leading an orderly life. Did the world fall apart because our shoes weren't ready in two weeks? Of course not. The world falling apart would take a little longer.

In Saigon, dinner parties were *de rigueur*. Every gathering became a celebration of what passed for normal life. One morning, Patty handed me an envelope delivered by messenger. Inside, I found a handsome invitation printed on heavy card stock. My friend Tini Wadjdi and her husband, Basheer, had invited us to a dinner party to celebrate their anniversary.

In preparation for the Wadjdi's party, I visited a beauty salon. The shop's entrance was through one of the small storefronts in the town center, but the interior took up more square feet than its façade suggested.

The décor consisted of silky columns of fabric the color of red grapes hanging from the ceiling to divide the space into work areas. A stylist ushered me to her chair for a trifecta of hair services—shampoo, cut, blow dry.

Next, the nail technician took over. She soaked, massaged, trimmed, and polished until my hands and feet looked like they belonged to someone who lived a privileged life. Finally, the manager presented my bill. I gasped when I saw the price . . . $5US for everything.

—

I stood in front of the bedroom closet, agonizing over what to wear to Wadjdi's dinner party. The invitation said casual dress. My mind whirred with possibilities—a guessing game.

What constitutes casual dress here? Is this too much? Is this too little?

"You worry too much," Steve said.

Finally, I settled on the pantsuit made for me by Alice Fabré and silver platform heels to complement the silver design in the suit's light blue cotton fabric. Steve wore gray slacks with a navy blue, open-collar silk shirt. He always had it easy.

We arrived at the Wadjdis' residence by taxi, and one of the uniformed guards directed us into the compound. Warm light spilled from the open doors and windows. We climbed the broad steps to the entrance, where a servant dressed in a fitted white jacket/blouse over a long batik wrap skirt ushered us inside.

Indonesian folk art covered the walls. Shadow puppets. Colorful batik fish prints. Fanciful animal carvings. I looked around for Tini and finally spotted her talking with a gentleman and another couple.

She wore a gorgeous, floor-length caftan of dark blue batik embroidered with gold. I felt I might have misunderstood "casual dress." Other women in floor-length dinner dresses drifted around us. Steve, however, seemed to have struck the perfect balance of tropical dinner party chic. *Stop stressing and enjoy yourself.*

When she spotted us, Tini and the gentleman with her hurried over.

"Karen, welcome," she said, squeezing my hand. "This is my husband, Basheer. We are happy you came."

"It's so nice to be here. Thank you for inviting us. And this is my husband, Steve."

"Please, make yourselves at home. Have a drink. Dinner will be served soon."

A waiter offered non-alcoholic drinks. The Wadjdis were Muslim. We mingled with the other guests. The buzz of conversation was interrupted now and then by a burst of laughter. The room vibrated with the carefree chatter of happy guests. I smelled the savory scent of curry wafting from the kitchen. A hint of musky incense teased my nostrils. Only the humidity and heat claimed more square footage.

BONNGGG!

The sound of a gong quieted the room. Basheer stepped forward.

"Dinner is served," he declared. "Please help yourself to the buffet."

The large dining table was brimming with platters of satay, grilled fish and chicken, *pepes* (packets of vegetables and herbs wrapped in banana leaves), coconut rice, curry, roasted vegetables, all kinds of fruits, loaves of bread, and cheeses.

Afterward, guests moved outside onto the veranda or relaxed in the sunroom's comfortable rattan furniture, cooled by a gently humming ceiling fan.

I joined a small group in the sunroom and sat on a loveseat. The lively conversation revealed an international group of well-traveled people full of fascinating stories. One woman delighted us with tales of the Yak cheese she'd eaten in Mongolia.

Wait, what? I'm out of my element here. Can I add anything to this conversation?

Just then, an Australian woman began talking about her experiences teaching at a private Montessori school in town. I had found my niche. For the rest of the evening, we pursued an animated discussion of the joys and pitfalls of teaching in a culture not one's own. No longer a shy newbie, I was an expat, just like them, with a story to tell. Some revelation for a farm kid!

On October 30, 173 miles northwest of the Wadjdis' dinner party, North Vietnamese troops began a battle in Quang Duc province that would rage into December. The goal was to clear the way for an expansion of their supply network from Hanoi through Cambodia into South Vietnam.

Chapter 11

If Life Were Predictable

November 1973

The rumble of nightly explosions rolled over our neighborhood like thunder. What had once been terrifying became normal. Steve, my fear barometer, had access to news that never reached me, and one day the information turned alarming.

"The VC are at it again," Steve said when he walked in the door from work. "They launched a rocket attack on Bien Hoa Air Base last night. That's only 18 miles from here. Three of the South's F-5A jets went up in smoke."

"What? That's not good," I said. "Any word from the embassy?"

"No, nothing, and USAID expects our work products to be delivered on time."

"Did you see anything happening in the city?"

"No, it's untouched, but we could soon find ourselves in a dicey situation. I'm sending those new stereo speakers home to your folks in case we're evacuated and don't have time to pack up."

A prickle of nerves radiated through me—not fear, exactly, more like an out-of-body experience. *Evacuation seems far-fetched, something that happens to other people in other parts of the world. What have we gotten ourselves into?*

I stood on the villa's second-floor balcony looking out over the rooftops of a brown city wrapped in a gray haze. On the street below, a man on a motorcycle transported furniture in a cargo carrier attached to its front fender. A Honda motorbike passed loaded front to back with a family of six. A bus, spewing exhaust, pulled to a stop in front of the villa. The driver climbed down and walked to the opposite side of the street. He stood facing a tall security wall and proceeded to relieve himself while his unperturbed passengers waited patiently in their seats. The street activity, though endlessly fascinating, bewildered and amazed me. Saigon had to be the strangest place I'd ever seen.

The Goethe Institute advertised a concert by classical pianist Peter Schmalfuss. I hadn't been to the Institute since I stopped taking classes two months before. Steve and I liked classical music and looked forward to the cultural opportunity. We took our seats in the small auditorium and greeted our seatmates. I assumed the woman next to me spoke German. *Great, a chance to use the language.*

"Guten abend," I ventured. Good evening.

"Comment allez vous?" How are you? She responded in French.

"Je vais bien. Parlez vous français?" I am well, do you speak French?

"Oui, je suis francaise," she said. Yes, I am French. *OK, I'll practice French.*

"Je suis Americaine." I am American.

Our brief conversation continued in English until the concert began. She spoke English so well it could have been her native tongue. So much for practicing a language. I had hoped she would indulge me with a short conversation in French. The beginning of the concert was a relief. I wrapped myself in the music like a warm blanket.

At the International English School, Mrs. Nguyen Noch Linh took exception to one of the children's books I bought for the school's small library, *The Five Chinese Brothers*, by Claire Huchet Bishop, with illustrations by Kurt Wiese. The popular retelling of a classic Chinese folktale first appeared in print in 1938 and received the Lewis Carroll Shelf Award in 1959. Every children's library collection in the States included copies. I thought donating an award-winning book would be well received, but Mrs. Nguyen dismissed it without hesitation.

"We do not need to know about Chinese," she said. "We already know enough about them."

I didn't get it. The ethnic Chinese made up a large part of the city's population. Moreover, many Vietnamese traditions originated in China. *What could she possibly object to?* I told Janet what happened, and she filled me in.

"That's normal," Janet said. "The struggle between China and Vietnam has been going on for centuries. Do you know about the Trung sisters?"

"I know about a street named Hai Ba Trung."

"Yes, that means two Trung women. In ancient times, the sisters opposed China's rule of Vietnam and became our first female military leaders. They are national heroines."

The light bulb flipped on. I'd naively chosen culturally insensitive reading material and would face repercussions. After that, nothing I proposed was acceptable to Mrs. Nguyen. She did not support me in the same way she did Carolyn, even though we both taught the same way.

"So, Mrs. Karen, whatever Mrs. Carolyn does you have to do?" she demanded.

"We are teaching the same program." I countered. "Everyone benefits from her experience."

"You have Janet. Perhaps that is enough. Yes?" she said, waving me off with a flick of her exquisitely manicured fingernails.

When I entered my classroom, I realized I'd been clenching my teeth, and my hands shook. The room seemed full of noise. Little Minh rushed over to show me a drawing he'd made, but I couldn't focus. Janet could tell I wasn't myself.

"Are you okay?"

"I'll be fine," I said. "Just need a minute to calm down."

Sandals slapped against tile as Patty carried our dinner into the dining room and placed the meal before us. Always soft-spoken, that evening, she seemed shy. I worried she had bad news for us.

"*Madame*," she said, hesitating, "my husband sister get married Thursday. *Madame* and *Monsieur* come to dinner after wedding?"

A relief! Nothing terrible. She just felt nervous asking us.

"Of course," Steve replied, "it would be an honor. We'd love to come."

The legal marriage ceremony took place at a courthouse. Afterward, the couple joined with both sets of parents and other family members at their respective homes for a private ceremony during which both the bride and the groom honored their parents by serving them tea.

They honored each other, their parents, and their ancestors' altar with a bow, a sign of respect and obedience to the first principle of traditional Confucian moral belief: responsibility to family. Then the banquet, *xi jiu*, pronounced "she joe," meaning happy wine, could commence.

The *xi jiu* for Patty's sister-in-law took place at a Chinese banquet hall in Cholon. Steve and I arrived to find a cheerfully crowded and inviting dining room. Colorful banners decorated the space: yellow and gold to symbolize wealth, and red, carrying the greater duty, as the symbol of love, success, happiness, luck, fertility, honor, and loyalty. Elaborately carved beams lined the ceiling, and decorative teak partitions divided the room into seating areas.

The bride was nowhere to be seen, but the animated groom commanded the center of attention. Perhaps he had just completed the "door games" or *chuangmen*, tests put to him by the bridesmaids to prove he was worthy of their friend. He smiled as he visited each table, talking and laughing with the guests.

The hostess showed us to an enormous round table with a proportionally large lazy Susan in its center. Thirteen of us, including two American men, sat around the table. We four were the only "round eyes" in the room. Chopsticks, napkins, plates, and soup bowls made up the place settings. Drinks arrived, followed by the first of eight courses. The number eight is symbolic. In Chinese, its pronunciation sounds like "good luck" or "prosperity."

Enticing odors emanated from the large platter of rice, vegetables, and fish carried to each table by a troop of servers. They placed the platters in the middle of the lazy Susan, and we helped ourselves using chopsticks.

All the food symbolized something—suckling pig, the bride's purity; chicken soup with the feet protruding from the tureen, peace, and unity. The savory soup was considered lucky because, in Chinese, the word "chicken" sounds like "good life."

Another delicacy presented a challenge. Thousand-year eggs,

made by covering hard-boiled eggs in gelatin and then burying them in clay pots for several months, tasted better than they looked and smelled. The white of the egg took on an almost solid black color, and they had the pungent odor of sulfur.

I hadn't spotted Patty when we arrived. After the meal, she approached us through the crowd. I hardly recognized her. Gone were her severe ponytail, pajama-style pants, *ao ba ba* (loose-fitting jacket), and rubber sandals. She looked glamorous in a traditional Chinese dress, *cheongsam,* made of blue and silver brocade. Her black hair framed her face in ringlets, and she wore silver high heels.

I stood to greet her as she neared our table. "Patty, you're so glamorous tonight. This is a lovely party."

A blush crept over her cheeks. "Come, *Madame*," she said, taking my arm. "You meet bride."

I followed her to a narrow teak door with Chinese symbols carved into its surface. Patty opened the door and led me into a dimly lit space the size of a broom closet. Being presented at court for a royal audience might have felt the same.

The bride sat on cushions surrounded by four older women who were close family members. She looked lovely in an embroidered pink silk gown, a sparkling tiara, and flowers in her hair. Patty introduced us, and we bowed to each other. I told her she looked beautiful, *ho lan*. The courtesies concluded, Patty returned me to the table for the dessert course—plump dumplings filled with sweet lotus paste, the symbol of fertility.

A slight commotion at the next table signaled the bride's arrival, escorted by one of the women who had been closeted with her. She had changed out of her elaborate gown into a short, tight-fitting pink *cheongsam*.

The guests stood to greet her, but she did not speak. Her companion said something in Chinese and gave everyone a red envelope from a tray she carried. We could guess what we were expected to do but looked for clues to be sure. When our table mates filled the envelopes with cash, Steve followed suit.

With Thanksgiving a few weeks away, thoughts of home and family celebrations brought waves of nostalgia. I'd taken all that for granted over the years. I now missed it more than anything—turkey with giblet gravy; candied sweet potatoes with marshmallows, which I ate too much of; bread stuffing moistened with juice from the turkey; my grandmother's pickled Seckel pears with cloves; cranberry sauce in the special cut-glass bowl; and Whitman's chocolates with the bottoms poked out by my mother looking for her favorites. I couldn't duplicate such things, or could I?

We had a family of sorts at church and decided to invite all nineteen American members for a more-or-less traditional Thanksgiving meal at the villa. But creating an American-style celebration in Vietnam came with one or two snags. Three days before Thanksgiving, I wondered if the dinner would happen.

Contractors like us had lost shopping privileges at the PX and commissary and no longer had easy access to traditional fixings. It made no sense, like everything else that happened there.

The temperamental refrigerator broke down . . . again. We had no ice or refrigeration. Each day brought more disasters. Then, church members stepped in to help bringing coolers of ice. Those who could still shop at the commissary cooked turkey, stuffing, and gravy for the feast. The single men arrived with pies their cooks had made. Others contributed extra plates and flatware. Patty candied sweet potatoes, and Yao helped prepare the other vegetables and served the meal.

The villa oozed merriment. We'd made a life in Saigon despite the stresses at work and the uncertainty of war. When everyone had gone,

I went to the kitchen to thank Patty and Yao. They, too, had left for the night. The kitchen was spotless. *Would I have been bold enough to invite so many if I'd had to cook and clean up myself? If I ever lose these two girls, I'll be lost.* Their next pay envelope included a big tip.

The post-Thanksgiving holiday seemed the perfect time to take a break and explore another part of Southeast Asia. Maps covered the dining room table. Where should we go first? So many intriguing destinations beckoned—Penang, Singapore, Kuala Lumpur, Bali, Bangkok, and Phuket. In the end, though, the obvious choice for our first adventure had to be Thailand. It was close and economical, and we'd already learned a little about it from friends.

We planned a one-week trip—two days in Bangkok, three days at the beach in Pattaya on the Gulf of Siam, and two more days in Bangkok before heading back to Saigon. Mr. Bei would get the exit/entry visas we'd need to leave and return. We trusted there'd be something to return to because, as far as we knew, nothing ever changed in Saigon. Until it did.

Chapter 12

Time is a Storm

December 1973

On December 3 at 2:30 a.m., the Viet Cong destroyed thirty gasoline tanks at the Nha Be fuel depot with rocket fire from across the river at Bien Hoa. The depot sat seven miles southeast of Saigon. Six hundred thousand barrels of gasoline went up in flames, eighty percent of South Vietnam's fuel. Black smoke from the fire spiraled high over the city and blended with the ever-present smog and billowing exhaust.

The effect on Saigon was immediate. Gas stations put up signs that read "*ngừng bán,*" stopped selling and rationing began. Taxi fares shot up. The price of a bicycle jumped from $70US to $100US. The number of motorized cyclos, cars, and motorbikes plummeted. Man-powered cyclos did a booming business, and the air became cleaner.

The city simmered with tension. But, news from the civilian-run American Radio Service reported nothing alarming, and we didn't have access to American newspapers. The embassy issued no statements. Consequently, we regarded the latest disruption as nothing more than a passing nuisance.

Worried friends and family wrote to ask if we were okay. Their news sources painted a dire picture. I understood their concern, but the media always dramatized everything. Saigon remained peaceful. We trusted our government's embassy to alert us of any danger.

One thing mattered to Mrs. Nguyen Noch Linh—money. By hiring teachers who spoke English as their native language, she could attract a large enrollment. Every week, she admitted more students and collected more tuition while complaining bitterly about the cost of supporting two sections of the Preparatory Class—mine and Carolyn Moore's.

By then, I'd come to believe Mrs. Nguyen purposely provoked me. The situation came to a head when Carolyn appeared at my classroom door one morning before the children arrived.

"Got a minute?" Carolyn asked. "We need to talk."

"Sure. What's on your mind?"

"Mrs. Nguyen. She's been asking me about some of the kids in your class. Wants to know how they're doing and if I think you're doing a good job. I don't know these kids. And I certainly can't comment on how you're doing. You should talk to her."

"Sure, but, you know, she and I don't get along. She seems bothered that you help me with lesson plans and gets her back up whenever I ask for the same support she gives you. But I can try."

"Listen, I'm happy to help you, but she needs to stop bothering me."

Mrs. Nguyen's insulting maneuver left me feeling belittled and ignored. Carolyn returned to her classroom, and I marched into Mrs. Nguyen's office, ready for battle. I couldn't do much about it if she didn't trust me. One way or another, though, I wanted the situation resolved.

"Mrs. Nguyen," I said. "Carolyn tells me you've been asking her about students in my class. Will you please come to me from now on? I interact with them every day. Either Janet or I can answer any questions you have. We know our students best."

"Why, of course. Is there anything else?' She could elicit anger easier than anyone I ever knew.

"Yes. If you want to know how the children and I are doing, you're welcome to visit my classroom and see for yourself."

"Thank you," she said, returning to whatever she'd been doing.

Mrs. Nguyen never visited my class or asked me about my students. She did, however, continue to question Carolyn. I couldn't think why I'd been sidelined. Was it because I lacked experience? Was it because of *"The Five Chinese Brothers?"* Or was it because I confronted her about overcrowded classrooms, an opinion I should probably have kept to myself?

With artifice and cunning, Mrs. Nguyen Noch Linh had made my job at the school untenable. She knew what angered me most and used it against me. I didn't see how I could continue to work there and decided to resign right after the Christmas assembly. Mrs. Nguyen accepted my resignation without comment. She had frayed my last nerve. Maybe that had been her goal all along.

I still had to come up with something for the Christmas assembly, a huge stress for me. I didn't have much experience with such things. The Girl Scout troop I belonged to as a schoolgirl sometimes put on plays, and I imagined myself having a part. Truth be told, when I auditioned, I flopped. I made it into my high school senior play, though, as one of the moon people in a production called "Mavis and the Moon Man," written by our math teacher.

Okay, think! Can I involve all the children somehow? Looking around the room, I spotted it. The whole class had created an art project we could use. Our packing box house. It reminded me of a children's song.

"In a cabin in the woods,
A little boy by the window stood.
Saw a rabbit hopping by,
Knocking at the door.

'Help me, help me, help me,' he said,
'Or the hunter will shoot me dead!'
'Little rabbit, come inside,
Safely we'll abide.'"

Hand movements accompanied the words, and the whole class could be involved. Their language skills weren't quite up to understanding what the words meant, but that presented another learning opportunity.

I taught them the song by drawing pictures on the blackboard to illustrate words like cabin and woods. I knocked on the blackboard to demonstrate what knock meant. For "help me," I threw my hands into the air, made my eyes very wide as if I were astonished to see a rabbit, and raised my voice a few octaves. The children loved it and got right into mimicking me. Janet and I designed costumes for the children to make—large cutout flowers, duck masks, and rabbit-ear headbands.

Next, we worked on acting out the story and positioning the children. The packing box house became the cabin, the main prop. The day of the performance, I stood on stage with the class as we sang and acted out our song. The audience applauded. Steve recorded the event for posterity with his Nikon. Although not strictly a Christmas theme, the performance did show compassion for the rabbit.

After the performance, one of Mrs. Nguyen's American male friends dressed up as Santa Claus and delivered gifts to all the children. I thought everyone would be excited to receive a present, but the fake beard and strange costume puzzled them. Mrs. Nguyen tried to give the children an American-style Christmas, but they hesitated to accept the brightly wrapped parcels. Did they understand the tradition?

Christmas assembly,
Saigon, 1973

Santa visits the classroom,
Saigon, 1973

With the administration's approval, I left my class at the Nguyen Noch Linh International English School in Janet's care. Although not a native English speaker—Mrs. Nguyen's preference—Janet was more than capable, and Carolyn offered her help should Janet ever need it.

I missed the children but knew they were in good hands. Coping with everyday Saigon life took emotional energy, and I needed every bit. Dealing with Mrs. Nguyen Noch Linh had taken too much of it.

In the American bubble that was Saigon, Steve convinced me to play tennis with him even though I warned him about my deficit in athletics. Anyone who knew me would agree. In school, I dreaded the obligatory gym class sports like badminton, volleyball, and basketball and endured them without much joy. Tennis offered something new. I felt ready to try, at least.

Steve bought equipment, and we went to the tennis courts at the Defense Attaché Office complex to try a game. My racquet was lightweight aluminum and felt solid in my hands as I swung it back and forth at imaginary targets. I almost looked forward to getting started. *Is it too late to reinvent myself?*

We attempted to play a game after Steve filled me in on the basic rules and scoring. He served, and I missed. He tried again and again, and I kept missing. When my racket finally connected with a pitiful pop off the rim, the ball hit the net. I wanted to play a decent game of tennis, but trial and error offered only slow going. Steve's impatience showed. He told me to take lessons.

I hired the tennis pro at *Cercle Sportif Saigonais,* Jean Pierre de Lulanier, a wiry guy of mixed Vietnamese/French heritage who spoke only French and Vietnamese.

To assess my skill level, Jean Pierre held the first lesson on one of the courts in front of the club's large veranda. He tossed a gentle serve over the net, and when I failed to return it, I blew my cover. No fancy tennis whites could hide the fact of my beginner status. He moved my lessons to one of the handball courts, and I viewed it as a relief and a kindness. I didn't care to embarrass myself, and him, in front of the general membership.

Inside the handball court, Jean Pierre tossed a ball to me. I missed.

"Regardez la balle," he said, pointing to his eyes and then at the ball to indicate his meaning—watch the ball.

I did as instructed and tried to aim so the ball struck the wall above the line painted there to represent the net. The ball was too low.

"Serrez la racket," he said. Tighten up on the racket. He tossed another ball, and I hit it better that time.

"Et maintenant, trois bonnes balles." And now, three good balls.

He tossed ball after ball until I returned three good ones, and the lesson ended. The same routine continued at every lesson. It appeared I would be practicing on the handball court for a very long time. I started out to learn tennis, but I was learning perseverance.

The people of Saigon possessed perseverance in spades. Despite the turmoil going on around them—the nightly bombings on the outskirts of the city, the fighting in the highlands and delta, sandbags and armed military on every street corner, electricity cut off one day a week, and a midnight curfew—the residents of that city continued to teach tennis, build buildings, go to school, run shops, clean houses, and patronize restaurants. An American woman I knew opened an antique shop in the center of downtown.

We, expats, filled our days with familiar routines, making a living, and maintaining traditions. The "Pearl of the Orient" still exuded some of its charm in cafés and restaurants like *Ramuntcho,* where we went for langoustines with rich Chantilly cream, *Guillaume Tell* for the delectable *Grand Marnier* souffle, and *Givral* for buttery *croissants.*

Meanwhile, the Viet Cong ambushed a joint U.S./South Vietnamese team fifteen miles southwest of Saigon. The team was engaged in a Missing in Action recovery mission. Captain Richard Morgan Rees and a South Vietnamese pilot were killed in the attack. Four other Americans were wounded. As a result, the U.S. suspended all MIA field recovery efforts indefinitely.

Things took a turn for the worse on the home front, as well. Patty surprised me early one morning with news that I hoped would never come.

"*Madame*, I no can work it," she told me. "I have to leave house."

"What? Why?" Only "devastated" could describe how I felt. Our trusted, loyal, capable Patty wanted to leave us? I didn't want to hear it. No!

"Yao no like work here. We have to go. I sorry. I like work here."

"Okay," I argued, scrambling for an alternate outcome, "if Yao wants to leave, couldn't you bring someone else to work with you? Why do you have to leave, too?"

Had I done something to offend them? Had Steve? What on earth would I do without them? They represented part of my Saigon family. Patty ran the villa perfectly. I trusted her absolutely. I didn't understand why Yao couldn't leave by herself if she wanted to. But Patty was firm, her mind made up. She explained that we were not the cause of her decision. Instead, I had run into a cultural impasse.

The problem had to do with ethics, culture, and family obligations. Those delicate Confucian rules balanced life's decisions. Patty brought Yao with her to the job. Yao had never done domestic work, and Patty directed her. Several problems existed with that arrangement.

Yao, being older, resented taking instructions from someone younger. They argued during the day. Moreover, Yao didn't like the work. When Patty went home to her family, Yao spent lonely nights by herself in the maid's quarters over the carport. Even her new, modern, private tiled bathroom didn't sway her.

Ultimately, it came down to the fact that Patty had convinced Yao to take this job and bore responsibility for Yao's unhappiness. If Yao wanted to leave, Patty had to go as well. If she didn't, there would be trouble between their families, for they were cousins.

Losing them felt like being abandoned at sea, but I couldn't quarrel with family loyalty. Patty told me privately that she would return to work for us if we someday had a smaller place she could handle by herself. At least I had salvaged her trust.

Patty did not leave us helpless. To take her place, as if that were even possible, she brought us a heavy-set, mature, ethnic Chinese woman named Aw Som, who spoke French, Chinese, and Vietnamese. She'd pulled her thin black hair into a tight bun that emphasized her round face. Shrewd eyes took my measure. *This woman has a mind of her own.*

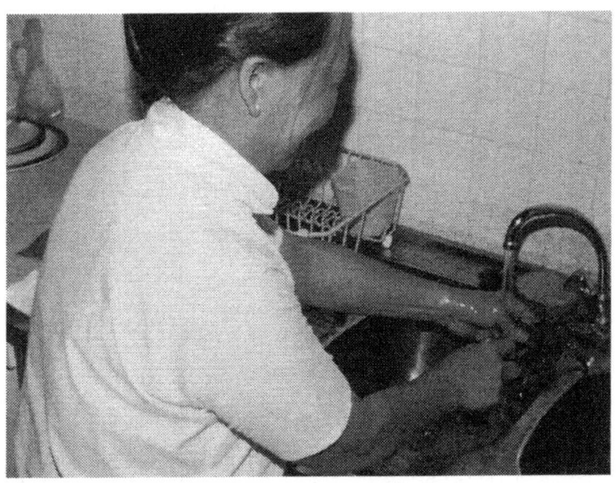

Aw Som cleaning crabs for dinner, Saigon, 1973

As part of a package deal, a young woman, Ching, and an older woman, Muoi, arrived with her to serve as maids. Muoi spoke Chinese, Vietnamese, and English sprinkled with French. Ching was taller than the others and slender. She spoke only Chinese and Vietnamese. The idea that these women could speak two or three languages bowled me over.

I assumed Aw Som managed the other two, but by this time, I just hoped for the best. Of course, I could reject them all, but then

I'd have no one. The timing couldn't have been worse. We had a New Year's Eve party already in the works. Time to shop for new help didn't exist. I was stuck.

Christmas had always been a special holiday for our families, and we thought putting up a Christmas tree would create some holiday cheer. The PX had them, but once again, we'd lost the privilege of shopping there, so we went local. The chosen tree stood four feet tall. Clever hands had fabricated it from thick rope frayed at the ends to suggest pine needles, then spray-painted it green. I put it on a rattan side table in the living room, a soldier ready to do his duty.

We found familiar decorations for sale all over the city and bought a few of everything— shiny glass balls the color of gemstones, strings of colored lights, garlands of plastic greenery. We also had some unique ornaments we'd purchased in Bangkok—miniature straw baskets perfect for holding pieces of candy, pink shrimp and green frogs made of straw, and a beaded Thai silk angel for the top.

Back home, we would have gathered with my family in my parents' cozy living room for a gift-opening ritual, one at a time, handed out by a young nephew or niece. With its high ceilings and tile floors, the villa was anything but cozy. I wanted to call my parents on Christmas, but we could make only collect calls to the States from the villa's phone. The time difference would mean reaching them in the middle of the night.

We could go downtown to the PTT (Postal, Telephone, Telegraph) office to avoid making a collect call. Due to the time difference, that would mean placing the call after the midnight curfew. It wasn't possible. Besides, if the connection were faulty, that would be more disappointing than not calling at all. We tabled the idea of a phone call.

A large crowd gathered at our New Year's Eve open house—Alice Fabré brought her husband, Carolyn Moore brought hers, people from church came, classmates from the French Institute were there, and Steve's co-workers all made an appearance. Aw Som and her helpers prepared a delectable assortment of *hors d'oeuvres* and sweets. We'd hired waitresses from USAID II to tend bar. The party rollicked on, but everyone remembered the midnight curfew and left for home as the magic hour approached. The festive spirit left with them.

"I feel like we're living in an alternate universe," I said to Steve when we were alone.

"Yeah, it's like we're actors in a bad war movie where only the audience knows what's happening."

"Wish we could see the future. Then maybe we'd know what to do."

"Well, we're here now. Happy New Year," Steve said and kissed me.

We rang in 1974, just the two of us.

Chapter 13

Opportunities Brilliantly Disguised

January 1974

Troop repositioning continued in 1974 as the armies of South and North Vietnam jockeyed for advantage. Spasms of Viet Cong guerrilla raids targeted lines of communication, villages, cities, and outposts throughout the South, with gains and losses on both sides.

Terrifying thoughts of an attack on Saigon filled my mind. Steve tried to give me perspective.

"What do you think would happen to us if the VC launched an all-out attack on Saigon?" I asked him.

"Where's this coming from? Have rumors been going around at the American Women's Association? Has Betty Ainsley been talking to you? You know she's a drama queen."

"No, it's just that, you know, we hear things. Nobody knows for sure, but what's to stop them? What if we couldn't get out of here and back to the States? Where would we go? Would we be refugees? Or would we end up prisoners, or worse, dead?"

Saying it out loud brought my fears to the surface. My mind raced in a confusing circle with no end and no answers. I scared myself.

"Maybe Thailand would take us in as alien refugees? Cambodia is out of the question. Thailand would be our only hope. Does anyone at the embassy realize how many of us non-government civilians are in the country? Are we accounted for?"

Steve took my hand. "Listen to me," he said, "no matter what you hear, the city is secure. Otherwise, I'm sure USAID or the mission warden would notify us. I'm sure there are evacuation plans in place if it comes to that."

He sounded so calm, so sure, so trusting. My emotions were too close to the surface, and my voice shook. I paced the floor in the upstairs den, too on edge to sit still.

"We aren't the only ones at risk here. What about the people in the highlands? How can they be safe in their own country? Where will they go if they're driven off the land they've farmed for generations? Into cities like so many of their countrymen, becoming beggars or gangsters? How much resentment must they feel towards foreigners, like us, who brought about the ruin of their country and their way of life? There could be riots."

"There aren't going to be riots. Stop making yourself crazy."

Of course, no one could know the outcome, but Steve, always cautious and pragmatic, prepared an inventory of our household goods, just in case. *We'll have plenty of time to pack up and leave. Won't we? Nothing to worry about.* Little did we know.

The fuel shortage caused by the attack on the Nha Be depot meant we ran out of propane for the stove. Aw Som fed us cold meals for a few days until a new supply arrived. Soon afterward, the scent of succulent chicken soup wafting from the open kitchen door filled the villa. I'd picked up a nasty upper respiratory infection and craved comfort food.

Dr. Lester Bush, an M.D., arrived the same day. Dr. Bush, a friend and member of our church, was attached to the embassy and made house calls for church members. He examined me and found nothing serious. He thought my infection developed because the air conditioner made the bedroom too cold at night.

"Try wearing socks to bed," he said. "Or turn up the AC."

I had to get well. My friend, June Eldridge, and I planned to leave for Bangkok in a few weeks.

June and I stood out because we were always the tallest women in the room. Her husband, Lou, worked for USAID, and they'd been posted to Bangkok before. The upcoming visit would be a sentimental journey for June.

Expats jumped in and out of war-torn Vietnam at will, their passports like golden tickets to Willie Wonka's chocolate factory. Only wealthy Vietnamese could do the same; most lacked the golden ticket. The disparity created a barrier between us that was difficult to cross. *What do they really think of us?*

June and I arrived in Bangkok in the evening. We stayed with a woman named Emma, whom we knew from church. She lived in Bangkok most of the time while her husband worked in Vietnam's central highlands. When he came to Saigon, she joined him for a few days. He said he was an AID worker but never talked about his job. We knew not to ask. He probably couldn't have told us anyway, but it was exciting to imagine him as a spy or a covert operative on a secret mission.

The first afternoon in Bangkok, June, took me on an adventure while Emma went to her volunteer job at a local school.

"I'm taking you to meet Walter," June said when I asked where we were going.

"Who's Walter?"

"You'll love him. Wait and see."

June hailed a taxi and gave the driver the address—5/10 Soi Nana Tai, Sukhumvit. Walter, a Thai national, was the proprietor of Walter's Gems, a jewelry store of international reputation. We entered the showroom to the tinkle of chimes, and Walter appeared from behind a curtain at the back of the showroom. His khaki trousers and linen shirt looked freshly laundered and ironed. He wore his full head of dark hair slicked back from his forehead.

A warm smile creased his face as he recognized his old friend, June, and scurried over to welcome us. June and Walter exchanged a bow and the usual pleasantries. Then he greeted me warmly as if I were also an old friend.

"May I offer you ladies a cup of tea . . . or something stronger?" he asked with a mischievous wink.

"Plain tea, please," we said. While we waited for him to bring our drinks, June and I admired the dazzling jewels in the display case. June chose an exquisite bauble, but I hesitated to commit. The prices, though inexpensive compared to the States, were still beyond what I felt comfortable spending.

June and Walter concluded their business, and Walter invited us to see his new house. He locked the store and led us to a Mercedes-Benz parked in the back. The drive to his neighborhood took only ten minutes. He parked the car, and we all stood in the road looking up at a structure resembling a traditional American frame dwelling, which was not what I expected.

The plain interior featured bland, ordinary furniture covered in plastic. The acrid smell of new construction hung in the air. That house was Walter's pride and joy. He pointed out that his two children had their own rooms.

His family was out of town, and after the house tour, Walter insisted we be his guests for dinner at one of his favorite restaurants. How could we refuse? At the restaurant, everyone seemed to know him. A hostess in traditional Thai dress—silk, floor-length wrap skirt, and short silk jacket in jewel tones—escorted us to the best table. I looked forward to one of the spicy Thai curries I'd enjoyed when Steve and I visited Bangkok in November and consulted Walter about which one to order.

"Oh no, *Madame*," Walter said. "You are much too delicate to eat such spicy food. I will choose the perfect dish for you, satay."

As his guest, I felt I couldn't argue the point. But his comment puzzled me. At nearly five feet eight, one hundred thirty-some pounds of sturdy German/English stock, I had never felt delicate a day in my life. I wondered what Walter saw that I didn't.

The satay couldn't have been more delicious—cubes of tender grilled chicken threaded onto bamboo skewers accompanied by a mildly spicy peanut dipping sauce. A cone of coconut rice, a side of vinegary cucumber relish, and slices of lime completed the heavenly meal.

June, Emma, and I spent the rest of the week shopping and sightseeing, usually ending up exhausted back at Emma's comfortable new apartment complex. An inviting swimming pool graced the back garden. On our final afternoon, tired and hot from tromping around Bangkok, I slipped into my swimsuit and went to the pool. It looked like I'd have it all to myself.

The water revived me. I floated on the surface, as weightless as a leaf, gazing up at the palm fronds swaying gently on a bit of breeze against the perfect blue sky. I couldn't help feeling astonished to find myself, a farm kid, in such an exotic place. From digging potatoes to a posh Bangkok swimming pool! Who would have guessed?

—

Tet, the three-day Lunar New Year celebration, began on January 23. It was the most important holiday of the year—a time to leave troubles behind, anticipate better times, and take steps to ensure good fortune for the family. My Vietnamese tutor, Pauline, had served as our guide to local customs since Patty and Yao left.

"Remember, your maids expect three days off for the holiday," Pauline said. "They will also expect one month's pay as a bonus. How long have they worked for you?"

"Only a few weeks."

"Okay, you can give them less."

"What else do I need to know?" I always worried about making a cultural misstep.

Tet involved many traditions—clearing one's debts, tidying ancestor's tombs, cleaning the house from top to bottom, cooking special food, preparing the five-fruits tray for the family's ancestral altar, and retelling legends.

One of the best-known legends told the story of the kitchen god, Ong Tao, who rode a carp to Heaven on the day before the new year and reported on the state of the household. Heaven would grant the family good fortune if the home were in tip-top shape. Pauline warned me not to sweep the house on the first day of Tet because I might sweep good luck away.

The importance of yellow and red in Vietnamese culture dates back thousands of years.

Yellow represented royalty, wealth, prosperity, and change. Red was the color of happiness, love, luck, and celebration. The nation's flag displayed three red stripes running through the center of a bright gold field to symbolize the common blood running through South Vietnam's three regions: north, central, and the delta.

It was no wonder that yellow and red were crucial to celebrating the Lunar New Year. An enormous flower market opened on Nguyen

Hue Boulevard, blocking it to all but foot traffic. Golden marigolds and red chrysanthemums stood in buckets of water, waiting to adorn homes. Nearby, vendors spread orange and yellow fruit on tarps lining the streets.

The mandarin oranges on the tree in our kitchen courtyard turned a vibrant color. Aw Som soaked the ripe fruit in salt water and then left it in the sun for a few days. Afterward, Muoi and Ching mashed it into a paste from which they made lucky medicine to treat a sore throat.

A small wild apricot tree called *hoang mai,* decorated the villa's front garden. If its bright yellow flowers bloomed during Tet, people believed the coming year would bring prosperity and good fortune. But the superstitious Vietnamese left nothing to chance.

To ensure the tree flowered, Patty explained before she left that all the leaves must come off the tree one month before Tet began. I thought nature would take care of that and was surprised when Patty insisted on showing me the proper way to remove leaves from branches.

A dirty film covered the tree's leaves because there'd been no rain for two months. As Patty and I worked together on the task, our fingers turned blacker and blacker. One month later, yellow blossoms appeared right on time.

The nuclear family reserved the first day of Tet for their private celebration. Friends and relatives visited on the second day, and the third day was dedicated to honoring teachers. The first person to visit a home during Tet determined the family's luck in the coming year.

No one wanted their first visitor to be someone who had been sick or suffered a business loss. Some heads of households left nothing to chance and exited the house shortly before midnight on the eve of Tet, re-entering just afterward to be the first person to arrive.

Children expected red envelopes full of lucky money from their parents. Mirrors, tied at the top with red velvet ribbons, hung in every house to catch lucky light. The bigger the mirror, the more lucky light one might catch. In the shops, a riot of lucky red decorations replaced Christmas ornaments—red lanterns, red banners wishing "*Chúc may mắn*," good luck, and strings of firecrackers.

Flower market on Nguyen Hue Boulevard during Tet,
Saigon, 1974

A parade on the last day of Tet, featuring bright-colored Lion/Dragon creatures and plenty of firecrackers to scare away evil spirits, would always weave along the main streets. The event drew huge crowds. I wanted to go, but it wasn't to be. Mindful of the Tet Offensive of 1968 and recent VC activity close to Saigon, Ambassador Martin directed Americans to stay away from the parade. Firecrackers could mask the sound of gunshots.

However, a visit to the flower market before the first day of Tet met with no objections. The Vietnamese believed that the more yellow and red they placed in their homes, the better chance they had for a prosperous future. Flowers offered one more way to accomplish that goal. Aw Som brought home a small bouquet of daisies dyed red. We hoped for a lucky year.

—

My relationship with Ching and Aw Som hadn't gone well. Aw Som smoked non-stop, even while she prepared meals. I couldn't be sure there were no ashes in our food, and I didn't like the smell of tobacco in the house. My request for her to stop went unheeded. Worse, she didn't account for the market money. I didn't trust her.

I came upon Ching one day cutting her fingernails with my expensive sewing scissors that she'd taken from the bureau in the den. *Has she been searching through our stuff?*

I couldn't catch my breath—a shimmer of suspicion and nerves burned beneath my rib cage. I confronted her. "What are you doing?"

Ching, startled, thrust her chin in the air and declared, *"Muoi nói dể làm điều đó,"* Muoi said to do it. All I understood was Muoi's name.

I put out my hand. Ching deposited the scissors into it.

"Don't do it again," I said through clenched teeth.

Muoi? The one I trust? I need to get to the bottom of this.

Laundry waved like colored prayer flags on the rooftop clothesline. Muoi turned when I called her name.

"Stop for a minute, please," I said. "I want to talk to you."

"*Nous* work okay?" My work is okay? *Nous* in French means "we," but Muoi used it to refer to herself.

"Your work is fine. I just talked to Ching. Did you tell her to take my sewing scissors?" I showed her the scissors.

"Che cha! No, *Madame*. Ching blame *Nous* all time. Say take more *Madame* things, too. *Nous* afraid tell *Madame, Monsieur*."

I went into my bedroom and closed the door. I needed time alone.

Who's telling the truth—Muoi, the reserved, industrious one, or Ching, already exposed as a culprit? Muoi doesn't make trouble and does her work well. I caught Ching in the act. A minor offense, but where will it lead if I let it go? Has Ching stolen from us before, and

I didn't notice? Steve and I live in a communication vacuum, and some or all of the women who work in our home are taking advantage of us. I have to bring this up with Steve.

After dinner, I told him about the incident with Ching, the problem with Aw Som, and my conversation with Muoi.

"Sounds like Muoi is the victim of the other two. What do you want to do?" he asked.

"I'd like Muoi to stay. I believe I can trust her and she likes working for us. The other two have to go, and soon."

"If that's what you want, it's okay with me. Want me to handle it?"

"No, I'll figure something out."

"Okay, but be careful. Remember what happened with Patty and Yao? I don't know if you can single out Muoi to stay. Aw Som and Ching will lose face if you try that. Then Muoi could be in more trouble."

After breakfast the following day, I told all three that I no longer needed them. I gambled that Muoi might find a way to stay on her own. They gathered their belongings, and I held the door open as they trooped out together. Muoi left last. As she passed me, she whispered in a voice barely audible, "*Nous* come back." She understood and let me know I wouldn't be without help. Heaven knew I needed it—both the help and the reassurance.

In the following weeks, I tried to keep up with the cleaning as best I could. We sent the laundry out and accepted invitations to dinner or went to restaurants.

What have I done? How will I find someone else? If Muoi comes back, will I take her back?

Dismissing the maids had seemed right, but their leaving left me feeling defenseless. *Is this how the Vietnamese felt when the American military left them to fend for themselves?*

Chapter 14

Times in the Darkness

February 1974

What the framers of the Paris Peace Accords created was, in effect, a cease-fire intended to provide breathing space for South Vietnam's military to resupply itself, supported by generous aid from the United States. Under the terms of the Accords, Hanoi would release American prisoners of war and agree that the South could choose its government by free elections. North Vietnamese troops would continue to occupy and control regions in the South they already held, and the United States would withdraw all remaining American ground forces. U.S. President Richard M. Nixon assured South Vietnam's President Nguyen Van Thieu that the United States would swiftly and severely retaliate against North Vietnam should the communist country violate the cease-fire.

—

South Vietnam's Highway Administration District Offices, located throughout the country, could provide Roy Jorgensen Associates engineers with the kind of information they needed to complete the reorganization plan: how many available staff, how much equipment on hand, how much more was needed, budget requirements, how much repair work the roads and bridges required.

Years of heavy bombing had damaged much of the South's highway system. The U.S. Army Corps of Engineers had maintained the country's infrastructure until the troop withdrawal, and then USAID hired RJA to pick up the slack.

An advisory issued by the embassy urged Americans not to travel outside Saigon. In early February, against the backdrop of a country where no territory was safe, Steve and fellow staff engineer, Dick Kline, planned a fact-finding trip to the District Office in Da Nang, 600 miles north of Saigon.

"I don't understand why Chittim approved a trip up there," I said. "Isn't he worried about safety? Besides, I thought everybody was supposed to stay in town?"

"He said that advisory is just a precaution . . . keeps people from leaving the city for no reason."

"You've heard the chatter. Hanoi and the Viet Cong have been active south of the DMZ lately. What about that?"

"Look, Karen, I know you're worried," Steve said, hugging me close, "but if Dick and I don't find out what the district engineers in that province need, we'll never get anywhere with the project requirements. It's only for three days. Knowing you, you'll find plenty to keep yourself busy."

"Keeping busy isn't a problem. If something goes wrong, there's no way for us to contact each other."

"Nothing's going to go wrong. You know how it is. People hear stuff, but the situation's been stable."

"Let's hope it stays that way."

I accepted that Steve had to make the three-day trip. What choice did I have? Still, I didn't feel comfortable about it. He'd be 600 miles closer to possibly hostile territory.

Is there any fighting around Da Nang?

I almost wished I'd kept my teaching job to occupy my mind with something other than worry.

They'll be back in three days. They'll be fine, surely.

The American Radio Service announced that South Vietnamese ground forces launched a successful preemptive strike on the Tri Phap, a marshy wasteland at the end of a maze of canals bordering Cambodia. The battle prevented Hanoi from establishing a base there and interrupted one of North Vietnam's many supply routes from Cambodia into the region. That section of the province lay forty-three miles south of Saigon in the Mekong Delta. Steve and Dick arrived back to the hopeful news.

Buzzzz! Someone waited at the front gate. I hurried out to open it, and there she stood, Muoi, true to her word. I was so happy to see her that I could have hugged her but refrained.

Is hugging acceptable in her ethnic Chinese culture? How well do you have to know a person before they are comfortable with a show of affection?

A younger woman peered over Muoi's shoulder, gazing at me wide-eyed as if I were from another planet.

"*Madame,*" Muoi said. "*Nous* come back work." She pointed to her companion, "This Jiao. She help."

"You'd better come in off the street before a Honda runs you over." I motioned them through the gate and into the villa. "We'll talk."

The women followed me into the kitchen.

"I'm happy to see you, Muoi, and your friend . . . Jiao, right? Tell me about her."

"Yes, Jiao. She *hai mươi*—twenty years old, I translated—and help *nous* clean house, cook little bit, too. She young. Work good. *Nous* old. *Nous năm mươi*—fifty. *Nous* cook, *allez* market, do laundry."

Muoi's long, salt-and-pepper hair intrigued me. It wound around itself several times to form a tight bun at the back of her head. *How does she get it to stay that way?*

She had a ready smile and delighted in chattering to me in her rich *mélange* of French, English, Chinese, and Vietnamese.

Taller than Muoi, Jiao seemed pleasant and spoke a little English. She might have been Muoi's relative but didn't say. Like Muoi, she kept her long black hair tied back. Her white work tunic and black pants were spotless.

Should I hire them? I don't know Jiao, but I do know Muoi well enough. Maybe I should talk it over with Steve first? Wait . . . no. We've been without help for two weeks, and we need someone. Whatever happens, I'll handle it.

I hired them both.

L-R: Muoi and Jiao, Nguyen Dinh Chieu villa, Saigon, 1974

"*Nous allez* market," Muoi announced before she headed out to buy food each day. She prepared basic fare but wanted to learn new dishes. I never knew where she found the French recipe cards. Beautiful, full-color photographs of delectable pastries illustrated each recipe.

"Look, *Madame*," she said, full of excitement. She fanned the cards for me to see. "*Nous* make *tarte*." Her finger pointed to a lovely-looking cream pie.

"That looks delicious. *Monsieur* and I would like that."

"*Madame* help?"

"Okay, but you have the directions on the card. Why do you need my help?"

"*Nous* no read French."

"Muoi, can you read Chinese or Vietnamese?"

"*Oui, nous* read Chinese, Vietnamese. No read English, no read French."

"Don't worry. We'll make pies together."

I knew how to make a mean pie crust and started by teaching Muoi my secret method. The shortening had to be chilled and then cut into the flour with two chilled knives in a chilled bowl. Pie crust is delicate and can't be handled too much, or it will lose its flakiness. Muoi learned fast, and together, we made all kinds of pies—apple, pumpkin, coconut cream—much to Steve's delight.

Foods I thought I didn't care for became favorites—earthy-sweet red beets accompanied by rich roasted chicken and the salty umami of cabbage soup. Garlicky fried rice with fresh, green snow peas and plump shrimp. Deep-fried pork spring rolls with pungent, spicy fermented fish sauce, locally known as *cha gio* with *nước mam*.

Muoi also served us tasty dishes containing ingredients from her culture, but soup with pork skin was far too different for either Steve or me. Sometimes, though, she'd ask before preparing a dish.

"*Madame* like dog?" Muoi said one evening as Steve and I finished the last bites of our meal.

Forks froze midway to open mouths. Brows shot up. Steve and I looked at each other, speechless. The air quivered with the possibility of a severe misunderstanding. Locals were known to eat dogs.

"Dog, Muoi?' I said as calmly as I could.

"Yes, dog . . . *dog*," she insisted, repeating the word louder each time.

"I . . . d-don't understand," I stammered.

"You know, dog . . . quack, quack."

Smiles . . . laughter . . . relief!

"Yes, Muoi, we like duck," I said, with emphasis.

A few days later, a succulent roasted duck with steamed water spinach, pickled carrot/parsnip salad, and soft, buttery rice graced our table.

Muoi, a dear soul devoted to us and trustworthy, went out of her way to please. Late one night, she noticed me scraping the last few cookie crumbs from the box and immediately went out to buy more cookies.

Roy Jorgensen and Associates had two projects in Vietnam, VN1 and VN2. Steve, at twenty-nine, was the youngest member of the VN1 team. Don Burgess, at twenty-six, was the youngest member of the VN2 team. They were two ships fighting against the current in a sea of older men whose outdated ideas, garnered from long years working in various state highway departments, were a constant source of shared frustration.

Don, a lean, serious, bespectacled guy with reddish-brown hair, first came to Saigon as a Navy ensign in 1969. In 1970, he met and married Dinh Thi Viet Nga, who worked in his office.

Nga came into the world in a suburb of Saigon called Long Bien. Her life played out against a backdrop of war where bits of bad news dropped along with the bombs. When she was thirteen, her oldest brother, Hung, an officer in the Army of the Republic of South Vietnam (ARVN), was killed in action. In 1970, when she was nineteen, Nga met and married Don. Three years later, she learned North Vietnam held her younger brother, Minh, an ARVN soldier, in a prisoner-of-war camp.

Don and Nga moved to the States in 1971 and started a family. Like most Vietnamese, Nga had strong ties to her parents and siblings still in Saigon and wanted to go home. When Don's tour of duty ended, he accepted the job with Roy Jorgensen and Associates because it meant returning to Vietnam.

By the time Steve and I met them in 1973, they had a daughter, Marian. An unusual name for an American/Vietnamese child, I thought. At twenty-three, Nga was a pretty woman with a broad, radiant smile who spoke English well. Her long auburn hair, an anomaly in Vietnam, identified her as someone who ventured outside her culture.

She and Don attended company functions, but I didn't see much of them otherwise. Nga preferred time with her family to dinner parties, and Don was fine with that.

Steve and Don, however, developed a camaraderie that turned into a life-long friendship. Their youth gave them something in common. Over lunch, they'd let off steam about the coarse and clumsy way Lew Chittim ran the projects. They talked about their families and discussed their hobbies. They created a safe harbor to share thoughts about the war, politics, and the project. In Saigon, having a close friend could save one's sanity.

Quiet days, filled with activity, replaced worried ones. Steve joined a weekly after-work bowling team, became the league president, and met with the other officers to rework the league's constitution.

At work, he labored to make headway. The Defense Attaché's Office unexpectedly restored our PX and commissary privileges. *Where is the logic?*

Tennis and *gymnastique* at the *Cercle Sportif* took up my mornings, afternoon French classes, consumed the rest of my days.

I found two sponsors and joined the *Cercle Hippique*, a riding club. The mount they saddled for me was, like the rest of the "Saigon ponies," so small I felt like I was riding a child's hobby horse, with my feet nearly dragging on the ground and my knees bent halfway to my shoulders. I was an experienced rider, comfortable on a horse, and wanted to prove it, but feeling absurd and foolish seated on that creature, I gave up the idea as a lost cause.

Muoi and Jiao settled in, and the villa returned to humming along. On weekends, Steve and I took advantage of movies at the DAO complex and swimming at the *Cercle Sportif.* There were dinners with friends and frequent visits to favorite restaurants. Hole-in-the-wall cafés served succulent grilled shrimp on sweet sugar cane, transparent rice noodles seasoned with fresh mint, delicate lemon grass soup, and, of course, the ubiquitous *phở*—robust noodle soup with pork. We relished all of it, surprised by the lavish side of life in the middle of a war.

The battle at Trí Phap, which began at the end of January, was still raging at the end of February, but the American Radio Service reported no new hostilities. A cautious sense of security permeated the city. It was a time of excitement and adventure, a time to savor, for beneath the scrim of dust and smog, the light of the exotic, romantic city that Saigon had once been flickered like a bulb about to go out.

Chapter 15

Worry Never Robs Tomorrow of its Sorrow

March 1974

The battle at the Tri Phap boiled over into March. In Saigon, the sense of normalcy we'd enjoyed took a setback. A month after Steve's commissary and PX privileges were restored, they were rescinded again. Perhaps the powers that be decided government contractors outside the United States who were allowed a hefty income tax break weren't eligible for more perks. Steve fell into that category.

How had we slipped through the cracks before?

Nothing made sense.

In reality, the PX and commissary had prevented us from acknowledging the whole truth of our circumstances. Regular, easy access to American goods masked the fact that we lived in a bubble. Like a hologram, the United States superimposed itself on Saigon to the extent that the city had become almost invisible. We existed in an alternate universe outside the realm of the Vietnamese and came together only on a superficial level.

The loss of privileges thrust Steve and me more firmly into the world of expats, trading in local currency, the *dong*—sometimes referred to by its former French name *piastre*—rather than dollars. Five hundred ninety *dong* equaled one U.S. dollar.

We frequented the black market for American products, household goods, and food items, like peanut butter, that fetched high prices. The bargaining technique I'd worked so hard to perfect didn't work anymore. I'd walk away after refusing a vendor's first price but wasn't always called back as before. If I wouldn't pay, another expat would.

Throughout our time in Vietnam, Steve and I experienced nondescript maladies that subsided over time, only to flare up again. Steve suffered from allergies, and he'd been complaining of sinus congestion, stomach cramps, loss of appetite, and exhaustion since the end of February. I'd never seen him so sick.

Dr. Lester Bush stopped in to check on him and diagnosed a bacterial infection of the stomach, a sinus infection, and a sore throat.

"These should make you feel better," Dr. Bush said, handing over a bottle of antibiotics from his embassy cache.

"Say, Lester, can you recommend a good dentist?" I asked. If we needed medical attention, we probably also needed to have our teeth checked. The last time we saw a dentist was over a year ago.

"Yvonne, my wife, uses Dr. Phuong. All the embassy wives go to him. He graduated from dental school in France and has an office not far from here," Lester said.

A cyclo took me to Dr. Phuong's office for a get-acquainted chat. The sprightly dentist, tall for a Vietnamese man, stood eye-to-eye with me at five feet seven and three-quarter inches. He combed his sparse black hair straight back over his round head. He looked younger than I expected. With a bounce in his step, he showed me around the office and explained his routine procedures in proficient English.

"Everything will be just like in America," he said. I made an appointment for a checkup the following week.

When I arrived, Dr. Phuong seated me in a comfortable examination room that was, as he claimed, just like in America. He cleaned my teeth, examined them thoroughly, tapping here and there, and said I needed three fillings. I felt comfortable with that, and he won me over by painlessly administering Novocain.

"You see," he said with great pride when he'd finished, "I have used the Johnson & Johnson product, just like in America."

Other than the *Army Times* and the *Stars and Stripes*, which published articles of interest to the military community, newspapers available in Saigon lacked news of the world in English. The *New York Times* and the *Washington Post* had bureaus in town, but those newspapers were published in the States.

Friends returning from home leave brought back American newspapers and passed them around. It didn't matter that the news was stale. It was the latest, as far as we were concerned. Sometimes, an article became the source of rumors.

The *New York Times* on March 20 reported, "The Defense Department is asking Congress for urgent new military aid to South Vietnam, and the American Ambassador in Saigon is warning that the 'people of the world' will be exposed to 'enormous dangers' if the

United States fails to provide wholehearted support for President Nguyen Van Thieu. 'Those who dare to question the continuing United States military effort,' says Ambassador Graham Martin, 'are only succumbing to the insidious influence of Communist North Vietnam.'"

An article such as that made us wonder why South Vietnam needed more assistance. *Isn't the war going well for them? What are the enormous dangers the ambassador speaks of?* It sounded dire to think people in Washington might succumb to communist influence. Did the ambassador believe that? It was a matter of opinion.

A week later, relaxing before dinner in the upstairs den, Steve had good news for me.

"How would you like to go home for Christmas?" he asked.

"C'mon, don't joke about things like that."

"No joke. We're eligible for home leave after six months in country. That's November, eight months from now. We could take all of December off. Chittim told me today."

"You know I would love that. It will be eighteen months since we've seen our families. If we had a month, maybe we could fit in sightseeing along the way."

"Sure, why not? Think about what you'd like to do. Don't mention it to your folks just yet . . . in case something comes up and we can't do it."

My mind swam with possibilities. I lost sleep. So many tempting scenarios presented themselves. Steve brought home a route map from the Pan Am office downtown, and I looked for places to stop over for a couple of days on our way to the States. My first choice was New Delhi, India, but Steve nixed it.

"No? How come?" I asked.

"India is dirty and crowded and chaotic. We have enough of that here. I want a peaceful vacation."

"Okay, then, let's go to Tehran."

"Iran? Fine. Then how about Frankfurt, London, and Philadelphia? We can catch a commuter from Philly into Allentown, and your parents can pick us up there. The British chapter of the Jaguar Drivers' Club has a meeting in December. We could go when we're in London."

Steve had bought his first Jaguar, an XK-120 sports car, in 1964. The current one, a sleek, 1966 silver-blue sport sedan, sat on blocks in a garage belonging to friends, who stored it for $5 per month. With its dark blue leather upholstery, burled wood dash, and chrome figure of a leaping jaguar on the hood, the vehicle had class. The stick shift made it fun to drive. Two gas tanks—right and left—surprised gas station attendants when we asked them to fill *both*.

A week after that happy news, I realized something was up between Jiao and Muoi. The two of them argued, but I didn't understand why. Also, the market money I kept in a drawer in the den seemed to have dwindled.

"You'll have to get Muoi to tell you," Steve said.

"I've tried, but, you know, she doesn't like to complain. She denies anything's wrong."

"Maybe Pauline can get to the bottom of it."

I asked Pauline, my Vietnamese tutor, to stop by and explained the problem. Could she find out the truth?

Tears filled Muoi's eyes when she told Pauline that Jiao tormented her constantly, picked fights, attacked her with a broom, and tried to convince her to pocket some of the market money.

Such behavior was particularly reprehensible in a culture that revered its elders. Muoi, being older, deserved respect from the younger Jiao. The lack of respect was terrible, but Jiao's attempt to talk Muoi into stealing was worse. Muoi vehemently denied ever doing such a thing.

"Let's find out what Jiao has to say for herself," I told Pauline.

I wouldn't say I liked confrontations, but I wanted to do the right thing. Nervous and upset, I clasped my shaking hands to keep them still. I was aware of a frown creasing my forehead. Butterflies fluttered under my rib cage. I had to sit down.

Pauline and Jiao talked for what seemed like a long time, but it was only fifteen minutes. From the tone of her voice and her expression, I could tell Jiao denied everything.

"What did she have to say?" I asked when Pauline and I were alone in the living room.

"She said Muoi took the money of her own accord."

"So, it was about money. But I'm not convinced Muoi stole from us."

"She didn't. Muoi is honest and very sweet. Don't believe Jiao. You shouldn't trust her."

I agreed with Pauline's assessment of Muoi. She didn't steal from us. Jiao did. Muoi's character showed in her work. She'd been diligent, eager to please, and kind. Besides, she told me she'd come back, and she did. I hated what happened to Muoi, but more than that, I hated that it took me so long to realize the quarrels between her and Jiao were not mere differences of opinion.

I fired Jiao on the spot, not caring whether she saved face. It was much too late for that. I asked her to collect her possessions from the maid's quarters and come back to the kitchen. When she did, I paid her what I owed her, and she turned to leave.

On her way out the kitchen door, she revealed her guilt by grabbing the broom and threatening Muoi with it. We watched her walk down the driveway, through the gate, and into the street. When the gate slammed closed behind her, air came back into the room, and we breathed again.

Jiao's gone, but now what? This villa is too big for Muoi to manage by herself. Something's got to give. Steve's announcement a day later provided the solution.

"I think we should find another place to live," Steve said.

"What? Why?"

"The lease on this place is up in July. I don't want us to spend another six thousand dollars to rent it for another year when the country is so unstable. Why don't we try to find an apartment that rents month-to-month? This would be a good time to start looking."

Remembering how long it had taken to find the villa and what the options were, house hunting didn't thrill me, but Steve's argument made sense. It would be a mistake to spend money on a year's lease. Mr. Bei could help us find something, but he had many demands on his time. I decided to ask around among my expat friends. We had three months to look. Who knew what might turn up?

The American Women's Association of Saigon started planning its most important social event of the year, the Spring Fashion Show, scheduled for April.

When I stopped by AWAS headquarters for coffee one morning, a woman I recognized but didn't know well approached me.

"How would you like to be one of the models in the fashion show?" she asked.

"Umm," I hesitated a beat. "Tell me more. Who else have you asked?"

"This year's theme is Silhouettes in Saigon," she said, "and . . . let's see, I've asked Ingrid McGuire, of course. I think you know her."

She listed a few other names. Of course, I knew Ingrid, one of the Jorgensen project wives. She seemed to have a subtle competition going with me. Depending on her mood, she could be kind or snarky, and she'd be an excellent model.

"Sure, why not?" I said, "Sounds like fun."

"Great! You're tall. You'll be good. Here's the plan. There are five categories—Early Morning, Sports, Travel, Afternoon, and Evening. Choose outfits for at least three of them."

"Do the clothes have to be new and made here, or can I wear something I already have?"

"They can be made here or someplace else in this part of the world—Bangkok, Hong Kong, or Singapore. They don't have to be brand new, but not something you've already worn in Saigon."

In the last week of March, 45 miles south of Saigon, units of the North Vietnamese army attacked Duc Hue, held by the army of South Vietnam, and laid siege to the city. In its last major offensive of the war, the South Vietnamese army broke the siege and forced the North Vietnamese to withdraw. Although the operation succeeded, severe constraints on ammunition, fuel, and flying hours meant they could launch no new initiatives. The decline in South Vietnam's ability to respond to further attacks proved irreversible.

Chapter 16

Gardens in the Midst of War

April 1974

Chi Linh Camp was a U.S. Army/ARVN base west of Dong Xoai in Binh Phuoc Province, seventy miles north of Saigon. In the first days of April, North Vietnamese forces attacked the camp. It fell in ten days. By the time the battle ended, half of the South Vietnamese defenders and twenty dependents had straggled into nearby villages. Unaccounted for were about fifty of the remaining ARVN soldiers. By conquering Chi Linh, North Vietnam gained unimpeded movement along Highway 14 and easy access to Saigon.

I lay awake watching a gecko scuttle across the ceiling. Morning sunlight spilled through the curtains. I felt comfortably at home. Nothing rattled me anymore, not the little lizards that shared the villa, not the crowds or the noise, dust or pollution, heat or humidity, or even explosions in the night.

I spoke enough Vietnamese and French to construct a full life. Taxi and cyclo drivers took me where I wanted to go since I'd learned to pronounce street names correctly. Being the tallest person on the street didn't faze me. I embraced the community and functioned within it.

The fashion show, three days away, occupied my mind. I opened the closet door and reviewed my choices—red and beige floor-length caftan purchased in Bangkok for the "Early Morning" segment; pink trousers, matching skirt, and coordinating print blouse topped off by a Panama hat for "Travel"; and a billowy, red dinner dress custom-made by Alice Fabré for "Evening"—I was all set.

The production details had not come together until a week ago when the chairwoman called a meeting at her villa. Models and crew gathered in the large, tropical living room. Fans whirled overhead. Servants offered tea and cool drinks.

"Welcome, everybody," she began. "Thank you all for coming today. We have a lot to go over, so I hope you're all comfortable. We need to decide several things: a rehearsal schedule, where and how to organize changing rooms for the models, and whether to repeat the show for the Royal Dutch Shell Oil Company Wives Club at their dinner meeting. Also, our Mistress of Ceremonies canceled, and I'm looking for a replacement. I've drawn up a schedule for rehearsals. Please let me know your thoughts."

"I have a conflict with French class," I said. "I might not be able to make all the rehearsals."

Ingrid sauntered over, leaned in close, and murmured in my ear, "If you can't come to rehearsals, maybe you shouldn't be in the show."

"Actually, I can rearrange some things," I said. I'll be there."

A new mistress of ceremonies stepped in. A pianist joined the crew, adding flair. Someone volunteered to organize the backstage space into changing areas. Of course, we would repeat the show for the Shell Oil Company wives.

The stage manager explained she would develop the "Silhouettes in Saigon" theme by opening each segment of the show with a silhouette of one of the models projected onto a life-sized scrim using a backlight.

She asked me to be the silhouette for the "Early Morning" segment opening the show, and I panicked. Shy by nature, I needed a bit of coaxing but eventually agreed to do it. When asked why she chose me, she said she liked my Egyptian profile. *Who knew?*

The big day arrived. Backstage, the models scrambled to find their changing areas and organize their wardrobes. Tuyet, the makeup artist, moved methodically from one model to the next, perfecting makeup.

For the first time in my life, I wore false eyelashes and yellow eye shadow . . . and so did everyone else. Tuyet made up every model the same way. *Do we all look alike to her?* With a last inspection in the floor-length mirror, it was time.

I stood backstage staring into space, summoning courage for my entrance as the first silhouette. The audience rustled in their seats as they adjusted chairs for a better view. The pianist played the opening piece, and adrenaline pumped through my veins. The room closed in on me. The stage manager called for "that Egyptian profile." *This is it!*

I took my place behind the scrim, balancing a China coffee cup on a saucer in my right hand as if offering it to a guest. I turned my head to the right, per direction, in what was meant to be a dramatic pose, and waited for the backlight to spring to life.

The pianist changed to a jaunty piece, beginning the Early Morning segment, and the newly minted mistress of ceremonies began her commentary. The backlight snapped on. My breath came in short gulps. My right hand shook. The coffee cup rattled against the saucer.

Good grief, the audience can hear that. Get a grip, girl! It's showtime.

Someone took the cup and saucer from my hand as I emerged onto the small stage. I paused, scanning the crowd of men and women. USAID II's large party room overflowed, every table full. It was happy hour. I could have used a drink to calm my nerves.

Coming back to myself, I turned and walked to the end of the stage, descended a few steps, and made a leisurely circuit of the room, pausing here and there to show the outfit, then hurried back to the dressing room for a quick change.

The pianist cued the "Travel" segment. Another model provided the silhouette, and I was having fun. Steve and Ingrid's husband, Jim, snapped photographs. The show received rave reviews. People speculated that the April 1975 show would be even better, but it would never happen. The era of AWAS Fashion Shows in Saigon ended that night.

Karen, AWAS Fashion Show, Saigon, April 1974

—

Dust rose in small clouds as traffic roared past on the street outside the villa. Even though it was already steamy, young women wore gloves and long sleeves to prevent their skin from tanning. They did not want to look like peasants. Face masks prevented dust particles from entering lungs as people maneuvered bicycles and motorbikes through traffic. Dehydrated gardens wilted for lack of rain. Air conditioners struggled. April in Saigon heralded the end of the dry season.

Steve and I considered Vietnam a place from which we could explore a part of the world we might not otherwise see. The USAID project gave us the means. As soon as Steve acquired enough vacation leave, we set off for New Zealand.

The first stop was Singapore, where we dined on skewered chicken satay with spicy peanut sauce purchased from a street vendor beside the Singapore River. A snake charmer performed for a crowd of locals that gathered in a little side street where I went to buy buttons at a shop overflowing with boxes of them in every shape, size, and description.

The Raffles Hotel provided shade and a cool drink on a hot afternoon. The establishment dates from the 1800s when the Raffles began life as a beach-front hotel. In 1902, the headmaster of a nearby school shot and killed a tiger in the Bar & Billiards Room.

Celebrities, including W. Somerset Maugham, were regulars at the Raffles' Long Bar during its heyday in 1915. During World War II, Japanese soldiers who had occupied the city encountered guests dancing one final waltz in the ballroom while the staff buried the hotel silver in the Palm Court.

Sydney, Australia, the next stop, surprised us with our first taste of reverse culture shock. We'd never been there before, yet we felt at home. The war in Vietnam wasn't the main topic of conversation. For all anyone knew, we'd just arrived from the States. The tension in my shoulders that I didn't realize I carried left me.

A tour of the shiny new Opera House began the four-day visit to Sydney. We relished eating in world-class restaurants and browsing in upscale stores. Shopping offered a perfect way to interact with local people when only spending a short time somewhere. One of the stores sold tennis clothes. I went in to have a look and talk to the sales staff.

"May I help you?" the clerk asked.

"Yes, I'm looking for something to wear under a tennis dress."

"Let's see. Many women wear Bond's Cotton *Tiles* under their whites."

"I'm sorry. Cotton *Tiles*? What is that?"

"These," she showed me the package with the name in bold letters, Bond's Cotton *Tails*.

Ah, yes, the accent! We all enjoyed a good laugh, and I bought several packages before catching the flight to New Zealand.

On the North Island, the customs agent in Auckland checked our luggage carefully for traces of dirt, debris, or seeds. Because New Zealand is an island, strict agricultural inspection laws are in place to prevent non-native species and invasive plants from entering the country. The agent found something objectionable on the soles of Steve's hiking boots and washed them. He then slipped the boots into plastic bags and repacked them. Released at last, we headed to the rental car kiosk, wondering what other regulations we might encounter.

Outside, a cool, sunny day replaced Saigon's heat, humidity, and smog. A chilly breeze blew off the water—autumn in the southern hemisphere.

Steve pointed the rental car south toward Wellington, where we would spend a few days before taking the ferry to Christ Church on the South Island. Along the way, we stopped to take in some of the sights.

The guidebook I had bought in Sydney described the geothermal activity around Rotorua as a must-see attraction. It was spectacular, but the underground grotto at Waitomo appealed to me even more. The guidebook said glow worm caterpillars covered the ceiling of a cave. I had to see for myself.

We paid the entrance fee at Waitomo and joined a small group of other tourists. A guide directed us down a flight of stairs, through a metal door, and onto a concrete platform where a boat waited in a pool of pitch-black water. When everyone was seated in the boat, the guide grabbed a cable strung across the ceiling of the cave, pulled the craft hand over hand into the middle of the pool, and stopped.

The walls of the cave and the water merged into a single blackness. It was completely dark. Motionless and silent, we waited, sightless, the water utterly calm. Gradually, the glow worms became used to our presence and lit the ceiling with a twinkling blue glow that reflected in the still water. A halo of bright, blue light surrounded us. I gazed in wonder at nature's mysterious creatures and hoped they stayed firmly on the ceiling. The guide explained that the glow worm's light is caused by a chemical reaction to attract insects to the sticky threads of its snare.

New Zealand's capital city, Wellington, is located on the southern tip of the North Island on the Cook Strait. There, we boarded the overnight ferry to Christ Church. The sturdy vessel pitched and rolled in rough seas. Too seasick to eat dinner, we spent a restless night in our cabin.

Bang! Bang! Bang! Someone pounding on the cabin door woke

us early the following morning. Steve went to see who demanded our attention at that hour.

"We're docked," the sailor barked. "Everybody's off the boat. You've got to leave. Now!"

We were the last to go ashore. Tired and hungry, we scrambled to dress and pack. The short walk from the pier into town took us through the commercial seafront area and ended at a main street, where we searched for a place to eat breakfast before picking up the rental car.

The South Island proved as scenic and interesting as the North Island but in a different way. The spectacular Mt. Cook, also known as *Aoraki*—roughly "cloud sky" in the language of the Māori—rises 12,218 feet above sea level in New Zealand's Southern Alps.

Steve had booked three nights at the Hermitage, a four-star hotel nestled high in the mountains, nine miles from the famous peak. Immaculate dairy farms, emerald fields, and pine forests lined the two-lane road to our lodgings. Every so often, palm trees splayed their fronds among the pines as reminders that this was a special place—European on the surface, Polynesian at its heart.

We met an older Australian couple in the Hermitage lounge on the first evening. When they learned we were Americans, the husband asked about the plight of our president, Richard M. Nixon. We avoided saying much of anything, not wanting to go down that road.

"Poor old Nixon," the wife said, "he certainly is having a bad time. I think he is courageous for not resigning and taking the coward's way out."

Before the encounter became awkward, that refined lady had offered a lesson in gracefully disengaging from a delicate situation. Four months later, Nixon would do precisely that.

Chapter 17:

Learning to Sail My Ship

May 1974

Mail from the U.S. arrived through the Army Post Office (APO) at Tan Sơn Nhut airport four days a week. APO privileges supplied a comforting connection to home, a conduit for American goods by mail order, and an efficient way to take care of stateside business. Standard domestic postage rates applied. More important, the APO bypassed the chaos of the local mail system.

With no reason that made sense, USAID notified us that our precious APO lifeline would be cut in thirty days. Steve scrambled to inform people. Friend Burt Foote, a pilot for Air America, agreed to receive our mail through his APO. It felt like the vast ship of state had sailed away, abandoning her crew.

—

The American Community School served children of American government employees in Saigon until February 1965. President Lyndon B. Johnson then ordered dependents of U.S. diplomats, aid missions, and military personnel to leave the country because of increased communist aggression, and the school closed. The Presidential order did not apply to dependents of Americans working for private firms.

A variety of private schools, established after the evacuation of 1965, provided education for those children whose families chose to remain in Saigon. One of the schools was the Phoenix Study Group. Like its mythical namesake, it rose from the ashes of its predecessor.

Dr. Norman Bottorff, the superintendent, occupied offices in one of the buildings that the United States rented. I heard from my friend, Avery, that teachers and staff would receive PX, Commissary, and APO privileges, as well as a salary of six hundred dollars US per month . . . and they needed a librarian. A job at the school would solve multiple problems. I just had to convince Dr. Bottorff to hire me as the librarian.

The superintendent's office, a nondescript space with grime-covered windows and walls the color of pea soup, greeted me when I went to apply. The only furnishings were a desk, chair, and a couple of file cabinets.

A thickset blonde occupied the chair. She gripped a half-smoked cigarette tightly between her prominent lips. An overflowing ashtray sat at her elbow. Her desk placard identified her as Bunny, administrative assistant to the new superintendent.

She glared at me from beneath thick eyebrows. "Who are you, and what do you want?" she barked.

"I'm here to see Dr. Bottorff," I said, attempting to project self-confidence in the face of her brusqueness.

"What for?"

Why is she interrogating me?

My pulse ticked up. A hot wave of adrenaline crept across my scalp. I took a deep breath to tamp down the anger that threatened to overwhelm me and continued with my planned opener.

"He'll need a librarian . . . and here I am."

Bunny glared at me. "Wait here," she said. Still scowling, she rose and lumbered into an adjoining room.

After a few minutes, she emerged and motioned me inside. The office was also devoid of personality and was outfitted with only a desk, a couple of chairs, and a bookcase. Behind the desk sat a rumpled, heavy-set, gray-haired man of about fifty, Dr. Norman Bottorff. Newly arrived from the U.S., he could be excused for appearing frazzled. He had a lot on his mind. I hoped to solve at least one of his problems and explained my business.

"You have experience?" he asked languidly, in a voice that pegged him as someone unused to heat and humidity.

I told him about my library science degree, my involvement with Head Start in Selma, Alabama, in 1966, and my work in school libraries. He said he needed to see transcripts.

Transcripts! In this place he needs transcripts? He should feel lucky I showed up.

"I'll have them sent from the States," I said. "It'll probably take three to four weeks. When are you planning to make a decision?"

"Once I have the transcripts, within a week or two . . . July or early August."

"That's fine. You can reach me through my husband's office. I look forward to hearing from you."

I gave him Steve's office phone number and, before our APO privileges expired, made one final request of my ever-supportive parents—please send copies of my college transcripts.

—

My British friend, Jane Jackson, taught at the American Montessori School run by a woman named Judith Nguyen, a New Zealander married to a Vietnamese man. Pregnant and with an imminent due date, Judith had decided to go home for the blessed event to ensure the child's New Zealand citizenship, given Vietnam's unstable political situation. Jane suggested I could fill in for Judith while I waited to hear from Dr. Bottorff about the job at the Phoenix Study Group.

"I'm not a trained Montessori teacher," I explained when Judith and I discussed it.

Judith grinned. "You know, it would be a big help if you would consider being a teacher's aide for Jane." I started work the following week.

The school, a palace compared to the Nguyen Noch Linh International English School, sat in a lush tropical garden. A riot of color welcomed me when I walked into the classroom. Toys and games of all sorts filled shelves and cubbies bordering the space. The furniture painted primary colors—red, blue, and yellow—made me smile.

Bright, happy children formed a lively international group that sent me home exhausted and sweating at the end of my three-hour shift. As much fun as the children could be, the non-stop attention that three- to five-year-olds required left me drained and longing for the sanctuary of my cool villa.

The rainy season arrived and scrubbed the dust and smog from the air. Almost a year had passed without my noticing, and life had become comfortable . . . enjoyable even. Regardless of reports in stateside newspapers, nothing threatening had happened in Saigon. The city's people went about their business as they always had, used to being at war for thousands of years.

Monday through Saturday, Steve went to work. I helped Jane at the Montessori school every morning and attended French class every afternoon. In the evening, we relaxed with books or the FM radio, not missing television. The villa ran smoothly. Muoi did her best to keep the basics under control with a pared-down routine.

On weekends, Steve and I rode the city bus like locals to practice tennis at the Defense Attaché compound. Even though I still took lessons with Jean Pierre at *Cercle Sportif*, my game hadn't improved. Frustrated and tired after an hour on the court, I couldn't wait to pack up the rackets and adjourn to the DAO restaurant. We couldn't have known then that, in less than a year, those tennis courts would become a helicopter landing pad to assist in the evacuation of Saigon.

The local movie theater ran a French-dubbed version of "*Funny Girl*," with Barbra Streisand. Lyrics to Streisand's songs were not dubbed. The projectionist stopped the movie four times to cut some of the songs, the purpose of which escaped me.

Saigon offered many ways to fill free time, but creative minds conjured up their own. A chance encounter with a colleague at USAID sparked, for Steve, memories from his youth—fishing in his uncle Bud's boat on Deep Creek Lake in western Maryland, sailing on Long Island Sound with friends from high school, cruising on the Potomac River with his father in the seventeen-foot motorboat his father had given him instead of a car when he turned sixteen.

Steve dreamed of owning a sailboat one day and sailing the Mediterranean, or any other body of water, for that matter. So, he and his friend, Don Burgess, decided to build a sailboat. He announced the plan to me one night over Grand Marnier *soufflés* at Guillaume Tell, our favorite French restaurant near the river.

"By the way . . . I meant to tell you," he said, between mouthfuls, "Don and I are going to build a sailboat in his garage."

"What? Why?" I asked, skeptical. "I thought you were going to commission a sailboat at one of the shipyards."

"I thought about it. In fact, I even talked to a couple of companies, but then I watched their work for a few weeks. It wasn't very good."

"Don't you need plans or something?"

"The boating magazines at the PX have design ideas—Don still has privileges there. It'll be great to make something we might be able to use. Besides, building a boat will give us something productive to do . . . take our minds off office politics and the war for a little while. We'll worry about sailing her later."

Using information they found in magazines and Steve's memory of a Sunfish that he had sailed in Thailand, he and Don collected enough data to give them an idea of the hull's proportions and the position of the mast.

They started construction in Don's garage, learning how to do the physical layout by trial and error and using materials available locally. Experienced working with wood, Don showed Steve how to shape the hull. They typically worked on Saturday or Sunday afternoons and enjoyed good conversations about everything from the status of the war to their family backgrounds.

They discussed hardware and a sail as work progressed on the wooden hull. Steve found a sailmaker on one of our regular R&R trips in Hong Kong who could construct what he needed. With numerous chandleries in Hong Kong, finding the hardware presented no problem.

Neither Steve nor Don thought about a name for their craft. I didn't doubt their sincerity about wanting, one day, to sail her, but somehow, their effort seemed destined for disappointment. The name I suggested, *Futility*, did not amuse them.

—

The strategic region known as the Iron Triangle encompassed 120 square miles of overgrown rubber plantations, thick jungle, and towering elephant grass. An abandoned chain of inter-connected tunnels and trenches crisscrossed the flat ground. During the height of the war, both civilians and soldiers used the tunnels as an underground refuge to escape bombs and artillery fire.

A system of trenches concealed under trees and bushes zig-zagged from the villages to the cleverly hidden tunnel entrances. People could ride bicycles through the deep trenches and still keep their heads below ground level.

Bomb craters from decades of battle and narrow, rutted dirt roads made the landscape of the Iron Triangle impossible to drive through. Its proximity to Saigon, which lay ten miles to the south, made the region critical to the city's defense. The Viet Cong had infested the area for decades.

South Vietnam's military held two towns at the edge of the Triangle. In the middle of May, North Vietnam launched a fierce attack on the westernmost town, beginning the Battle of the Iron Triangle. The prolonged campaign would last until November and end in a victory for South Vietnam. However, the strength of the enemy that pushed against Saigon's outer defenses could not be overlooked. The final, decisive attack on the capital would be organized in the Iron Triangle.

Chapter 18

Threatened by Morning Light

June 1974

The People's Army of [North] Vietnam fired rockets into Bien Hoa Air Base, destroying five hundred napalm canisters but no aircraft. Runways received minor damage. Stray rockets exploded in hamlets surrounding the base, killing and wounding civilians.

The familiar sound of the explosions carried eighteen miles to the villa on Nguyen Dinh Chieu Street, startling Steve and me awake.

"That sounded close," I muttered.

"Yeah, they're at it again. Probably nothing to worry about," Steve reassured me. "Go back to sleep."

But sleep wouldn't block out the noise.

What are we doing in this place?

The American Women's Association asked if I would be responsible for planning and coordinating the organization's monthly events as program chair. I'd been in Saigon less than a year, but having no other commitments at the time, I gave the idea a few days to gel *(thankless job . . . time-consuming . . . could be interesting)* and accepted.

First order of business: build a portfolio of program ideas. Being relatively new in town, I needed help and remembered hearing that Dorothy Martin, the ambassador's wife, knew several people who could present exciting programs. One obstacle blocked my way, however. She and I had not been introduced. Our paths did not cross socially, as I wasn't associated with the embassy.

I debated with myself. *Is approaching her out of order? Why? She's one of us, isn't she, an American woman in Saigon? Being program chair gives me some credibility, doesn't it?*

Finally, I decided there was no harm in trying. What would be the worst that could happen?

My mind made up, I paid a visit to the ambassador's residence one afternoon. A maid answered my knock, and I asked to speak with Mrs. Martin.

"You wait here," the maid said, indicating the foyer. "I go tell *Madame*."

The French colonial building had been home to America's ambassadors for years. Light from the stunning chandelier shimmered on the polished tile floor. Colorful artwork pulled me in. A riot of colorful flowers spilled from a large white vase decorated with swimming goldfish.

After a few minutes, a small, elegant woman with a halo of white hair and warm Southern manners entered the room. A flicker of surprise crossed her face at her unexpected visitor, especially one she'd never met. A true diplomat, she recovered quickly.

"I'm Dorothy Martin," she said, extending her hand. "How can I help you?"

"Thank you for seeing me," I said after introducing myself as the new program committee chair. "I won't take up much of your time. I'm relatively new here and need help getting started. I understand you might be able to suggest some program ideas."

"All right, let's sit and talk. Would you like tea?"

She invited me into a large, bright, high-ceilinged space with cool white overstuffed sofas and chairs. Oriental antiques and art sat on carved stands around the room. Hand-painted porcelain urns, gilded figurines, a portrait of the Nixon family displayed on the piano, and a stuffed ocelot mesmerized and terrified me at the same time. I prayed I wouldn't accidentally break something. Gracious and kind, Mrs. Martin spent an hour discussing a few possibilities over tea. The meeting went well, I thought.

A few days later, one of the embassy wives let me know that I had committed a serious *faux pas.* One does not just drop in on the ambassador's wife out of the blue and especially not to ask for help planning programs.

The floor seemed to slip out from under me. How naïve of me. Embarrassed and confused over being reprimanded, I felt the criticism was unjustified. Mrs. Martin hadn't appeared displeased, only surprised. She could have declined to speak with me. I took the criticism for what it was and forgave myself.

The lease on our villa would end in little more than a month. After weeks of searching independently, neither Steve nor I had found anything but rat traps. Pressure mounted.

We explained our dilemma to church friends Jeannie and Burt Foote during dinner one night in their cozy two-bedroom, one-bath apartment. They lived on the second floor of a five-story building along a quiet lane off busy Ky Dong Street. In the States, it would have been referred to as the third floor; the ground floor didn't count.

"There's a unit one floor up for rent . . . same layout," Jeannie said. "Come, I'll show you around our little hideaway."

The space offered good-sized rooms, although far fewer than the villa. There was even a small space off the dining room that could be a place for ironing or sewing.

"What do you think?" Steve asked, raising his eyebrows at me to emphasize the question. "Will this do?"

"I like it," I said. "It's the best we've found. Whom do I talk to?"

"That would be *Monsieur* Allard, the owner," said Jeannie. "He lives next door. He's not always in town, but you can stop by his house. You might catch him. By the way, how's your French? He doesn't speak English."

Oh, boy! Renting this apartment depends on how much I want it. Am I brave enough to do this on my own? In French?

The next day, I found myself in the lane off Ky Dong Street. *Monsieur* Allard's bungalow was easy to identify. Masses of bougainvillea vines spilled over the walls, dropping their luminous magenta blossoms like confetti. Oddly, the gate stood open. The unmistakable citrusy-sweet scent of frangipani's porcelain-like white flowers drew me into the garden like a siren's song. A tall jackfruit tree, its exotic, knobby green fruit hanging in clumps like enormous grapes, shaded the front porch where a cat sunned itself.

Have I left Saigon? Am I in a Disney movie?

I moved slowly through the garden, taking in the scents and visions surrounding me. When I returned to the dusty streets outside,

I wanted to remember the most exotically beautiful place I'd ever seen.

Monsieur Allard opened the door before I had a chance to knock. He had that elegantly casual look perfected by the French, and I stared into the handsome face of a tall, fifty-something gentleman with dark hair progressing to gray.

I introduced myself and asked about the apartment. With the manners of a cultured aristocrat, he invited me into a large front room filled with plants and antiques. Light filtered through Bahama shutters. Fans whirled. With a gesture and a slight bow, *Monsieur* Allard offered me a seat, then signaled a servant to bring us tea. I wanted to get right to the point, but clearly, pleasantries had to be observed before we could talk business.

He asked how I liked living in Saigon, how long I'd been in town, if I was married, and how I spent my time. I mentioned Jeannie and Burt to let him know that I hadn't just wandered in off the street.

After finishing our tea, *Monsieur* Allard and I walked next door to see the apartment—seven small rooms, tile floors, no telephone. The front door opened into a dining room with a table, six chairs, and a buffet. To the left, almost hidden from view, an arch opened into the unfurnished living room, tucked out of sight like a treasure.

Through the galley kitchen, to the right of the entrance, a back door opened onto a catwalk with a spiral staircase at one end that led to the maid's quarters behind the building.

French doors at the end of the dining room accessed a narrow balcony protected by a thick wire screen. A clothesline crisscrossed one end. From the balcony, I had a view of rooftops and trees. I could make out the Presidential Palace to the south if I stood on my toes.

Opposite the entrance, double doors set in a second archway provided privacy for the two bedrooms and bath beyond. A small room next to the kitchen would become a place for Muoi to iron and for me to sew. Plain white walls begged for character, and I couldn't wait to begin supplying it.

We returned to *Monsieur* Allard's bungalow and completed the transaction. I left with a new home leased on a month-to-month basis. The space would work, and the unit, although dated, looked well-maintained. It was charming.

I couldn't wait to tell Steve about my success in managing a small conversation and renting an apartment in French. I felt almost like a native *Saigonaise*. Almost.

"We got the apartment," I told Steve. "Lots easier for Muoi." I babbled on and on in excitement, describing all the rooms and plans for decorating the place. When I finally stopped to breathe, Steve had news for me.

"Patty came to see me at work today," he said.

The amazing Patty, our first cook. She always said she'd return to work if we moved into a smaller place.

"How did she know where you work? What did she want?"

"Don Smail told his cook, Wong, we were looking for a smaller place. Wong's a friend of Patty's, and he passed along the office address to her. She wants to come back to work for us . . . and she's pregnant. She thinks she'll be ready to start work again in January."

"Wouldn't it be great to have her back? But do we need a cook and a maid in the apartment? What about Muoi?"

"Let's wait until we get there to decide. I told Patty to contact us when she's ready."

The new information presented an impossible choice. We planned to move in early July and take Muoi with us. Maybe by then, I'd know what to do.

To celebrate our new home and Steve's thirtieth birthday, I organized a surprise party for him. All our friends came to share the cake. It was our last party in the villa.

The small group of American women in my class at the *Institut Français* met for lunch at Restaurant Ramuntcho, a cozy French bistro on Le Loi Street. We asked to be seated on the second floor in the less crowded dining room, where larger tables accommodated all of us.

"Nice place," said Linette. "I've never been here before. What's good?"

"Langoustines with Chantilly cream are my favorite," I told her. "But everything's good here. We like the relaxed atmosphere."

"When are you moving?" Sara asked me.

"First of next month. Steve hired Bekins to pack everything," I told her.

"Did you have to pay a year in advance?" asked Jean.

"No, month-to-month," I answered.

"Smart move," Jean said. "Honestly, we're beginning to wonder how much longer we can stay."

"Did Tony hear anything at USAID about the explosions last night?" I asked Sara.

"My husband doesn't talk about that. Unfortunately." She answered. "I wish I had something reassuring to tell you."

The space served no other diners until two well-dressed gentlemen arrived and settled at a table near the stairs. I recognized one of the men as the owner of the restaurant. His companion seemed familiar in a distant sort of way. He wore a black suit. His bald head almost glowed with sweat, yet he projected a confident, self-assured image. From their demeanor, I could tell they had serious business to discuss.

Then it clicked. The bald gentleman looked exactly like film star Yul Brynner, who may be best known for portraying the King of Siam in *The King and I* opposite Deborah Kerr.

My camera sat on the table, but I hesitated to use it. I'd need a flash and didn't want to risk intruding on their privacy. After all, he had chosen to sit upstairs, away from prying eyes.

"Don't look now," I whispered across the table. "I think that's Yul Brynner over there." Of course, everyone looked.

"I'm going to find out," said Linette. She stood and walked toward the powder room, pausing at the table by the stairs.

"Excuse me," she said, "are you Yul Brynner?"

"No," he replied sarcastically, "I'm Shirley Temple."

And just like that, one of my favorite film stars fell from grace. Later, I read that Mr. Brynner had been in Saigon to finalize the adoption of a Vietnamese orphan, his daughter, Mia.

L – R: Tini, Jean, Karen, Linette, Sara, Restaurant Ramuntcho, Saigon, 1974

—

The Defense Attaché to South Vietnam, Major General John E. Murray, criticized the Pentagon for reducing military aid to South Vietnam and predicted that without more support, the country could never survive a major attack. He believed the U.S. should "write off South Vietnam as a bad investment and [a] broken promise."

CIA station chief Polgar and Ambassador Martin believed the Army of the Republic of [South] Vietnam to be in good shape. Others in the embassy knew better. The Army was in serious trouble.

Chapter 19:

The Way You Look at Things

July & August 1974

Although South Vietnam had superior weapons and manpower, the fuel crisis, lack of spare parts, and motivation rendered these resources ineffective. The United States Congress voted to reduce aid to South Vietnam from $1.1 billion to $750 million. Worse, Vietnamese officials frequently redirected military aid to individuals and other agencies, hampering the ability of the army to resist future attacks. Some became wealthy while the country suffered.

On July 2, a Bekins van pulled away from the Nguyen Dinh Chieu Street villa, holding our household belongings. We bid farewell to the showy villa and moved to the modest two-bedroom, one-bath apartment off Ky Dong Street. I loved the cozy, Old-World ambiance, but it came with a few quirks.

Muoi sometimes had to coax the ancient gas stove to life. Running water could be erratic. If we lost power, days could go by before the city restored it. Screens covered unglazed kitchen and bathroom windows, but the afternoon rains soaked everything. Steve arranged for someone to install window panes. As if to make amends, the landlord graced the dining room with a cheerful potted red poinsettia the size of a dogwood tree. The apartment would turn out to be my favorite Saigon home.

With the new accommodations came an ancient, French-speaking Vietnamese groundskeeper, Mr. Ngo, who lived in a small house behind the parking area. Besides sweeping the parking lot and doing some gardening, he monitored comings and goings by acting as gatekeeper. The gate, set into a concrete wall surrounding the grounds, served as our security. He and a group of neighborhood children swarmed around me whenever I left or returned.

Mr. Ngo also controlled the apartment's erratic water supply from a cistern mounted on the roof. One day, the water stopped when I was in the middle of a shower. Still wet and soapy, I threw on a beach dress and ran down three floors to confront him.

"Mr. Ngo, *Pourquoi n'y a-til pas d'eau*?" Why is there no water? I glared at him, hands on hips.

Mr. Ngo with neighborhood children, Ky Dong apartment, Saigon, 1974

"*La citerne est vide.*" The cistern is empty, he said with a shrug. "*Que pouvez-vous faire?*" What can you do?

An uninterrupted water supply was a luxury. I went back upstairs, dried off, and got on with the day.

The building that housed our new home sat across the lane from a Buddhist temple and school. When Muoi opened the windows and French doors in the morning, the lilting voices of children reciting their lessons in unison filled the air. In the afternoon, a slight breeze carried the rhythmic chanting of monks and the deep tone of brass temple bells, creating a feeling of order, normalcy, and peace.

Furnishing and decorating the apartment became my *raison d'être* of the moment. For this project, I planned to use all local products. I clipped pictures from magazines of the rattan pieces I wanted—three tall bookcases, a sofa, a matching side chair, two high-backed chairs for the dining room, two more as occasional chairs in the living room, and a chaise lounge. Armed with measurements and photographs, Steve and I took one of the ubiquitous blue and yellow taxis in search of someone to build them.

The tree-lined furniture street spread out wide and dusty. Narrow storefronts stood crammed side by side. Precarious-looking masses of electrical wiring hung from poles and sides of buildings overhead like spaghetti drying on a rack.

Proprietors sat on the sidewalk in front of their shops, shaded by canvas awnings. Surrounded by their wares, they cooled themselves with paper fans. Everything, from footstools to futons, could be found there.

The taxi let us out at the curb. Steve paid, and we made our way along the street, searching for a shop selling rattan furniture. We found what we were looking for, and I was relieved that this shopping trip would be short. The heat and humidity had already begun to take their toll.

We made a deal with hand signals, a little show-and-tell, and a combination of French, English, and even a little Vietnamese. Our custom furniture would be made by hand.

A week later, Muoi told me I had a visitor waiting on the landing. A workman from the rattan shop stood there with one of the chairs I'd ordered. It looked finished except for the seat. *It's a big chair. Did he bring it here on his motorbike?*

He said something to Muoi, which she translated for me. He wanted to measure how high off the floor the seat of the chair should be for Steve's and my long legs. To figure this out, he'd placed a stool where the seat would be and asked me to pretend to sit in the chair. Then he raised and lowered the stool so that when seated, my legs were bent 90 degrees. Custom-fitted chairs, a first!

Besides furniture, I bought fabric for curtains, slipcovers, a bedspread, and pillowcases.

We purchased another air conditioner to install between the living room and dining room. Steve hired a handyman to do the installation. Like the workers at the Smail's villa months ago, the man began by creating an opening through the stucco and brick wall with a hammer and chisel. A thick cloud of white dust settled over everything that Muoi worked so hard to keep spotless. I told her not to worry. We'd clean it up together.

Steve and Karen, Ky Dong apartment, Saigon, 1974

—

Don Burgess, his wife, Nga, and their three-year-old daughter, Marian, stopped by to see our new digs. A precocious, pretty little girl, Marian was also a poignant reminder of Steve's and my unsuccessful attempts to start a family.

Although Steve expressed doubts occasionally, we'd planned to have children. We'd failed. Neither of our families pressured us. I didn't think about the consequences of a pregnancy in the middle of a war, isolated from it as we were, but I wanted answers.

On a friend's recommendation, I sought advice from Dr. Pham, a French-trained Vietnamese OB/GYN. He ran some tests that were inconclusive and suspected a blockage somewhere. The next step, he told me, was insufflation, whereby carbon dioxide gas was introduced into the fallopian tubes to determine if they were open.

I arrived for the procedure and took a seat on a bench outside the doctor's office. Seated beside me, a young, hugely pregnant American woman, whose baby was overdue, waited to be induced. A nurse called her in. We wished each other good luck.

Shortly, my turn came. A nurse showed me into an examination room and prepped me for the procedure. It took only a few minutes. Apparently, blocked fallopian tubes were not my problem. Dr. Pham could tell right away, for excruciating pain caused by the gas escaping into my abdominal cavity and diaphragm seized me whenever I moved.

The nurse rolled the litter on which I lay into a large operatory where several other patients waited and told me to lie still. Eventually, the gas would dissipate. Then, she handed me a tube connected to an oxygen tank, saying that breathing oxygen would help.

Meanwhile, Dr. Pham busied himself with my friend from the waiting room. She lay on a litter a few feet from mine. Labor had been induced, but the baby was taking its time.

"The baby is coming!" Dr. Pham exclaimed, at last, with a burst of excitement and genuine glee.

I turned my head just enough to witness the amazing miracle of childbirth. It took my breath away, for there he was with ten tiny fingers and ten tiny toes, a perfect little boy right away.

But wait! Something was very wrong!

Dr. Pham called for the nurse, who rushed to his side. The umbilical cord had wrapped itself around the baby's neck three times. He wasn't breathing! A tense few minutes passed, and then I heard the doctor's voice again,

"Have you seen that? Have you seen that?" he cried, "I have saved him!" His excitement spread and the rest of us cheered, as well.

The nurse whisked the infant away. After a few minutes, she returned with a cleaned-up and clothed baby. Instead of taking him to his mother, the nurse headed toward me.

Wait! What's happening? Has the nurse confused me with the mother? Is she bringing the baby to me because she knows I hope for one?

I panicked for a second but snapped out of it when I realized the baby needed oxygen, too, and I held the only source. In a spirit of compassion for us, the nurse held the newborn while he and I shared oxygen from the only supply in the office. The baby looked as mystified as I had been.

This would never happen in the States!

Six hundred miles from Saigon, the battle of Duc Duc in Quang Nam Province began. It would last until October 4, and South Vietnamese troops would suffer 4,700 casualties. On the same day, the Battle of Thung Duc commenced when a regiment of the People's Army of [North] Vietnam overran the An Hoa Industrial Complex and attacked the town of Thuong Duc, a key entrance to the Quang Nam Province lowlands and essential for extending the Ho Chi Minh Trail. Although South Vietnam stopped the advance of the North, it suffered extreme losses of personnel and ordnance that could not be replaced because of reduced funding.

President Richard M. Nixon's national security advisor, Henry A. Kissinger, had brokered a deal that would play Russia and China against each other and both of them against North Vietnam.

The upshot—an agreement to withdraw all American ground forces in exchange for Hanoi's releasing all American POWs and agreeing to wait a decent interval, eighteen months to two years, before overtaking South Vietnam, which no one in the higher echelons of the U.S. government or military doubted would happen eventually.

In return, Nixon assured Hanoi the U.S. would not interfere in its conquest of the South after the decent interval had passed. At the same time, he promised South Vietnam's president just the opposite.

On August 9, the one deterrent to robust aggression by the North Vietnamese into South Vietnam, President Richard M. Nixon, resigned. No one elected President of the United States had ever resigned from that office. Hanoi was then free to pursue its goal without waiting.

Aid workers, district advisors, and others who came in from the northern provinces brought stories of fierce battles there. The belief, held by some, that the fighting would end within a few months of the Paris Accords collapsed like an airless balloon. More than a year had passed. Nothing had changed.

Our apartment's walls vibrated with sound waves from shelling somewhere outside Saigon, yet the American Radio Service did not mention it. Reality closed in all around us. Neither side was giving up. Still, the city remained unchanged, and no one in authority to do so ordered an evacuation.

My anxious parents sent letters filled with concern. I wrote back to reassure them that none of what they read or saw on TV happened in Saigon, regardless of the news. "We'll be home for Christmas," I wrote to cheer them, referring to the month-long respite known as home leave. I wished I believed it myself.

Home! Where is home, anyway? Can I click my heels and go there? Is the apartment on Ky Dong Street home? When I had a rough day, I thought there was no place I'd rather be.

We were going on home leave at the end of November, three months away, and needed to prepare, both mentally and physically.

"One problem with home leave," Steve said. "It's winter. It's cold. We need proper clothes. Let's go to Hong Kong and have some made.

"Sure, I'm all for going to Hong Kong, but we can have clothes made here," I argued.

"Yes, but here they don't have that nice *vicuña* wool."

"Ahhh . . . I see where this is going. You and your luxury fabrics. Okay, book it."

The Peninsula Hotel in Hong Kong recommended a tailor, and we placed our orders. The next day, we took a hydrofoil to Macau, the Portuguese colony on the Pearl River Delta. Riding along the Malecon bordered by faded mansions, it was easy to imagine this place had once been a prosperous trading port. Macau had changed. It wanted to become the Las Vegas of the East, and its gambling casinos dominated the downtown.

Steve rented a car the following day for a drive outside Hong Kong proper to the New Territories, one of the three main areas of Hong Kong. After driving for a while, we came to the border with mainland China.

"Stop the car," I said. When he did, I got out and walked toward the border crossing.

"What are you doing?" Steve asked.

"I want to step one foot in China."

"No!" Steve called out. "Stop! Karen, come back!"

The young Chinese guard with a menacing firearm glared at me. Then, that small, still voice that some call intuition stopped me in my tracks.

A chilling thought occurred to me as I joined Steve in the car. I could have found myself in a headline: *China Detains American Tourist for Illegal Border Crossing.*

We drove back to the city in silence, Steve exasperated by my carelessness. He had definite opinions about how people should behave and present themselves to the world. Although he could be overbearing sometimes, I appreciated that about him most days.

He also displayed a sophisticated worldview. Something I lacked. His taste in everything, from apparel to cocktails, influenced many of my own decisions. Where I could be foolish and headstrong, he was cautious. He would never have approached the Chinese guard the way I did.

I had to admit he was right. The gravity of that situation and its potential consequences were no laughing matter. I'd have another story to tell when we got home in November.

CHAPTER 20:

Resistance Becomes Duty

September & October 1974

At the end of August, 621 miles north of Saigon, communist troops captured a series of hills at Phu Loc and installed artillery that closed Phu Bai Air Base and stopped traffic along Highway 1 between Da Nang and Hue. South Vietnam's army recaptured the hills, but the fighting depleted its reserve forces.

On an early September afternoon, I stopped by the American Women's Association headquarters to finalize plans for an upcoming program I'd planned.

"Hi, Karen," a familiar voice called out to me. I turned to see my friend, Avery, walking my way.

"Congratulations," she said. "I hear you're the new librarian at the Phoenix Study Group."

"What? Where did you hear that?"

"The committee met last night. Dr. Bottorff, the superintendent, announced the teachers' names, and you got the job."

"That's great news," I said, "but I haven't gotten confirmation."

I appeared at the superintendent's office the next day. Bunny seemed in a more pleasant mood than on my first visit. She greeted me with half a smile.

"Karen, good morning," she said. "What can I do for you?"

"Hi, Bunny. I need to see Dr. Bottorff. Is he in?"

"Yeah . . . umm . . . hold on a minute. Listen, I'm sorry about being gruff with you before. I'm always tough with people until I know who I'm dealing with. I lighten up later."

"Well, I guess it pays to be careful."

"He's here. Go ahead in."

I tapped on the office door and walked in. The room looked like a crazed squirrel had gotten loose inside. Folders lay scattered over the desktop, contents spilling out. Piles of textbooks slumped onto the floor.

Dr. Bottorff sat at his desk looking as frazzled as ever. He squinted up at me like I'd interrupted a complex thought process.

"Good morning," I said. "Do you have a minute to talk?"

"Uh . . . sure. Have a seat." He indicated the one empty visitor's chair. "What can I help you with?"

"I heard through the grapevine I'm going to be PSG's librarian, but I haven't gotten a confirmation letter and just wanted to be sure the rumor is true."

"Oh, well, that's right. You have the job. I'm surprised you didn't get the letter. Bunny was supposed to contact everybody."

"Nope, no letter, but I don't care about that. I'm happy to have the position." I stood to leave.

"Hold up a second," Bottorff said. "I'll walk out with you."

At her desk, Bunny concentrated on the paperwork before her.

"Bunny," Dr. Bottorff said, "what happened to Karen's confirmation letter? She didn't get it."

"I paid that messenger guy to deliver it," Bunny said. "Oh, no . . . he must have kept the money and disappeared. Damn! That's the last time I hire him."

With Avery's information confirmed, I prepared to go back to work.

The Phoenix Study Group served English-speaking children at three locations: Kindergarten met at 66 Doan Thi Diem, first through 4th grade at 192/194 Cong Ly, and fifth grade through high school at 209 Hien Vuong.

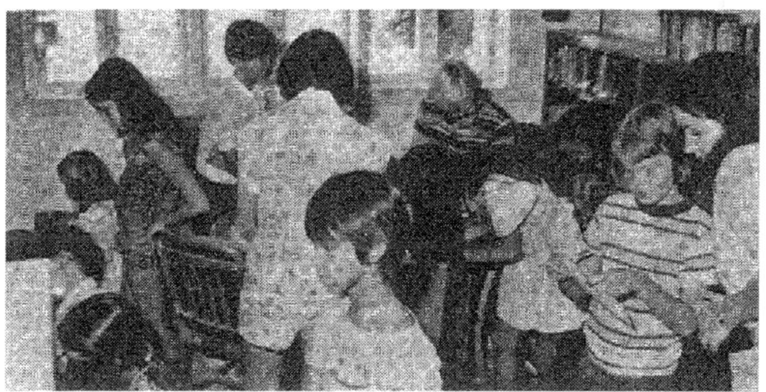

Karen (far right) working with a student at the Hien Vuong location, Saigon, 1974

The library occupied a sizable second-floor space in a building at the Cong Ly location. A small room was set aside at the Hien Vuong location, and I transferred selected books there to create a library for the higher grades. Besides managing the book collection, I taught library skills to each class and presented book talks.

The existing card catalog looked adequate, but I would need to compare it to the library's actual holdings at some point. Supplies were few, and the room needed furniture—tables, chairs, and bookcases. Dr. Bottorff asked me to put together a supply order and specifications for furniture. Coming up with a list of the basics presented no problem. As for the furniture, I had to wing it.

One week later, the carpenter and his assistants delivered sturdy but slightly out-of-proportion tables, chairs, and bookcases built precisely to my specifications. The seats of the chairs were too wide, and the legs of tables and chairs too long—like something out of *Alice's Adventures in Wonderland*— but they worked. The shelving looked a little off, too, but it served the purpose. I could not complain.

A corkboard on one wall demanded a mural, which I created from construction paper left over from my previous job at a different school. When I'd finished, the room resembled a proper school library.

The Phoenix Study Group, Cong Ly, Saigon, 1974
(Photo credit: Phoenix Study Group—Find Alumni, Yearbooks, and Reunion Plans (classmates.com)

My routine changed with the new job, which consumed the mornings. After school, I flagged down a cyclo to take me back to the apartment. Hot, sweating, and tired, I puffed and shuffled up three flights of stairs. By the time I reached the landing, Muoi held the door open for me. She knew I arrived home at the same time every day and listened for my footsteps.

I dumped my bag of library work in the second bedroom/office and sat down at the dining room table where lunch waited—half a sandwich and a tall glass of diet cola with lots of ice. While I devoured the food, Muoi turned on the bedroom's air conditioner and ceiling fan. Afterward, both Muoi and I went to our separate quarters for *siesta*.

At four o'clock, I headed back outside and down the lane to Ky Dong Street. On the way, I passed sidewalk barbers, soup vendors, scrap-paper sellers, school kids, and women balancing poles on their shoulders with baskets of produce swinging from each end. Out on the street, I searched for a cyclo to take me to French class.

The same routine continued for a week or two. One day, I noticed three young cyclo drivers lined up with their vehicles at the entrance to the lane, all waiting to be chosen like debutantes at a ball. They all smiled at me, and then one of them pulled his cyclo forward slightly as if to say, "Pick me." I climbed aboard, gave him the address, and he pedaled off.

Feeling the breeze in my hair and the exhaust in my lungs from the cars ahead of us, I felt like a human bumper. However, I never had a bad experience riding in a cyclo. The contrivance amazed me with its maneuverability as my chauffeur, perched high on the bicycle seat behind me, angled us smoothly through traffic and around corners.

After class, I repeated the routine to find a ride home. One day, I recognized the driver who had delivered me to the *Institut* sitting at the curb with his cyclo. When he saw me, he waved me over. He'd figured out I kept the same daily routine and waited for me after class. From then on, he drove me there and back every day.

A few weeks later, I went out to the street after class one day, expecting to see my regular driver and his cyclo, but he wasn't there. An anxious minute passed before I noticed one of the other drivers from the triumvirate on Ky Dong signaling to me. He let me know in Vietnamese and broken English that my usual driver sent him. I wanted to ask why, but, of course, I couldn't. My Vietnamese didn't stretch that far, and neither did his English.

After dinner in the evenings, Steve updated his work diary or took care of other business, and I sewed. Creating curtains or pillow covers for the apartment or a dress for myself relaxed me. The paper dress patterns I'd brought from the States intrigued Muoi—the tailors of Saigon never used them. The fact that I knew how to sew in the first place interested her even more than the patterns. I tried to explain that, in America, women did all sorts of things that we hired other people to do in Saigon. She had no idea how differently we lived in the States.

My mother's letters, full of concern, arrived every week, the news coming out of Vietnam ratcheting up her protective instincts.

Why don't we know any of this? If things are as bad as they say, why hasn't anyone told us? What are we still doing here?

Saigon's hustle and bustle didn't change. Talk of U.S. plans to open a larger American school the following year circulated among the teachers. The expats I knew trusted the embassy's party line that South Vietnam would survive, even without American boots on the ground.

—

Steve's work included inventorying South Vietnam's roads and bridges, which meant travel to provinces outside Saigon. An upcoming trip to Vietnam's fourth largest city, Can Tho, in the Mekong Delta, required him to investigate the possibility of augmenting the one bridge across the Hau River with an expanded ferry crossing.

Even though the area was a Viet Cong hot spot, Steve and his colleague, Dick Klein, once again received USAID approval for the trip. Dick's wife, Sally, and I assured ourselves the men would be all right, that things couldn't be as bad there as people said. After all, why would USAID send them if they'd be in danger?

We were right . . . that time.

Before we had moved to the apartment, Steve and I discussed rehiring Patty now that we had a smaller place she could handle by herself. However, we hadn't heard from Patty since the day she visited Steve at his office. So, we took Muoi with us.

Then, two months after the move, Muoi answered a knock at the apartment door and called me.

"*Madame,* lady come . . . see *Madame.*"

What in the world?

"Hello, *Madame.*" Patty stood on the landing dressed in the loose tunic Vietnamese women wore during pregnancy. Her shy tone and down-cast eyes revealed how tentative she felt about the visit.

Muoi retreated to the kitchen.

"Patty! What a nice surprise," I said. "Come in."

I took her to the living room and asked Muoi to bring tea for us.

"Did *Monsieur* tell you where we live?"

"Yes, *Monsieur,* tell me."

"How are you? When is your baby due?"

"Baby due four months," Patty got right to the point. "In January, I can come back work it. Do you have work for me?"

"Patty," I said, as gently as I could, not knowing if Muoi could overhear the conversation, "I don't know. We would be happy for you to come back, but we have someone else now." I felt like I was rejecting a lover who wanted another chance.

"I know . . . but . . . maybe need two?"

"I have to think about it. Okay?"

What an abysmal dilemma! The agonizing encounter tormented me that night. Sleepless, my mind churned with possibilities.

Muoi—who proved her loyalty and trustworthiness day after day, who would go out late in the evening to buy me another package of cookies when she saw I'd eaten the last crumbs—had devoted herself to us.

Muoi, unmarried and childless, had taken it upon herself to raise and educate a young orphan girl who would care for her in her old age, as was their custom. Steve and I provided Muoi's livelihood. To let her go would be cruel. I believed it would break her heart.

Muoi in Ky Dong Apartment, Saigon, 1975

On the other hand, we could have the excellent Patty back, who cooked like a dream, knew what we needed before we did, and would help bathe a kitten just because I asked her to, even though she thought cats were bad luck.

We had become attached to both of them.

Can I rehire Patty and keep Muoi, too?

In the small apartment, it didn't make sense. The issue wasn't cost. It was compatibility. If I'd learned nothing else from the experience of having help, it was that hierarchy ruled. Who would take charge in that situation—Patty, because she had more experience, or Muoi, who had risen to the challenges of managing the household? Muoi hadn't been with us long, but I couldn't betray her. Still, I didn't want to let Patty down.

"What do you think we should do?" I asked Steve the next day.

"It's a tough one," he said, "but Patty can't work right now, anyway. Let's send word to her through Wong that she should come to see us again when she's ready. If Muoi doesn't work out, we can rehire Patty. If Muoi does work out, we can help Patty find another job. New guys coming in are always looking for cooks." My husband was a practical man.

"Perfect . . . we won't have said 'no' to Patty, and we're still taking care of her and Muoi. I knew you could solve this. Thanks," I said, hugging him.

In October, the fragile façade surrounding life in Saigon showed signs of cracking. An episode involving Wong, the Smail's cook, shook everyone's sense of invulnerability.

Don and Alice Smail, who had hosted us when we first arrived in Vietnam, were reassigned to a project in Indonesia. Another Jorgensen engineer, Bob Taylor, his wife, Betty, and young son, Burt, newly arrived from Maryland, took over the lease on the Smail's villa and retained their staff, including Wong.

The family of three soon settled in. Betty played tennis and paid attention to her health. Bob, whose powder-blue safari suit belied his serious side, worked with Steve. Betty invited the project wives to a get-acquainted luncheon at the villa.

Wong's dishes never disappointed. I arrived anticipating a memorable meal and a pleasant afternoon. Too many minutes passed after my knock before a visibly distraught Betty opened the door. There would be no luncheon that day, she told me.

The night before, South Vietnamese soldiers had come in the wee hours demanding to see Wong. When Wong roused himself and shuffled to meet them, he was arrested for desertion and taken away. The connection to Patty disappeared with him. We would never see Patty or Wong again.

A subtle but conspicuous shift in mood settled over the city. The usual rumble of traffic coming from Ky Dong Street sounded more like a hum. Temple bells made the only sound at the pagoda across the lane; the chorus of children's voices was silent.

Steve's Work Diary

> ***21 October 1974:*** *Dropped by Lew's office this morning . . . He related that Mr. Jorgensen had asked if I could be transferred to another job as soon as possible. He [said] Mr. J did not identify the job. Lew showed me [the] telegram he had received . . . asking about my status. He read the telegram. I did not look at it.*

The puzzling conversation between Steve and Lew Chittim made us wonder about our status and raised a multitude of questions.

Steve hadn't asked to be reassigned, but he knew Lew was more his adversary than his colleague. Was Lew sabotaging him?

"What are you going to do?" I asked.

"I told him I intend to stay here until the work is finished," Steve said. "That'll probably mean at least another year. Besides, I'd need more information before I'd agree to another move. I will talk to Roy Jorgensen when we're on home leave."

The International School in Bangkok, Thailand, a sister school to the Phoenix Study Group, employed a children's librarian named Betty Van Dyne, an American. I corresponded with Betty for a few weeks, and she invited me to visit her at the school. I accepted eagerly and planned a four-day visit to Bangkok over a long weekend when the PSG would be closed to celebrate Confucious Day.

The week before the trip, I developed, not for the first time, an infection that left my sinuses so congested that I could hardly breathe. Determined to go anyway, I packed my bags. The morning of my departure, Steve asked Mr. Pho to take me to Tan Son Nhut Airport on their way to the office.

Steve's Work Diary

> ***31 October 1974:*** *Took Karen to the airport to go to Bangkok. Gave her instructions to stay there in case something happens.*

The incident with Wong and the battle at Phu Bai finally pushed "pause" on the normal life we'd constructed in that chaotic city. Leaving felt like an escape, but from what? A nagging uneasiness that I could not name hung on the fringes of my mind.

I'll be back soon, no worries.

I kissed Steve goodbye, untroubled by his instructions, believing nothing would happen because it never had. Nothing disrupted Saigon's busy life.

Steve's Work Diary

> ***31 October 1974:*** *We [Pho and I], of course, had problems getting to work. The police have blocked off all of downtown to avoid people demonstrating. Therefore, this caused large traffic jams. The police would not allow people to enter the area. We were lucky in that we were able to talk our way through.*

Demonstrators brandished signs and shouted slogans that Pho translated for Steve, "They don't like the government."

Police allowed no one through the area, but Pho eventually convinced an officer to let them pass. When they finally got to the office, Steve discovered he was one of many who had problems getting to work. Few others had arrived.

Later that night, the American Radio Service reported that the mob was part of a protest rally led by Tran Huu Thanh, a Catholic priest, to confront government corruption. Skirmishes between the protesters and police resulted in injuries to policemen and civilians alike.

Confidence in the government deteriorated, and President Nguyen Van Thieu needed help filling his cabinet for lack of qualified individuals willing to serve. Some anti-government activists called for President Thieu's resignation.

Closely linked to the issue of corruption was the issue of censorship. The press that reported the corruption came under scrutiny.

Saigon's police attacked Vietnamese and American journalists and thousands of supporters, who were protesting the police confiscation of *offensive* newspapers, a practice that proved costly to publishers. The government justified its methods by saying the country was at war and cracked down on citizens who possessed documents deemed detrimental to national security.

Air Vietnam flight 706 took off from Da Nang bound for Saigon, but one of the passengers had other ideas. Hijacking the flight and demanding to go to Hanoi, he jeopardized the lives of the 75 souls on board. The pilot, attempting to land at Phan Rang Air Base, 200 miles north of Saigon, overshot the runway. He executed a go-around maneuver to set up a second approach, which also failed. All 75 aboard perished in the ensuing crash.

Chapter 21

Faith, And Trust, And Pixie Dust

November & December 1974

Saigon calmed after the riots, but nightly artillery fire continued. Rumors of brutal fighting in the Mekong Delta and Central Highlands signaled trouble elsewhere. U.S. Ambassador Graham Martin considered the South Vietnamese Army to be in good shape, able to hold the line and thought there would be a negotiated settlement to the war. Other embassy officials predicted serious trouble ahead.

In Bangkok, to visit the International School, I settled into my room at the Erawan Hotel. The elegant establishment hosted clientele from all over the world. It amazed me to be among them. No longer a teenager curled up on her parent's sofa, seeing the world through *National Geographic* photographs, I was living it!

Traveling the world, however, was not without risks. Since Steve had dropped me off at Tan Son Nhut Airport yesterday, his instruction to stay in Bangkok if something happened in Saigon nagged me. *Why? What does he think could happen?* I stored Steve's words in the back of my mind and prepared for the school visit.

Betty Van Dyne, the children's librarian at the International School, set aside an entire morning to show me around. A mature, energetic, and friendly forty-something, she surprised me—I'd expected someone closer to my age. Her enthusiasm for the job radiated like a heat wave. I wanted to emulate her.

The school featured a modern, American-style library with up-to-date furniture, audio-visual equipment, and rows of stacks filled with books.

Could Phoenix Study Group's library hope to match this?

Betty's main concern was the unique needs of expat American kids.

"Adjusting to a foreign culture is a real problem for some of them," Betty said. "The families move every few years. Relocating within the U.S. isn't too hard on them, but coming to a place like Thailand is another story. It's all new and very, very different."

"Yes, I've seen that in my school, too. They have to learn a whole new way of operating—a new language, making local friends, learning to appreciate a new culture—it's hard enough for adults, let alone kids. I experienced that myself." I said.

"There's a lot of stress on the families. The more information they have, the better the chances they'll adjust well. Let me show you my favorite tool. The kids love it, and they share it with their families. It helps."

I expected an elaborate program or piece of equipment, but Betty's favorite tool was a simple four-drawer vertical file cabinet. Folders, arranged alphabetically by the names of the countries that made up Southeast Asia, filled the drawers. Inside the folders, travel brochures, postcards, and colorful literature offered an easy and creative way for students to begin an exploration of their new home.

The tour over, I thanked Betty for her time and offered to return the favor should she venture to Saigon. If I'd felt better, I would have accepted her invitation for dinner at her home. "Another time," I told her. I needed to head back to my hotel and rest. Lightheaded, realizing that my dream of seeing the world was coming true, I fell into a deep sleep until morning.

The following day, I treated myself to shopping at the Nightingale Olympic department store, a treasure trove of elegant objects and delicious goodies not available in Saigon. I bought good cheese, a few toiletries, and my favorite Guy LaRoche perfume, *Fidji*.

Later, I ordered dinner in my room. Women's lib notwithstanding, I felt uncomfortable eating alone in the dining room. Besides, my sinus infection left me exhausted and constantly blowing my nose. Not good company.

In the morning, I returned to Saigon with my treasures and a batch of travel brochures and postcards to begin a vertical file like Betty's.

Even with its wonky furniture, the Phoenix Study Group library looked like a school library. Still, I needed to address the guts of the operation—the book collection and the card catalog—so it would function like one.

The school had recently moved, and the books remained in their packing boxes. Before I could order new titles, I needed to undertake the painstaking job of inventorying the books on hand, checking their titles against the card catalog, and organizing them. Nothing brought me more satisfaction than creating order out of chaos, and I dug in with gusto.

One morning, while I was head-down, deep into the project, Dr. Bottorff appeared in the library. He carried a large cardboard box full of donated paperbacks and informed me he wanted them processed—fast.

Donations of books don't always thrill librarians who spend several years learning to be discerning in book selection. I didn't understand why he'd made these particular books a priority. Maybe the donor was an influential parent or board member. I didn't ask.

The interruption felt more like an intrusion. Tamping down a few choice words, I told him I'd do my best. He left the box on the floor next to my desk. A few days later, I looked over the contents.

Most of the paperbacks turned out to be too adult for the age group the school served, and, like a sorcerer, I made them disappear. I held no power over most circumstances surrounding my life in Saigon, but I had control over that small thing, which made my day.

The Catholic orphanage served as an indication of how desperate and miraculous life could be for some. A couple we knew adopted a baby girl from the orphanage; she was the most pitiful child I'd ever seen. Sores covered her emaciated little body. During the first week out of the orphanage, the new parents discovered she had pneumonia and needed to be hospitalized.

The doctors at the Seventh Day Adventist Hospital resorted to shaving her head to find a spot to insert intravenous lines, her arms and legs being too thin. She was one of the lucky ones, though, and would get the care she needed to thrive.

Her adoptive parents had already taken in three other girls who were turning into lovely young women and a little boy they found abandoned in the market in equally bad shape. This couple had transformed him into a healthy, energetic child.

The idea of taking on such a challenge terrified Steve and me. I could fix a damaged library, and Steve could fix a damaged highway department, but taking responsibility for a damaged child was frightening. What if we made huge mistakes? They wouldn't be so easy to correct. As much as we admired our friends, adoption wasn't for us.

Home Leave. *Leave home? Leave for home? What is home? Where is home?*

Steve and I had made a home in Saigon and had a housekeeper for whom we provided a home. *Home* equaled the apartment on Kỳ Dong Street. A trip to the States equaled just another vacation. We'd be gone for a month. A lot could happen in a month in Vietnam.

On November 23, our plan to see more of the world unfolded as we traveled back to American soil. We left Muoi in charge of the apartment, and a parent volunteer took care of the Phoenix Study Group library.

After an overnight flight from Bangkok on Pan American Airlines, the first stop was Tehran. The welcoming Intercontinental Hotel offered a haven after we'd been aggressively interrogated at the airport as to the purpose of our trip and taken into separate enclosures for a thorough body search. *I don't get it. We're Americans. We are not a threat. Why are they harassing us?*

Wanting to put the unpleasantness behind us, we asked the concierge to arrange something more enjoyable—a tour of the Grand Bazaar. She put us in the hands of a friendly gentleman named Immanuel, who showed us to a big American sedan. To make sure we knew he was a Syrian Christian, he repeated that information several times.

Tehran's wide, tree-lined boulevards reminded me of Washington, D.C. The enormous bazaar stretched over six miles. Dusky alleyways branched off the main corridors. Shops filled with carpets, gold jewelry, bins of spices, antiques, clothing, fabrics, meat, vegetables—it was undoubtedly Grand.

From Iran, our itinerary took us to Germany to visit *Herrischried am Sackingen*, a village at the southern edge of the *Schwartzwald,* where I hoped to find information about my father's side of the family.

Fresh snow made the roads dicey. As we drove into the tiny village, I spotted a shop with a snow-capped sign above the door that read "KAISER," my family name. The dry goods store also housed the office of the town clerk. I thought he would be the person who could help me.

Entering the building, I approached a gentleman who looked like he worked there. Using my best college German, I asked to see the town clerk. The gentleman informed me that Herr Detweiler was not in. I explained that I only had one day in town and that I'd come from America via Vietnam to do research.

Herr Detweiler, he said, was probably at home and directed us to a white house nearby. Back outside, I looked around for a white house only to realize that all the houses were white. The tiny town had few streets, though, and after searching street by street, we saw a mailbox with the name Detweiler painted on it.

A man wearing house slippers and a heavy cardigan over woolen trousers answered my knock. He looked stunned to see two strangers at his door.

"Ja was wünschen sie?" he asked. Yes, what do you want?

I introduced Steve and myself and stated my business. He invited us into the foyer of his tidy home but didn't offer us refreshments or a seat, wanting to get right to the point of this surprise visit. He told us that Father Eügene Rüd, at the Catholic church down the road, kept a record of all births, deaths, marriages, and baptisms in the parish. We should go there.

At the church, I pounded on the locked door to no response. Then, the creak of a window opening overheard drew our attention. Peering down on us, the ruddy-faced cleric called down,

"Ja?"

"Ich suche Florentine Kaiser," I said. *"Mein Urgroßvater. Taufregister."* I'm looking for Florentine Kaiser, my great-grandfather's baptism record.

"Ich lasse dich rein. Werden Sie bald fertig sein?" replied Father Rüd. I will let you in. Will you be finished soon?

"Ja, sehr bald, vielleicht," I said. Yes, very soon, maybe.

In an upstairs room of the church, I found the christening record of Florentine Kaiser, my great-grandfather. The words *"Nach Amerika ausgewandert"* were handwritten next to the entry. Immigrated to America . . . a goosebumps moment. Father Rüd transcribed the information on an official form, applied his stamp, and showed us out.

On a whim, Steve suggested we drive on to Zürich. Not far. Barbed wire barricades left over from World War II bordered the road. We bought cheese, bread, and ham in a village for a picnic lunch. The Hotel Zurich had a last-minute room available, and we debated whether to pay the exorbitant rate of $50 US per night. It was late, and we did.

We arrived in London on December 2 and rented a car. I had lived in East Anglia in the late 1960s and wanted to return to see how it had changed. We drove north to Woodbridge and Ipswich, two small towns near the North Sea. Steve stopped at every chandlery, hoping to find fittings for his and Don's sailboat. They hoped to launch her in January when we returned from home leave.

An avid Jaguar owner, Steve planned our time in London to coincide with the annual Jaguar Drivers' Club UK meeting, which took place in a restaurant that looked like it had occupied the same ground for centuries. Golden light from the multi-paned, mullioned windows seemed to welcome us on a cold evening, and we won the prize for having come the farthest for the event.

From London, we flew to Philadelphia and, finally, to Allentown, Pennsylvania. My parents picked us up at the airport and took us to their home in Kutztown. Leaving Saigon hit hard. An unexpected feeling that we'd abandoned our home overwhelmed me.

Were we so cavalier as to think we had no obligation to the people who shaped our daily lives there? We could hop in and out of the war-torn country with American passports. It seemed wrong to enjoy peace and cheer while people like Muoi, Patty, and Pho faced endless turmoil.

However, an element of turmoil for Steve and me still overshadowed our lives—the mysterious transfer telegram Lew Chittim claimed originated at Jorgensen's home office, just two hours away by car in Gaithersburg, Maryland.

"I'm going to drive down to Gaithersburg today," Steve said early one morning, "try to get some answers about the transfer. You want to come along?"

"Thanks . . . I don't think so. Mom and I have some Christmas shopping to do. You go. Now's the time to get to the bottom of this," I said, kissing him for luck.

I went shopping with my mother and got reacquainted with my younger sisters, Karol and Kristine.

Karol, nineteen and the baby of the family attended the small state college where our father headed the geology/geography department. Twelve years separated Karol and me, but they felt like generations.

Married with two small children, Kristine, twenty-eight, lived in the Poconos. Our lifestyles couldn't have been more different. Finding common ground among the three of us wasn't always easy. Still, we all agreed on Christmas traditions—a holiday scene painted on the living room picture window by my sisters, the Kingston Trio Christmas album playing on the hi-fi, and helping our mother cut fruit for the twenty-four-hour, ambrosia-like salad.

"How did it go in Gaithersburg?" I asked Steve when he got back that night. "Did you get a chance to ask about the mysterious transfer?"

"Yeah. You-*bet*-I-did." He fired the words like bullets, wrestling his shaking voice to submission.

"Jeez! Take a minute. Breathe. Calm down. Tell me what happened." I'd seen him angry before, but not like this.

"I talked to Roy Jorgensen himself. He told me the transfer idea didn't start with him. The first correspondence came from Lew, who told them my work in Vietnam was done. Gaithersburg assumed I was ready to be reassigned."

"That snake. How did you leave it with Mr. Jorgensen?"

"I told him I wanted to stay in Saigon until further notice. The work isn't finished. I'm just starting on what we originally planned because things were disorganized when I arrived. There's so much left to do . . . and I told him about your job with the school. Neither one of us is ready to leave."

"What did he say?"

"He had no problem with us staying in Vietnam."

"What about Lew? Any idea why he's trying to sabotage you?"

"We don't agree on a lot of things, and I push back on his pet solution for every problem, 'If it's good enough for Montana, it's good enough for Vietnam.' Well, it's not. I challenge him. He hates that."

"Can you live with it?"

"Guess I'll have to. I don't want to leave until the project is finished."

The home visit came to an end, and I felt apprehensive. I thought I'd adapted to Vietnam. Still, after a month of reliable American plumbing and electricity, daily mail delivery by the postal service, and the comfort of my family, I realized what a struggle Vietnam had been. The relentless, day-to-day pressure of maintaining a life there had taken its toll.

At the airport to catch the flight back, we said goodbye to my parents and thanked them for their hospitality. I tried not to let the tears show. The exciting, happy, adventurous life I'd been portraying in letters covered up the reality. Although Saigon did have its charms, life there was hard.

Our small family group congregated nearby while Steve checked our bags with the gate agent. The process was taking longer than usual.

"That's a first," Steve said, joining us.

"What?" I asked.

"I mixed up the departure time. We just missed our flight and all our connections."

For a moment, I felt a reprieve. *We can stay here longer!*

No, we can't. Saigon needs us, but for how long?

The efficient ticket agent worked her magic. We'd leave in an hour.

"Don't worry," my father said, giving me a tight hug, "you'll be back soon."

He had no idea how soon.

North Vietnam's fierce attack on the radio relay station atop Nui Ba Den mountain in Tay Ninh province, sixty-six miles west of Saigon, near the Cambodian border, lasted for weeks. Attempts to resupply the company of indigenous forces that operated the station were unsuccessful because of heavy missile and rocket fire. Unable to hold on, the company gathered its wounded and descended the mountain to friendly lines, crippling the ARVN's communications ability.

Chapter 22

Reality Continues to Ruin My Life

January 1975

On January 6, North Vietnam captured Phuoc Binh, the capital of Phuoc Long Province, 75 miles north of Saigon, gaining control of one of South Vietnam's provincial capitals for the first time. The lengthy battle decimated the ARVN forces defending Phuoc Binh, who ran out of supplies and ammunition. Morale was low, desertion high.

The Politburo in Hanoi realized the lack of U.S. response signified it would not intervene militarily and that an opportunity existed to destroy South Vietnam's Army, which seemed to be rapidly deteriorating on its own.

The trip back to Saigon was a nightmare of missed flights and bad weather, but Muoi welcomed us home with a bouquet and a happy smile. We were two days late, and she had worried we wouldn't come back at all. She'd heard the whispers circulating among the maids in our building—trouble on the way. Steve and I returned to a city on low boil. Everything still looked normal, but somehow the hologram had shifted.

Steve's Work Diary

> ***7 January 1975:*** *Went to work. Received word on the news that Phuoc Binh had fallen. No other news. Everyone said that it is dangerous to go out on the road. Security is a day-to-day situation.*

"Remember that hot landing yesterday?" Steve asked me, referring to the plane's speed on touching down at Tan Son Nhut airport. "Did you notice the fortifications at the ends of the runway?"

"Yes . . . and no," I answered. "Why?"

"Well, I think I know what happened. According to the guys at the office, a battle erupted at Phuoc Binh, which is on the flight path into the airport. When the pilot started his descent, the tower must have warned him about stray artillery fire. So, he came in high and dropped down fast for the landing. The fortifications were to stop the plane if the pilot couldn't. We were pretty lucky."

"Jeez! Do you really think that's what happened?"

"It's a definite possibility. And, last night, the VC pumped shells into Phu Lam near Cholon."

Phu Lam, situated on the western outskirts of Saigon, had once been the U.S. Army's communications base. In 1972, the U.S. unceremoniously turned the base over to the Army of the Republic of [South] Vietnam.

"Cholon? That's where Patty lives," I said. "Can we find out if she's okay?"

"I doubt it, now that Wong's under arrest. He was the go-between."

"I hate this! Why didn't we find out where she lives . . . or at least her Chinese name?"

"Don't worry," Steve said. "Things will probably calm down again. Saigon seems the same."

Despite Steve's assurance, the city felt different in subtle ways. The signs of change accumulated, one after another—more military vehicles on the streets, fewer cyclos, more aggressive panhandlers, and fewer tennis players on the courts at *Cercle Sportif*. Something was brewing, and we were perfectly positioned to get a ring-side seat.

Steve's Work Diary

> ***8 January 1975:*** *Work as usual with discussions about the 6-month report. Heard on the news that the [aircraft carrier] U.S.S. Enterprise was moving toward Vietnam.*
>
> ***9 January 1975:*** *There is, of course, a lot of discussion at work about evacuation. If, when, etc. Don Burgess . . . checked with the consul and seemed to be satisfied with any evacuation plans that had been made.*
>
> ***10 January 1975:*** *Work as usual. Traffic blocked off at Le Loi for a pro-government demonstration about the fighting at Phuoc Binh. Last night, the lights went out at 4:15 a.m. and came back on at 6 a.m. This was a result of an explosion at the Tu Duc generating plant, we later found out—also, a lot of shelling last night.*
>
> ***17 January 1975:*** *On the way to work this morning, we passed a bomb that the VC had placed. This was on Hong Thap Thu Street in front of the Health Ministry. I don't think it ever went off.*

What . . . where am I?

I stopped at the top of the stairs and looked around, confused. It took me a minute to realize I'd climbed past my floor and arrived, instead, at the roof of my apartment building, something I'd never done. I headed back down to where Muoi stood, holding the apartment door open for me. She looked as bewildered as I felt.

"Chee-chaa! *Madame, ou allez?"* Muoi said, concerned. Where are you going?

"Ugh, Muoi, I don't know," I said, trying to laugh it off. "A silly mistake."

I didn't want to alarm her by saying what frightened me—evacuation plans, the fall of a provincial capital, an aircraft carrier cruising toward us, unexploded bombs in the city, heavy shelling at night. I fought to keep a clear head.

Later that night, after Muoi had gone down to her room, Steve and I sat in the privacy of the back bedroom/office and talked about what had happened.

"It was the weirdest feeling," I said. "For a minute, I didn't know where I was, must have walked right past Muoi without seeing her."

"That's not like you," Steve observed.

"No, it's not, and you know what's odd? When we first moved here, I'd be exhausted by the time I climbed three flights of stairs to the apartment in this heat, but today, I whizzed by without thinking about anything except the latest developments . . . didn't think I was on our floor because the climb was so easy."

"That's called conditioning."

"Might be good to be in shape. What did Don find out about evacuation plans?"

"As far as he could tell, the mission has designated assembly points around central Saigon. Everybody's supposed to go to the closest one when they give the signal. Buses will take us to the airport to fly out, probably to the Philippines or Guam."

"What's the signal?"

"Whoever Don talked to didn't say."

"You're not making me feel much better, you know."

"Relax. I doubt it will come to that."

One hot, super-steamy night when the line between clean-sticky and dirty-sticky was all too thin, we attended a dinner party at the home of Lynn and Bob Bell, American expats like us. I had met Lynn through the American Women's Association. Bob worked in the Saigon office of Price-Waterhouse, an accounting firm.

They were about our age and had two young children who frolicked about the house, excited by the unusual swarm of activity. In addition to dinner guests, a van carrying a crew with microphones, video cameras, and studio lights arrived.

Bob greeted us on the front porch and explained the reason for the hubbub. We'd be joined that evening by a team from ABC News, Tokyo, reporting on a day in the life of an American businessman and his family in exotic Saigon. Would we agree to be filmed? Neither Steve nor I had a problem with that.

The Bells' attractive dining room, with its spotless white linens, fine china, and gleaming flatware, called to us like a siren. Their maid held a match to the wicks of the tall, white candles. Flames sprang to life and lit the room with a soft glow. The fan on the high ceiling hummed, doing its best to relieve the heat. We took our seats.

The TV producer urged everyone to act naturally during dinner and ignore the cameras and the microphone dangling overhead on a boom.

"We'll just hang out in the background.," he said. "When the lights come on, you guys go ahead and talk normally. Don't pay any attention to us." *Pay no attention to the man behind the curtain.*

"Ready! Action!" he called out.

Click, buzz. . . . Blinding, white light flooded the room, rendering the candlelight invisible. The hot night became even hotter. Somewhere, people would be watching six American expats sweat on the evening news.

"It's not going to be easy ignoring them, is it?" Bob said, referring to the TV crew.

"Interesting they're here now," said Steve, "with all the new security measures. Do you think they might have a reason besides producing a piece about your life?"

"Who knows? Your guess is as good as mine, but we probably should save our opinions until after they've gone."

"Yes," said Lynn. "Let's talk about something else. Karen, who's your dressmaker these days?"

Small talk accompanied the rest of the meal. Eventually, the film crew packed their gear and left.

Among the guests that night were Al and Jan Topping. Al was Pan Am's director of operations for Vietnam and Cambodia.

"So, Al, what do you make of the latest developments?" Bob asked, refilling glasses with French wine.

"I don't know," Al said. "Could be something, could be nothing. At Pan Am, we're watching and waiting. This war's been going on so long that conflict's become a way of life."

"I wonder what these people could do if they weren't fighting each other," I said.

"Boy, I'd sure like to find out," said Jan. "The Vietnamese are industrious. They could do almost anything."

"What d'ya think about the TV crew? Are they really just here doing a story about the Bells, or do they have a different angle?" Steve asked.

"My opinion," said Al, "is they're here to cover any story that breaks. Surely they know about the USS Enterprise and the fall of Phuoc Binh. They're anticipating something, and a good producer is going to want to be first on the scene for what happens next. I seriously doubt they're on a covert mission."

Faced with a dubious future, Steve and I packed our important possessions to ship back to the States for storage. The ordeal tested our nerves, already under duress.

Important possessions included things on which we'd spent a great deal of time and money—a set of Royal Crown Derby porcelain, bronze flatware, electronics, and oriental rugs. Southeast Asia had been like a regional grand bazaar, and we'd taken full advantage.

At United Service Packers, Steve picked up air and surface freight forms. Because Steve worked on a USAID contract, the bureaucrat at USAID couldn't sign off on the shipment request without a copy of the contract. He told Steve to go to Embassy Shipping. There, Steve found out they couldn't approve the request without clearance from the contracting officer. Steve finally acquired the necessary signatures only to be told that he also needed a shipping list . . . in triplicate. Red tape followed us everywhere, even in these uncertain times.

Vietnamese artisans learned the ancient Chinese lacquerware-making technique sometime during the thousand years that China ruled

Vietnam. Products of this ancient art, lacquerware boxes and bowls, had been found in tombs to ease the departed into the afterlife. Families passed the skill from generation to generation. When Vietnam was a French colony, artisans studied at *École des Beaux-Arts* in Paris or the Indochina School of Fine Arts in Hanoi and began to create new designs using eggshell, mother-of-pearl, and gold leaf.

Lacquer, from a small tree of the same name, produces a toxic sap containing *urushiol,* the same oil found in poison ivy. The juice makes a highly durable, waterproof sealant. Considering that lacquerware is hand-crafted, artisans risked a nasty rash if careless.

Steve and I talked about buying a piece of Vietnamese lacquerware for weeks.

"I'd like to have a small chest or something," Steve said. "It's unique, a nice souvenir."

"True, but I don't really like it," I said. "It looks tacky, cheap."

"The fake stuff is cheap-looking, but authentic lacquerware is exquisite. Each item has to be sanded and painted by hand. Sometimes, it takes fifteen to thirty layers of painting and sanding to create a finished piece. Let's look at some."

We went to the furniture street and soon came across a stunning black cabinet, thirty-five inches tall, with a delicate goldfish design shimmering below layers of transparent lacquer. Its two doors locked with a brass bar shaped like a tiger. And like the big cat, Steve leaped and bought it.

The cabinet, likely worth more than our other treasures combined, added panache to the humble apartment and forever changed my opinion of lacquerware. It was such a delight to look at that Steve decided not to include it with the current shipment of important possessions so we could enjoy its beauty for a while longer before sending it to storage.

U.S. President Gerald R. Ford, ignoring the advice of National Security Advisor Henry Kissinger and that of the Joint Chiefs of Staff, took no significant military action to support South Vietnam's struggle against the communist invasion. However, he asked Congress for $300 million in military aid for the country. In no mood to keep throwing money at a lost cause, Congress rejected Ford's request.

Chapter 23

Life Can Only Be Understood Backwards

February 1975

With the success of the offensive against Phuoc Binh, North Vietnamese general Van Tien Dung took command of the People's Army of [North] Vietnam. His next objective was to capture Ban Me Thuot, the capital of Dak Lak Province, 198 miles north of Saigon.

In Saigon, yellow blossoms on the *hoang mai* trees announced the upcoming Tet holiday that would usher in the Year of the Cat. Red lanterns and decorations of all kinds appeared in the shops, along with firecrackers and red-dyed daisies. The flower market reopened on Nguyen Hue Street, which was blocked off to allow pedestrians to browse among the blossoms.

The apartment building on Ky Dong Street sported a new coat

of paint. Throughout the city, the citizens of Saigon prepared to welcome the new year with hope. Saigon had been as quiet as ever, but the embassy again advised Americans to stay away from the downtown area during Tet.

Most of the Vietnamese staff in Steve's office were away for the two-week holiday—work slowed to a near standstill. We gave Muoi her New Year's bonus and time off to celebrate.

With everyone on holiday, Steve and I went to Bangkok for a long weekend. Shopping there boggled the senses. Merchants crammed small shops from floor to ceiling with their merchandise. Imagine a shop filled top to bottom with shiny pots and pans or a toy store showcasing nothing but fanciful patchwork creatures. I spent a few *baht* on two—a turtle and a caterpillar—to amuse students in the library. We took the bus to Pattaya, on the Gulf of Siam, for a day at the beach. The world was our playground, full of fun, discovery, and adventure. What a life!

Returning to Saigon brought us back to reality like a slap.

"Got an angry call from Lew today," Steve said. "He's furious that I left the country without telling him."

"He had to know you got the exit visas," I said.

"I tried to reason with him, but he wouldn't listen. I just let him rant until he ran out of steam."

"There'll probably be consequences."

"Yeah, and that's not all. Lew is so paranoid and suspicious that he grills everybody who goes on home leave about where they went and why. The man is sure good at schmoozing the customer, though."

In no time at all, fallout from the confrontation manifested itself. Without giving him an explanation, Lew took over Steve's responsibility for writing the project's monthly progress report, not a task usually handled by someone in Lew's position as chief of party. He intended the move to rankle Steve. Even though the country seemed in crisis, Lew needed to make a point.

Meanwhile, the Phoenix Study Group library buzzed with activity. I trained a group of parent volunteers to process new books delivered from the States and wrote procedures to help them.

My rush order of library skills workbooks arrived. They would provide a basis for lesson plans. I asked one student from each class to act as class librarian, take charge of the date due stamp, and check out books for their classmates.

When I wasn't working with students or parents, I spent my time reconciling the cards in the card catalog with the books on the shelves. Excited by our progress, I submitted my supply order for the 1976 school year two months ahead of schedule.

Running into the kids outside of school happened all the time. A child's voice called out during a Saturday afternoon swim at the DAO pool.

"There's my librarian."

I couldn't see the speaker, but a second voice piped up, "She's my librarian, too." I liked being known as their librarian. The smile stayed with me for the rest of the day.

One morning, the second-grade teacher came to me with a question.

"I've assigned my class a story-writing exercise," she said. "Can you think of a way for the kids to use some of the better stories in connection with the library?"

"Well, your students could read their stories to another class,"

I suggested. "Fourth grade is coming tomorrow morning. Would you like to bring your group in then?"

"Good idea. Yes. We'll be here."

The next day, both groups sat around the library anticipating this new twist on story hour. The second graders amazed me with their confidence. One after another, they stood and read their words in clear, expressive voices.

The stories held no surprises until one little girl took everyone's breath away with a story about the life cycle of a rose that couldn't have been more timely. I summarized it in a letter to my parents:

> *A tiny bud grew bigger and bigger until it blossomed into a magnificent rose. The maid went into the garden and chose that rose, over all the others, to take into the house. The rose brought joy day after day until, one day, the edges of its petals turned brown, and its head drooped. Then, the beautiful rose wilted. Its petals fell to the floor. At last, it died. The maid carried the rose outside and threw it in the trash.*

The seven-year-old had written a story about life and death, about the impermanence of everything. I wondered what experiences she must have had in her seven years to write a story like that. She could just as well have been writing about South Vietnam.

The inhabitants of Saigon, expats included, remained innocent of the fact that 198 miles to the north, South Vietnam was unraveling. I continued doing what I'd been doing—planning programs for the American Women's Association, going to French class every day, sewing clothes for the April fashion show, teaching Sunday School, running the library, and making plans to attend the International Conference of School Librarians in Berlin the following July.

LaSalle Extension University awarded me a certificate stating I had completed the correspondence course in interior decorating I'd been working on in the evenings. Steve and I played tennis and taught church members to square-dance in our dining room as if riots hadn't happened and explosions every night were normal because, for that time and place, they were.

Late afternoon. The sun sat on the shoulders of the trees. Muoi called me from the kitchen in the breathless, urgent voice she used when something upset her.

"*Madame, madame*, come quick . . . outside!"

I ran into the kitchen. Muoi stood on the catwalk outside the kitchen door. I joined her.

"Look, boy in tree . . . fall."

Three stories below, a small gaggle of people congregated around one of the coconut palms. Everyone talked at once. Harsh Vietnamese tones rattled against each other. Thin arms waved wildly. Whatever happened took place only moments ago.

"Go!" I said, horrified. "Find out what happened!"

The expression on Muoi's face when she came back signaled sad news.

"Boy, die," she said.

One of the youngsters who hung around the compound had climbed the tree and fallen to his death. My heart pounded. I couldn't breathe. I'd never experienced anything like this.

What should I do? What could I do?

"Oh my God, Muoi," I cried. "We need to do something!" I started for the stairs.

"No, *Madame*," Muoi called. "You no help. Family come, take boy home, take care of him."

Reluctantly, we went back inside, but it was impossible to concentrate on anything else. *Why did he climb that tree? Was he showing off for his friends? Maybe he just wanted a coconut because he was hungry. Will these people ever find peace?*

People poured into Saigon from the provinces—American advisors, missionaries, and government workers—bringing horror stories about heavy troop buildup near Ban Me Thuot. Word traveled fast among expats. For the first time, we glimpsed an impending disaster.

The coming battle would begin Campaign 275, a limited offensive to capture the Central Highlands, with diversionary attacks near Kon Tum and Pleiku. At the same time, North Vietnamese General Dung built up forces near Ban Me Thuot, his main objective. The hologram that was Saigon started to pixelate.

Chapter 24

The Worst Thing

March 1975

One week after the assault on Ban Me Thuot, North Vietnamese troops controlled the city and the province. South Vietnam's President Thieu unrealistically ordered General Phu to retake Ban Me Thuot and withdrew all ARVN forces from Kon Tum and Pleiku in the Central Highlands to assist him.

The units at Ban Me Thuot suffered heavy losses, and General Phu abandoned his attempt to retake the city. The retreat to the coast began. Rather than report for duty, many soldiers deserted to save themselves and their families. Senior officers departed the highlands by helicopter, leaving a leaderless mob mixed with fleeing civilians trying to make their way to the coast—the convoy of tears. Relentlessly attacked by the North Vietnamese, hundreds died along the way.

As deputy chief of the CIA office in Saigon, Conrad La Gueux received reports of the poorly executed retreat and viewed the tragic situation from a seat on an Air America helicopter. At that moment, his long experience in intelligence told him that the ARVN could not win the war. It was over for South Vietnam, and he needed to convince the ambassador.

Steve's Work Diary

> *19 March 1975: . . . With the fall of Ban Me Thuot and the pullback of ARVN troops from the Central Highlands, things could get a bit hectic. . . . Haven't noticed any change in mood in Saigon.*

Da Lat, in the southern section of the Central Highlands, provided fresh fruits and vegetables to the markets of Saigon until the chaos of war disrupted transportation to the city.

Ambassador Martin transferred part of the embassy staff elsewhere, reducing the size of the mission. The U.S. government closed some of its facilities and eliminated jobs. The faculty at the Phoenix Study Group hosted a farewell luncheon for one of the teachers whose husband's government job no longer existed.

Even so, government officials agreed to provide a larger building for the school at the end of the school year. I felt like the "Push me, Pull you" statue on Le Loi Street. On the one hand, rumors about moving to a new school suggested smooth sailing. On the other hand, the talk didn't mesh with North Vietnam's capturing provincial capitals one after another.

The pros and cons of going or staying chased each other around in conversations with Steve. A revolving door of possibilities circled my brain and pushed sleep away for hours.

"Hear anything from Don since he and Nga went to the States on home leave?" I asked Steve.

"Just that they'll be back in April. They will stop in Guam to finalize Nga's US citizenship."

"Should we think about leaving, too, just 'til things settle down? We don't know what will happen, maybe nothing, but all we get is bits and pieces of news. I'm starting to worry."

Steve sighed heavily and shook his head, "I've got to finish the project . . . unless USAID decides to close it down, which it won't do as long as Ambassador Martin insists that South Vietnam can somehow survive. Look, whatever's happening in the highlands isn't affecting us."

It was always all about the project for Steve.

"Maybe USAID will put the project on hold," I said. "If they did, we could go to Bangkok or somewhere and return when things are less iffy."

"What about your job at the school? Has anybody talked about closing it?"

"Nothing from the embassy about the school, either. If it were dangerous here, wouldn't someone say something about pulling families out?"

"You'd think so."

"I don't want to give up my job—it's the first one I've had that I like, but I could take a leave of absence."

"I think we're okay for now . . . at least until somebody tells us otherwise."

We stayed.

Steve's Work Diary

> ***20 March 1975:*** *More bad news today about the war. Kon Tum, Dar Lac, Quang Tri, and Thua Thien-Hue provinces seem to be giving up. The ARVN is moving back to consolidate positions. Da Lat appears to be in danger, and*

> *the rumor is that all Americans are being pulled out of there. New curfew tonight @ 2200. Office morale is rapidly going downhill. The Vietnamese resent very much that we ask why the people aren't willing to fight. I look for this to cause problems later on. It is difficult to get any work done with an objective point of view. Personnel in VHA are more worried about their families, and their attention is on this rather than work. [Neither] USAID nor the embassy here has made any statement.*

A series of unrelated events chipped away at our feelings of security. Steve came into my sewing room and sat in the extra chair. He held a finger to his lips, signaling he had something to tell me but didn't want Muoi to overhear.

"Just heard the USS Enterprise reached the South China Sea off the coast," he whispered. "Something about evacuating Americans."

"What! We're being evacuated!" I whispered back, a swarm of bees buzzing under my ribcage.

"No, no, I don't think so. It's probably just posturing. We'll see, but I wanted you to know in case."

Air America friends Burt and Jeannie Foote had allowed us to use their APO address to send and receive mail until the Defense Attaché's Office rescinded their APO privileges for no apparent reason. At the same time, the DAO mysteriously restored Steve's access to the PX and commissary—even more bizarre, the PX stocked fashionable Vogue dress patterns for the first time, and the commissary offered goodies not seen there before.

I attributed low attendance at the American Women's Association March program to disinterest until I discovered how many American women had packed up their children and left the country. *What's happening? Nothing makes sense!*

British friends Jane and Pete Jackson would return to England soon and invited Steve and me for a farewell dinner at their favorite curry restaurant.

I hadn't seen much of Jane since we worked together at the Montessori school. Pete, a non-commissioned officer in the British Army attached to the embassy, spent most of his career in Southeast Asia. He loved to tell how he and Jane married in Malaysia, Jane wearing a sari.

They picked us up in a Land Rover and drove us through the crazy Saigon traffic into a dodgy part of town I'd never been to before. Grime-covered street lights clicked on, turning the night into a film noir set. He stopped before a seedy-looking eatery, and I wondered if Pete had made a mistake.

The restaurant's open front revealed a poorly lit, shabby interior furnished with a collection of crudely made round tables and stools crowded together near the entrance. A glimpse of the kitchen in the back didn't instill confidence in the quality of the food, but our friends recommended it.

How bad can it be?

We piled out of the car into the street before I spotted them. Standing in front of the restaurant, two solidly built, swarthy men carrying menacing-looking knives in their belts stared at us.

Oh boy, now what?

Pete took in the situation immediately and didn't hesitate. He walked up to the men, looked them in the eye, and . . . shook their hands! He knew them—Kulbir and Ganju—Gurkha soldiers employed as guards at the British Embassy. Pete was their commander.

The British Army first encountered *Gorkhali* soldiers during the Anglo-Nepalese War between the British East India Company and what is now Nepal. As the British refer to them, Gurkhas were closely associated with the *khukuri*, a forward-curving Nepali knife, and had a reputation as fierce fighters. There is an adage: *If a man says he is not afraid of dying, he is either lying or he is a Gurkha.*

The six of us took a corner table, and the grungy restaurant turned into a cozy, exotic eating place. The Gurkhas were not reticent, and the dinner conversation was lively and exciting.

The evening proceeded comfortably until a commotion at another table disturbed our good time. A group of Vietnamese men became loud and unruly, alarming the owners, who didn't know how to disarm the situation.

While the rest of us tried to ignore the noise, both Gurkhas rose slowly and deliberately from the table. They approached the offending group with the force of a slow-moving tidal wave. Staking out positions on either side of the troublemaker, they towered over him like giant sequoias. One of the Gurkhas leaned down and whispered something so calmly you knew he meant business.

Immediately, the noise ceased, and order returned to the dining room. The Gurkhas strolled back to our table and resumed their meals without another word, as if nothing had happened.

"What was that all about?" Steve asked.

"I don't know," said Pete, "but I would not want to make these guys mad."

"*Bonjour*, Karen."

A familiar French accent wafted across the parking lot of the *Institut Français*. I turned to see Guy Nandillon walking my way. He worked in the administration office and had helped me register two years before when I was new in town. Always gregarious and friendly, he was the antithesis of most Americans' opinions of the French.

"*Bonjour*, Guy. *Comment ça va*?"

"*Bien, Bien*. I need a favor, he continued in English. "Do you have apples?"

"Apples? No, but I might be able to find some at the commissary—fruit is scarce these days. Why?"

"My daughter is sick. The doctor thinks apples will be good for her."

I was happy to help Guy in return for his kindness to me and, a few days later, delivered a bag of apples to his apartment, where I met his wife and daughter.

I wanted to get to know them better, and hosting a casual dinner at the Ky Dong apartment lingered on the edges of my mind for a week. The French were a close-knit community and rarely socialized outside their sphere, but Guy and Maddie seemed different, and I decided to venture an invitation.

My primary concern was Maddie, who spoke only a little English; my French could have been more fluent. To avoid a stressful evening, I invited my friend from the *Cercle Sportief,* Catherine, an American woman who spoke beautiful French, and her husband, Armand Malo, a Frenchman who spoke beautiful English.

Both couples accepted, and the evening was a lot of fun. My nervousness disappeared. Stretching beyond our usual social circle with those people created a feeling of belonging in that strange, foreign place like nothing else possibly could. I hated to think we might lose it all.

The People's Army of North Vietnam marched into Quang Trị, South Vietnam's northernmost city, prepared for battle. They were disappointed. Its defenders had abandoned the city days before. It fell to the invaders without a fight.

The Imperial City of Hue, thirty-four miles south of Quang Tri, followed six days later as PAVN forces rolled over the ARVN units, picking them off one by one until they retreated to the coast. The Army of the Republic of [South] Vietnam in the I Corps Tactical Zone disintegrated. Deserters joined the panicked mob of refugees taking to the sea to save themselves.

Da Nang, fifty miles south of Hue and six hundred miles north of Saigon, sat in North Vietnam's crosshairs. Half a million refugees had already been evacuated, and 16,000 ARVN soldiers forced themselves onto barges and transport planes, pushing foreigners aside in a mad attempt to escape south to Na Trang or Phan Rang for safety.

PAVN troops captured one coastal city after another without firing a shot. ARVN officers and men deserted by the hundreds. U.S. Army Chief of Staff Frederick Weyand assessed the situation in light of such intelligence.

"It is possible that with abundant resupply and a great deal of luck, South Vietnam could survive. However, without U.S. strategic air support, it is doubtful."

Colonel William Le Gro, senior staff officer at the U.S. Defense Attaché Office, agreed and predicted that without strategic bombing, South Vietnam would fall within ninety days.

My mood soared when Muoi handed me the dinner invitation the Toppings' maid delivered.

Why not throw a dinner party? It's better to fret among friends than stay home and worry alone.

I'd struggled to put on a cheerful face at school while swallowing my fear, but the Vietnamese staff at Steve's office had no problem showing how terrified they were, making conditions there barely tolerable. A pleasant evening with friends was just what Steve and I needed.

The Toppings, Al and Jan, lived in a beautiful, modern villa and owned an impressive collection of blue and white Oriental porcelain. Each stunning piece sat in a lighted niche, like a museum display.

Lynn and Bob Bell and another American known only as Mike also attended the dinner. We didn't know Mike or why he was in Vietnam, but he'd just come in from the Central Highlands bringing with him first-hand intelligence about the state of South Vietnam's army.

"The ARVN," Mike said, "hate Americans for leaving. They blame us for the situation they're in. I once saw a pissed-off ARVN soldier pull a gun on an American guy, screaming it's his fault they're losing the war. The dude was lucky he didn't get his head blown off.

"Then a couple of congressmen spend two days in Saigon and think they know all about the situation . . . that the ARVN don't have the will to fight and that President Thieu wants someone to bail him out."

"What's your take on it?" Al asked.

"The Vietnamese could be fierce fighters if they were motivated. The problem is their commanders failed them."

"What do you mean?" Steve asked. "Why don't they fight for their country?"

"Look," Mike continued. "For generations, traditional Vietnamese lived life focused on three essential priorities—family first, then the village, then their emperor who set the example of proper behavior—a very orderly system.

"The ARVN is an army of individuals with guns, but not with a broad sense of obligation to the group. The concept of loyalty to their entire country is unnatural to them.

"The officers and generals failed their men when they abandoned them at Ban Me Thuot to save themselves like they think America abandoned them. It's a vicious circle. That's why the soldiers see no reason to keep fighting. Their main objective is to save themselves, their families, and their village because that's their first loyalty."

"I never thought of it that way," said Bob. "But it makes sense."

"Read *Fire in the Lake*," Mike added. "Frances Fitzgerald wrote a remarkable book that explains it all."

Steve must have read my mind. "Wish I'd read it before we came to Vietnam," he said.

Gloom settled over everyone at Steve's office. All reasons to get on with work vanished. Some of the senior engineers became physically ill and stayed home. Project bosses at Jorgensen's home office advised Don Burgess to delay his return from home leave in the U.S. until the situation in Vietnam calmed down.

Jorgensen's Vietnamese staff at the VHA worried more about their families than their jobs. Their attitude frustrated Steve. Neither of us understood their mindset.

"It's nuts at the office," Steve said, walking into the apartment at lunchtime, earlier than usual. "Work's at a standstill. All the Vietnamese want is to stay home with their families. I might as well be home, too."

"They're really worried, aren't they? Any word from USAID?"

"Nothing," he said, "and Lew is acting crazy, ranting about how '*we have to stick to the schedule*.' I'm thinking about taking a few days off to get some relief from him. I don't give a damn about the schedule."

"Wow! Okay . . . look, things are good at school. I can take some time off. What would you think about getting out of the country for a week? How about Penang? Maybe things will settle down by the time we get back." An excuse to travel suited me just fine.

"Yeah, I like that idea. I'll ask Mr. Bei to rush through our exit/entry visas."

With paperwork processed in record time and itineraries on Lew's desk, we arrived at Tan Sơn Nhut Airport and found it operating as usual. On the tarmac, workers loaded rice onto a civilian DC-8, leased by the US government to airlift rice to Phnom Penh, Cambodia's capital city, under siege by the Khmer Rouge.

Penang Island popped up in the Malacca Strait, eleven miles off the coast of the Malaysian Peninsula. Our flight landed at the airport in Butterworth on the mainland. A hired driver took us across the eleven-mile bridge to our lodging, the Rasa Sayang Hotel on Batu Ferringhi Beach, thirty minutes away on the island.

The resort welcomed us as soon as the driver turned off the two-lane road into the entrance gates. Ahead, the hotel extended a *namaste* with its sweeping roofline shaped like prayer hands. The lush grounds and beachfront location promised serenity, something neither of us had felt in weeks.

"Look at this place," I said to Steve. "It's a tropical paradise. I'm so glad you got them to change our room. From this balcony, we can see the bay. It's gorgeous."

"Yeah, it was more expensive but worth it, I guess. What d'you want to do now? Explore the gardens, go to the pool? The beach?"

"Let's walk around, get the lay of the land."

Not one, but several pools curved through the gardens. One featured a swim-up hot tub area. Betel nut palms lined a white-sand beach, and a palapa roof made of palm fronds announced the location of the tiki bar nearby. Mist-gray mountains hugged the bay. Magical.

As often happens at a resort, people start to chat, and the next thing you know, you have new best friends. This happened to us at dinner the first night. A group of lively Germans who occupied a table next to ours at dinner struck up a conversation. They adopted us, and we'd meet them for after-dinner drinks in the lounge.

One couple in the group, Edie and Gerhardt Eckert seemed particularly intrigued that we lived in Vietnam and intended to return. *Why wouldn't we go back to our home?* That two armies battled each other was nothing new, and the conflict hadn't impacted Saigon. We believed that everything would have been handled and life would have returned to normal when we returned.

During the day, we toured the island. At the Tropical Spice Garden, nutmeg—the same spice that filled little glass jars on grocery store shelves in the US—grew on trees. Tapioca dried in the sun after being extracted from cassava roots. We watched local women making batik, first outlining a floral design with paraffin wax and then filling the design with color from paint pots using a fine brush. After the paint dried, they boiled the fabric to remove the wax. The entire process could take days.

We sampled fresh banana chips, suffered sunburns when we stayed too long at the beach, and rode a cable car through the lush jungle to a scenic overlook with a view of the Malacca Straits that separated the island from Indonesia.

In the evening, we dined under the stars and walked along lantern-lit garden paths while making pie-in-the-sky plans—graduate school in New Zealand, sailing the Mediterranean, starting a family. Options seemed endless. Saigon's stress slipped away.

On our last day, Steve stopped at the concierge desk in the hotel lobby to grab a newspaper. Before he could look at it, Gerhardt, our new German friend, rushed over.

"Have you seen the headlines?" He yelled. "Da Nang is captured. Vietnam is falling apart. Sure you want to go back? Maybe you should stay here."

Steve looked up from the newspaper in his shaking hands, his blue eyes cheerless.

"My God, Karen . . ." Steve said, his voice hoarse.

"What happened? Let me see!"

I crowded in, reading over his shoulder. On the front page, a photograph of the airport runway showed a mass of humanity swarming over a transport plane like ants on sugar cane. The reality caught us off guard.

"Da Nang and every city on the coast has fallen to the communists," Steve said. "And no one's stopping them. Where are the ARVN units?" The question was rhetorical. We knew the answer to that.

"Why did it take leaving the country to find the truth?" I asked. "Maybe the report is exaggerated. We're out now. What if we stayed here for a while . . . wait to see what develops?"

"Not possible; we only have tourist visas," Steve answered. "Besides, I have to get back to the office. There's still work to do. We have to get back there."

"You're right . . . too many loose ends. It was a crazy idea."

Little doubt remained about South Vietnam's fate after the terrible news of Da Nang's fall and the melee to get out of the city. The restorative effects of a serene tropical paradise vanished.

Conflicting emotions on the flight back to Vietnam erased any chance of catching a quick nap, which would have made the trip easier. *What on earth are we going back to?*

The city sounded different, more agitated, with fewer taxis and more army trucks. At the Ky Dong apartment, Muoi fussed over her chores and muttered to herself, trying to hide her fear.

When I arrived at the Phoenix Study Group, I didn't know what to expect, but I was unprepared for the TV news crew lying in wait at the front door. Annoyed at the intrusion and dreading the choices we had to make, I tried to ignore the reporter until he stuck his microphone in my face.

"What d'you think's going to happen? How do you feel about the fall of Da Nang? Will the school stay open? How many families are still here?" He peppered me with questions.

I hadn't had a chance to process what the fall of Da Nang meant in terms of the school or anything else. I dug my fingernails into my palm to keep from screaming, *"Get out of my way!"*

My mind flashed on thoughts of Pauline and the other church members, Muoi, Patty, and the people who worked for us or interacted with us daily in restaurants and shops, teaching French or tennis or driving us around town. *What will happen to them?*

I had no words to describe how I felt about America's betrayal of its citizens, keeping us in the dark to rely on rumors and suppositions. We wouldn't have known how serious the situation was if we hadn't left the country for a week.

"It's all just so sad," was all I could muster by way of a civil response.

Welcome back to Saigon!

Steve's Work Diary

> ***31 March 1975:*** *... Lew said he had cabled the home office with some questions and would try to call and get answers at the end of the week ... Situation doesn't look too good for Nha Trang right now. The people [Vietnamese staff] at the office are all shaky and say they are going to die. Most of the day was spent trying to find out more information about Da Nang and the Central Highlands.*

In Hanoi, the government changed the name of Campaign 275 to the Ho Chi Minh Campaign and ordered General Van Tien Dung to "liberate Saigon before the rainy season," which occurred in mid-May.

South Vietnam would keep half a country if it won the war. If it lost, it would lose everything. North Vietnam would either keep half a country or win it all. There could be no tie.

Chapter 25

Blind Faith Will Get You Killed, Part 1

April 1975

The American Consul General in Nha Trang ordered all American personnel to evacuate the city. In the mad scramble, one hundred of the consulate's Vietnamese employees and one of the five U.S. Marine security guards were left behind. Air America dispatched a helicopter to rescue them. Contrary to what they'd been promised, the consulate's Vietnamese employees and their families were abandoned.

South Vietnamese General Phu broke his promise to defend Nha Trang against all odds, ordered his troops not to retreat, and departed secretly by helicopter. He did not inform his men or officers of his departure, and order quickly broke down.

Nha Trang fell with little or no opposition leaving the communists firmly in control of South Vietnam's northern provinces. The drive toward Saigon, one hundred and ninety miles away, began.

Steve's Work Diary

> ***1 April 1975:*** *APRIL FOOL—beginning to wonder if it isn't on us. Went out to Air America to find out if there was any news from Nha Trang. The guys told me about the last flight out of Phan Rang. Not a pretty picture, also Nha Trang. The ARVN wouldn't let Americans into the airport to board the planes. Riot situation with no control.*

> ***2 April 1975:*** *I went to work with apprehension today. The people from Nha Trang came in last night and confirmed what I heard at Air America. Lew Chittim came over this morning and told Bob Taylor and me we'd probably be going to the Philippines. I decided today to get Karen to Bangkok on the 12th or 13th. I also checked on getting air freight shipped out. ARS stopped broadcasting the news from the States. We heard that seven hundred Marines were off the coast to conduct an orderly evacuation of the Vietnamese refugees.*

Two comfortable rattan chairs furnished a small den tucked into a private corner of the apartment away from kitchen noise. When I wanted quiet, I went to the den.

I sat there trying to make sense of the latest news when Steve came in from work. He dropped his briefcase on the desk and plopped down into the other chair.

One look at my husband's face told me something was up. "What happened?" I asked.

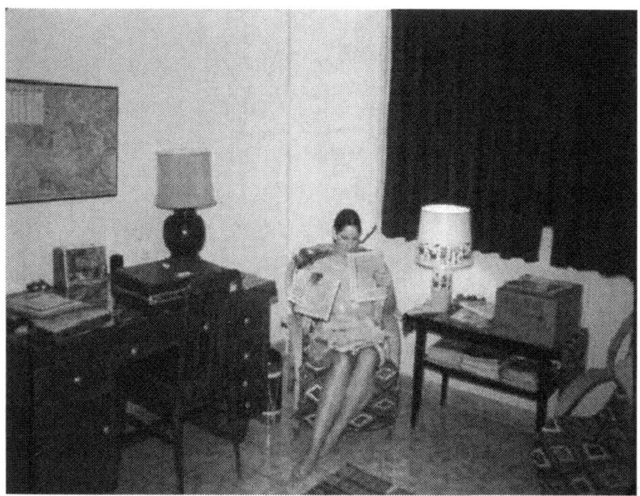

Karen, Ky Dong Street apartment, Saigon, 1975

"Chittim came over for a meeting this morning acting a little nuts. I think the pressure from USAID for us to continue working on schedule is getting to him."

"Uh-oh."

"He said he knows it looks bad, but Ambassador Martin refuses to order an evacuation of Americans because he believes there's no danger in Saigon, and a sudden exodus of Americans would alarm the Vietnamese, who would turn on us and riot in the streets. He also thinks the ARVN can still prevail with enough U.S. aid to back them."

"That doesn't make sense. The embassy must know how unstable the country is, yet no one thinks we should leave?"

"Nope, it's up to us to find our way out, and I'm getting you a ticket to Bangkok for the twelfth or thirteenth. Chittim said I'll probably go to the Philippines. You can wait in Bangkok until we know for sure. Things might settle down here. Then you can come back."

"Wait a minute . . . do I get a say? What about you?"

"Look," Steve said, his mind made up, "I've got to wrap up this project in whatever way I can, and I'll have to arrange to have our stuff shipped back to the States if it comes to that. Besides, the Vietnamese employees are pretty shaken up. Over at the VHA, they're refusing to work, they want to be home with their families, and we're expected to take up the slack."

Steve's Work Diary

> ***4 April 1975:*** *This will be Karen's last day at school. I went to work, and things seemed to be a little more relaxed, anyway, better than yesterday. Lew reneged on his deal to set a date for closing down the project. He did get the word from project services to get dependents out of here. . . . they [dependents] weren't to go to Bangkok. Karen has a ticket to Bangkok on Saturday, April 12. Bill Funk is trying to put her on a plane going to Singapore. I will also try to get her on an earlier flight. Worked on the training report, which I will arrange to get printed tomorrow."*

American families left in droves, including students and teachers from the Phoenix Study Group. With neither students nor faculty, the school board had no choice but to close the school.

I spent an emotional day shutting down my beloved library. The out-of-proportion tables and chairs, the shelves of books, and the card catalog that I never finished organizing might fuel a bonfire in the courtyard for all I knew.

Before turning out the lights and closing the library door for the last time, I packed new books that had arrived a few weeks before into boxes with some of the better titles from the original collection.

I moved the boxes to a workstation on the school's veranda and helped Dr. Bottorff and Bunny organize documents for students to take with them. As the children filed past to process out, I invited them to take a book or two. Perhaps part of the library would live on somewhere else.

While I handled the paperwork, I overheard two American parents talking about Operation Babylift, a US government project to fly hundreds of Vietnamese orphans to the United States. The organizers wanted volunteers to accompany the children. The flight would leave that afternoon.

Should I volunteer? I could leave immediately and relieve Steve of the stress of getting me a ticket somewhere. No, it's too soon. I'm not ready to go yet—not emotionally, not physically. I need to finish what I'm doing.

As Americans packed up and left Saigon, Steve considered ways to ship our remaining household goods home. His employer covered the cost of a move, but Steve had to figure out the details. Local shipping companies would pack and ship our household goods, but there was no guarantee we'd see them again. Everything could be lost. Losing the stunning lacquered chest, however, was unacceptable.

USAID designated one of its buildings as a secure depository for employees' household goods to be packed and shipped. USAID's shipments would be safe, and Steve's friend from the agency agreed to include the lacquered chest with his shipment.

Steve delivered the prized piece, locked the doors decorated with shimmering goldfish, and dropped the tiger-shaped brass key into his pocket. At least one precious reminder of our interval in Saigon could survive.

—

Friday evening. Someone hammered on the apartment door, frantic to get our attention. Muoi flung it open to see Bert Foote, our downstairs neighbor.

Steve and I rushed to see what was going on. "What is it? What happened?" Steve asked.

Bert's voice shook with emotion. "The C-5A orphan flight crashed on takeoff . . . not sure if it was shot down or something else. Mrs. Tho, from across the hall, and her two kids were on the plane . . . they didn't make it."

I gasped. *"No!"* The shocking news exploded in my brain. I pictured the hopeful family packing for their flight to freedom, rushing to board the American transport, feeling saved, and then plowing into a rice paddy on takeoff. How capricious life is. It turns on a dime. One wrong choice, and you're dead. My heart sank to my toes. *I could have been on that plane!*

"Jeez . . . when?" Steve wanted facts.

"About 1700. I'd just come into Air America from a mission. There were over 300 people on the plane—babies, escorts. They haven't identified all the dead yet."

"Any survivors?" Steve asked.

"Some. The medics are still working on triage."

"Can we do anything? Do they need help out there?" I asked, feeling I had to do something to earn the right to have survived.

"It's a madhouse right now," Bert said. "You're better off here. Jeannie and I are staying put, but I will check out our roof. I can land a helicopter there if I have to get us out in a hurry."

Steve's Work Diary

> ***5 April 1975:*** *The news said there was heavy fighting in the delta. I will admit I got pretty scared. The only way*

> *out of our area is to get to the USAID building on Yen Do. Karen and I discussed the possibilities before going to sleep.*

Our assembly point was the USAID building on Yen Do Street. It wasn't far from the apartment, but we would have to get there on foot. All cyclos had been banned because some drivers were suspected of being Viet Cong. Taxi drivers could turn on us. Not safe.

Are my three French-class chauffeurs among them?

We each packed one small bag with essentials in case we had to move fast. The photograph from the newspaper in Penang flashed through my mind. We could be that desperate at any moment.

"We have to be ready to grab our bags and get to Yen Do when the time comes," Steve said. "We can't tell anyone."

"How will we know when?" I asked.

"I think I'll hear something at the office."

"How will I know if you're there and I'm here? We don't have a phone."

"I'll come get you," he said.

"What if there's no time? You have to make it to the evac site. It's going to be dangerous." Panic . . . those bees began buzzing in my chest.

I can't think straight. Anything can happen. What will happen?

Steve pleaded with me not to worry, "I promise I'll come for you. I would die for you."

Speechless, I stared at him. *I would die for you.* In five words, he'd expressed a level of feeling I hadn't known he possessed. *Is this what fear does to you? Is this what fear feels like? We're in danger. The streets are full of people who hate us. Nothing matters more than the people you love. Please, God, don't let it come to that.*

Sleep eluded us after that, and by morning, we'd decided I could not wait until the twelfth. I had to go to Bangkok right away, but there were still procedures, even in the worst times. Mr. Bei had to take my passport to the immigration office, which was becoming increasingly overwhelmed, and try to get my exit/entry visa. The wait seemed endless.

Meanwhile, the ARVN's tenuous ability to hold back the enemy might falter. Orders to head for the evacuation site could come at any moment. If I wasn't afraid before, I was then.

While I waited for a flight out, Sunday morning slipped in with no bad news, so we went to church. The mood among the members was grim. They were surprised to see me still there, and I almost felt guilty about it.

"If you go, who will teach us?" Pauline asked me.

"I don't know, Pauline." *How can I tell her that finding a teacher might be the least of her worries?*

Most of the other Americans had left the country, as had the six missionaries. At first, the missionaries didn't want to go, believing instead, like the rest of us, that the situation would blow over. But a phone call from my friend June Eldridge, urging them to get their visas in order and "get out of here," changed their minds.

Muoi had the day off, and we went to the restaurant at USAID for lunch and dinner to see who else was still in town and to hear the news. U.S. Air Force pilots in flight suits arrived for a meal—a new development. For the past two years, there'd been no evidence of U.S. military personnel apart from the Marine guards at the embassy.

The restaurant's manager, Leon, said people had been by to check out the roof as a helicopter landing pad. *Helicopters on roofs, assembly points, buses to the airport? Drama or reality?* At dinner, the band played until 7:30 p.m., the new closing time.

Tuesday morning. The force of the explosion rattled the bedroom windows. I looked out to see what had happened—not the thing to do with gunfire in the area. Black smoke billowed into the sky a few blocks away and drifted over the city.

I grabbed my camera, fired off a shot, and rushed to finish dressing. Muoi banged through the kitchen door. She hadn't made it to the market. Her basket was empty.

"*Madame*," Muoi's voice, shrill and shaking, echoed the sound of fear. "Airplane drop bomb. *Peut-être* Americans come back?"

"No, Muoi, I don't think so," I said, regretting that no one was coming to help us.

Smoke rising over Saigon, April 8, 1975

The farm where I grew up sat on top of a hill in upstate New York, where winter came early, and heavy snow meant we often lost power for days. I learned then that the priority in an emergency was water.

Is Saigon under siege? It might be!

As Muoi and I prepared for a siege situation, potable water took precedence. Tap water wasn't safe and had to be filtered through charcoal to purify it after boiling.

I asked Muoi to get out all the liquor bottles and pour me a Coke. She did as I asked, then was astonished when I told her to pour all the liquor down the drain. We needed bottles for drinking water.

I didn't drink liquor, but, being in panic mode, I opened a bottle of rum and, before pouring out the contents, added a hefty amount to my glass of Coke. Out of the corner of my eye, I saw Muoi doing the same—desperate times.

Next, I took stock of our pantry. *How long can we exist on peanut butter and crackers?* There wasn't much more in there. Muoi shopped every day for that day. It would have to do.

The radio announced a new, 24-hour curfew. I couldn't go out, and Steve couldn't come home. I had no way of finding out if he was okay or getting an account of what was happening. The lack of a telephone never felt more nauseating.

Ralph Hill, one of Steve's coworkers, lived just down the lane from us and had a phone. I decided to risk leaving the apartment to go to his house, hoping to call Steve's office.

"No, *Madame . . .* you stay here," Muoi begged me not to go out.

"It's okay. I'll be right back." *I hope.* "Don't worry."

I'm not just going to sit here and do nothing.

I crept slowly down the stairs to the lobby. Nobody there. Moving carefully along the driveway to the entrance gate, I peeked out and scanned the lane — empty, of course, with the curfew — and then stepped through. Hugging the outside wall of our compound, I made my way to Hill's house, only a few hundred yards away, but it seemed like miles. I kept my head on a swivel, scanning the lane and the street beyond like a spy on a covert mission.

American bucking curfew. No one will see me. Am I going to get shot? Is this for real?

Ralph's wife, Pat, let me in. The phone worked, but the call didn't go through. With no choice left, I crept back to the relative safety of the apartment building and waited.

Chapter 26

Blind Faith Will Get You Killed, Part 2

April 1975

Steve's Work Diary

> ***8 April 1975:*** *Went to work early to get a head start on things. I decided to go to the PTT [post office] with Bob Taylor. As we drove up Tu Do Street, a jet flew low overhead. By the time we got to the PTT, it had made a second pass and dropped a bomb on the [Presidential] Palace. The ARVN fired into the air, and people ran. I'm sure most thought it was an attack.*
>
> *I directed the driver to take us back to the office. The Minister [of Public Works] heard a news broadcast [about the bombing] and locked down the compound. I called around and got conflicting reports. MPW finally agreed to let us out at our own risk.*

> *Mr. Pho took me home. The curfew was lifted at 3 p.m. I went back to the office to see if it was secure. Bill Ainsley was there and said Mrs. Truc [head secretary] wanted to resign. Problems, problems, and the day isn't half over. Guess I'll try to finish the progress report.*

The Jorgensen office compound, Saigon, Vietnam, 1975

While we waited for more news, Muoi and I fussed in the kitchen, making up work to keep our minds occupied. We needlessly organized the meager supplies in the pantry, bottled drinking water, and filled the mop buckets when we ran out of bottles. Finally, I went into the living room and sat by the radio. I tried to read but couldn't concentrate. After a while, I stood on the balcony, looking over the city for answers. Silence. The minute hand took its time circling the clock's face.

Muoi was about to serve lunch when Steve came through the door.

"Steve!" I ran to meet him. "ARS reported a curfew. How did you get here? What's going on out there? Is Saigon under attack?"

"*Chee-chaa*," Muoi muttered from the kitchen door.

Steve filled me in, and I told him about going to Hill's.

"So we're not under siege?"

"Not that I've heard, but I sure could use a drink."

I glanced at Muoi, who ducked back into the kitchen.

"Um . . . sorry," I said. "Seems we're all out of booze."

—

Steve's Work Diary

> ***9 April 1975:*** *Karen leaves for Bangkok today. I went to the office at 8 a.m. Traffic was terrible because the roads were blocked around the palace. We now have a problem with too many people in the office. It's a mess. Also, nobody feels like working.*

The morning arrived quiet and already hot. My luggage sat by the door, ready to go; just a few last-minute items remained for me to stuff in somewhere. I'd cleared my toiletries from the medicine cabinet and my clothes from the closet. It looked like I'd never been there.

That apartment had been my refuge, and every room held a memory. Of course, I had known one day we would leave, but leaving like this felt cruel. Looking around the home we'd made, I said a silent, painful goodbye.

Muoi, upset and anxious, shuffled around the apartment, trying to do her chores. She knew I was leaving, but I didn't tell her that I might not be coming back. She knew anyway. Neither of us spoke about it. It was not in her character to complain. I acted blasé but, inside, my heart sank.

I was abandoning Muoi, the loyal helper and companion who chattered merrily to us while we ate the meals she cooked, told us about her life, and always asked at the end of every meal, *"Madame, Monsieur fini?"* like a litany. Muoi's seven-year-old adopted daughter,

Ham Nuoi, used to sit at the kitchen door doing her schoolwork. I'd invited her inside. "You can use the dining room table," I said, but she was shy and never accepted.

What will become of them? They're part of the masses. They'll have a chance to survive if they stay under the radar.

"What d'you think about bringing Muoi and her daughter back to the States with us?" I'd asked Steve weeks before.

"I don't know . . . how old is she?"

"She says she's fifty."

"I think she's too old to adjust to American life. It wouldn't work."

We never asked her if she would come with us, and she never asked to go. I gave her extra money and left my sewing machine for her because she'd taken an interest. It was too little, but all I could think to do. Maybe she could sell it, if nothing else.

At 11 a.m., Steve and Mr. Pho picked me up for the trip to Tan Son Nhut Airport. Muoi, all the other maids in the building, the children, and the ancient watchman gathered on the front steps of the apartment building to see me off, all of us trying to put on a brave face.

Muoi had never been demonstrative, but she reached out to me as if she meant to shake hands. Instead, she bent forward and lightly kissed the back of my hand in a poignant act of understanding, respect, and affection.

We didn't hug. Sobs rendered me speechless, and grief painted itself across Muoi's face as we looked at each other. Before I dissolved into tears, Steve guided me into the waiting car.

I can't believe I might never see Muoi again. Maybe I'll be back.

Mr. Pho pulled out into the empty lane heading for Ky Dong Street. A shape flashed up ahead as a male figure materialized from behind a building. His black clothing signaled Viet Cong. He stood blocking our way and glared. The pistol he held in his right hand was aimed directly at us.

Before anyone could react, the man in black disappeared so quickly that I wondered if I'd imagined him. Mr. Pho stomped on the gas, and we flew out of the lane into the flow of traffic. Steve wrapped me in his arms to stop me from shaking. On the verge of panic, we finally understood the danger we were in. Saigon had turned on us.

My luggage held everything I owned and was overweight. Steve paid the extra fee, and we said our unsentimental goodbyes.

"Call me when you get settled," he said.

"I will. Stay safe, and please, don't linger too long in Saigon." With a hug and a kiss, he turned and was gone.

How long before he gets out of here?

What do I do now?

The so-called departure lounge looked more like a holding cell. Its wall of chicken wire kept us separate from the curious local children and others who hung around outside as if they were looking for a chance to stow away.

End-to-end benches lined the walls and filled the rest of the space. Anxious passengers waiting to board various flights sat packed together. I recognized several faces in the crowd. One inconsolable American couple told me their daughter had perished in the baby lift crash a few days ago. She'd been in town on holiday. Another said their daughter survived but lost an ear—grim news. No one wanted to be leaving under such awful circumstances.

Tan Son Nhut Airport, April 9, 1975

The Air Vietnam Boeing 727 sat on the tarmac. An agent called for boarding, and I joined the line of other passengers proceeding through a dim hallway leading out of the terminal. The curious Vietnamese onlookers stared at us as if to say, "Why are you leaving us?"

We should be ashamed of ourselves.

Every seat in the aircraft was occupied, and the flight was uneventful. I had only a two-week tourist visa and planned to bide my time in Bangkok until things settled down in Vietnam, and either I could go back, or things fell apart, and Steve joined me. I hoped one of the two would happen before my visa expired. We still didn't know for sure which way it would go.

A taxi took me to my hotel, the Chao Phraya, which became the gathering place for us refugees. The TV in the crowded bar broadcast the news all day long. People sipped Thai beer and discussed the details of their departure and the desperate situation in Vietnam.

In the hallway, I ran into a ten-year-old Burmese boy I knew from school. The awful purple bruise on his face looked recent.

"Hello, Kung Sang. What happened to you?" I asked.

His sweet little face looked back at me, dazed and confused.

"I was in the plane that crashed," he said. "My mother died."

My God! He survived the crash. Will he survive losing his mother? What can I do for him? I don't know.

"How did you get out?" I asked.

"I was in the lavatory." *The enclosure must have acted like a shield.*

"Where are you going now?"

"Home . . . to Burma," he stammered, giving me a wan smile.

Just then, a woman wearing a First Aid badge appeared. She took his hand, bowed her head to me, and led the boy down the hallway.

God bless you, Kung Sang.

The following day, I stopped by the International School library to say hello to my friend, Betty Van Dyne. She'd been following the news and wasn't surprised to see me.

"Don't stay in that depressing hotel where you'll have to listen to gossip about the situation back there," she said. "Come stay at my house. I have room, and my cook is excellent."

"That's a generous offer, but I might be here a couple of weeks or more. I don't want to inconvenience you."

"Nonsense. You're coming to stay with me." Betty was steadfast. "You can earn your keep by playing a game of Scrabble with me in the evenings."

Betty picked me up from the hotel. If I could have conjured the perfect Thai house, it would have been Betty's, tucked into a *cul-de-sac* off the main road at 32/1 Prom Sri, Soi 39, Sukhumvit Road, Bangkok.

The sweet suntan-lotion scent of frangipani blossoms drew me into the garden when I stepped out of the car. Bright yellow flowers cascaded from a tree near the entrance. Fuchsia lotus blossoms floated in a pool at the base of a small fountain.

Mango and lime trees bordered the property. Bright red hibiscus lined a path leading to a two-level teak structure perched atop stilts in the center of the lush garden. The building's roof swept to a ridge at the apex, and the tips of its eaves curled upward to resemble the wings of Garuda, an eagle-like Hindu demi-god of Southeast Asian culture.

It wasn't a large house, but the rooms were spacious enough. Teak floors gleamed—traditional teak furniture with jewel-colored Thai silk cushions invited lounging. At breakfast the first morning, I learned to cut papaya and eat it with hand-squeezed lime juice. I loved it there.

I'd stop by the Chao Phraya once in awhile to watch the television news. Reports out of Vietnam confirmed that Hanoi controlled the Central Highlands and major coastal cities. President Thieu ordered all remaining ARVN units to Saigon in a last-ditch effort to defend the capital and save the country.

"The ARVN aren't fighting back," someone said.

"President Ford asked Congress for more aid," said someone else, "but no one, including the Vietnamese military, believes that more US aid could save South Vietnam."

A fellow, who claimed to have confidential information from within the US Embassy, said,

"Ambassador Martin thinks there's going to be a negotiated settlement to end the war. He won't order an evacuation of Americans because he's afraid of anti-American riots."

Our recent incident with the gunman proved his point. The Vietnamese public hated America and Americans for deserting them. Being an American on the streets of Saigon was asking for trouble.

"How many Americans are still there?" Someone asked.

"They think about 6,000, but there's no roster. They're using things like the membership list at the *Cercle Sportif* to figure it out."

The hologram that was Saigon had dissolved at last.

Betty and a girlfriend planned a weekend trip to Pattaya and invited me to join them. I knew Pattaya from previous trips to Thailand and looked forward to returning, thinking the beach town would erase some of the anxiety roiling in my mind.

The hotel was perched on the edge of a cliff overlooking the Gulf of Siam. It seemed like I'd entered a parallel universe, the opposite of the disintegrating country I'd just left. After checking in, we lounged by the pool. For some crazy reason, my strongest memory of the place is ordering a bowl full of sliced bananas and eating them at the swim-up bar . . . safer than a bottle of vodka.

That night, the three of us attended a party at the home of one of their friends, an American expat couple. The dwelling took up minimal space among palms and wild orchids on a clean-swept patch of sand. Inside, clusters of guests gabbed cheerily in the yellow glow of lanterns.

Betty introduced me to a few guests and then left me to circulate on my own. A gentleman in a batik-print shirt, tropical linen slacks, and brown leather Thai sling-back sandals wandered my way.

"Can I get you a drink?" he asked.

"Thanks," I said when he handed me a tonic and lime.

"Where are you visiting from?"

"Vietnam."

"The war's going badly for the South, I guess. How could you stand living in that place?"

"It has its charms. My husband's still there."

"Ugly situation. We try not to think about it."

"The war isn't important to you because it hasn't affected you . . . yet."

Ironic. That's how I felt until last week. So why do I find this man so annoying?

Being at the beach didn't help after all. The beautiful hotel, the gorgeous views, and the gaiety of the party were lost on me. It all felt wrong. I couldn't even pretend to socialize and wandered away from the party into the garden. I'd always preferred being alone in the dark when I had something on my mind. That night, my only thoughts were for Steve.

My two-week Thai tourist visa expired in eight days. If that happened before Steve arrived, Thai immigration law required me to leave the country and apply for a non-immigrant visa, which permitted a stay of up to thirty days. Since I had no idea how long Steve would remain in Vietnam, I went ahead with plans to acquire the necessary documents.

I've got to stay in Thailand because I'm not leaving without Steve.

"You can take the train to Laos," Betty suggested. "It's relatively safe to travel up there. Cambodia and Burma are out of the question, of course."

"Relatively safe?" I asked.

"You'll be fine overnight. Stay in the hotel by the train station and don't go sightseeing. Have you thought about going back to the States?"

"Not my first choice. If Vietnam quiets down by some miracle, I'll go back."

I tamped down my fluttery nerves and booked a seat on the train to Vientiane for the next week, then stopped by the Laotian embassy to pick up an overnight visa and reserve a room at the Pearl Hotel near the station.

I'll be safe. Why wouldn't I be?

Chapter 27

Blind Faith Will Get You Killed, Part 3

April 1975

South Vietnam's remaining mobile forces moved into Xuan Loc, fifty miles east of Saigon, in an attempt to stop the People's Army of North Vietnam from advancing on the city.

Steve's Work Diary

> ***Thursday, 10 April 1975:*** *With Karen gone, things are quiet around the apartment, and I can concentrate on work. Went to PX in the afternoon. Saw a few GIs there. Marines are also at the Defense Attaché Office. Chittim gave us a rundown of a briefing by the Mission Warden. Chittim will call us "when the time comes [to evacuate]." Not a very good system to have to rely on the telephone. I got a call from Karen saying a couple we knew from church was killed on the baby lift last Friday. It seems like I really don't care anymore. I hope the Vietnamese start fighting soon. Everyone is waiting for Ford's address to Congress.*

Friday, 11 April 1975: Finally got the monthly progress report finished. Chittim's suggestion that USAID suspend the project didn't go over well. I could hear shelling tonight. A big battle is going on at Xuan Loc. If the Viet Cong break through, Saigon is doomed.

Saturday, 12 April 1975: Went to Cercle Sportif for lunch w/Bob Taylor. Then went back to the office for the afternoon. Called Karen in Bangkok. She had gone to Pattaya and will be back Monday. Just when everybody's relieved that all the wives are gone, Nga Burgess, Don's wife, comes back. I went to Don's, and Nga was there. She was surprised to see me. She said RJA's home office told her nobody was here except Chittim. She thought I was in Europe! Nga said she came back mainly to get her sister and cousins out of the country. I told her it was useless but to see what she could do, and I would make a reservation for her return to the U.S. Sporadic outgoing artillery.

Sunday, 13 April 1975: Went to Hill's for a party at 4:30. Jack, Charlie, Travis, Lawes, Reg, Bob, Bill, Ralph, and I were there. Wives have all left. We discussed the situation and how long we should stay. Bob, Ralph, and I decided privately that we would leave by the weekend.

Monday, 14 April 1975: Got a copy of new evacuation procedures along with a "coded message." What a bunch of crap. Chittim brushed it off as unimportant and asked who wanted to leave. I raised my hand. Everyone had pretty much decided after the party yesterday. Chittim tried to use that old chestnut, "The company will never *get another AID contract again if everybody goes home." I made a reservation for Bangkok on Friday.*

Should it be felt necessary for U.S. personnel to report to their designated assembly areas, a coded message will be broadcast over American Radio Service. This message will consist of a temperature report for Saigon of "105 degrees and rising" followed by approximately the first 30 seconds of "I'm dreaming of a white Christmas". This message will be broadcast every 15 minutes for approximately two hours.

If you hear the above message, report, with travel documentation, to your nearest assembly point. Stay tuned to American Radio Station FM 99.9 (primary) or FM 90.1 (secondary) for further announcements.

Evacuation Instructions: "Should it be felt necessary for U.S. personnel to report to their designated assembly areas, a coded message will be broadcast over American Radio Service. This message will consist of a temperature report for Saigon of '105 degrees and rising' followed by approximately the first 30 seconds of 'I'm Dreaming of a White Christmas.' This message will be broadcast every 15 minutes for approximately two hours. If you hear the above message, report, with travel documentation, to your nearest assembly point. Stay tuned to American Radio Service FM 99.9 (primary) or FM 90.1 (secondary) for further announcements."

Tuesday, 15 April 1975: *Not many people at work and not much work being done. Tried to get typing done on the organization manual and training needs appendices. Bob Taylor and I decided to delay our departure until Sunday. The VC started shelling Bien Hoa tonight. Set off explosions in ammo dumps.*

> ***Wednesday, 16 April 1975:*** *Stayed home this morning because the packers were supposed to come. They didn't, so I went to the office. Got packers to come out in the afternoon. Worked on manuals while I watched them work. Went back to the office and had to explain to the girls about leaving.*

The Foreign Ministry of North Vietnam announced it would not interfere with the U.S. evacuation provided it was done immediately.

> ***Thursday, 17 April 1975:*** *Chittim handed out emergency phone number stickers and new assembly point maps. The packers picked up my stuff. Told Chittim I plan to go to Bangkok on Sunday. I said I would return if the situation was stable and I was allowed to return.*

A CIA spy within the inner circles of the North Vietnamese government told the U.S. Embassy in Saigon that Hanoi would never negotiate and was committed to a military victory over South Vietnam before the end of April.

President Ford, over objections from Ambassador Martin, ordered all non-essential American employees of the United States in South Vietnam to evacuate.

> ***Friday, 18 April 1975:*** *Chittim came in at 10:30 and said "they" had decided that a number of us should leave this afternoon. I was among them. I went home, got my bags ready, and returned to the office. We were not to say anything to the Vietnamese staff. Got the word to be at*

> *the DAO (Defense Attaché Office) theater at 4 p.m. I was processed out through MAC (Military Airlift Command) personnel. Flew out of Tan Son Nhut at 6:45 p.m. I called Karen and went to the house where Karen's staying.*

Processing out at Tan Son Nhut, April 18, 1975

At Betty Van Dyne's house, Steve slept for twelve hours. I was overjoyed and relieved to have him out of Vietnam. I wouldn't have to take the train to Laos after all. If I'm honest, though, part of me felt disappointed to miss that adventure.

"Muoi sent this for you," Steve said, handing me a tissue-wrapped package.

"What in the world?" She'd never given me a gift before. The package weighed almost nothing, but when I pulled back the tissue, it was almost too heavy to hold. In my hands lay a gold chain gleaming in the sun, each link resembling a tiny gold bar. I could hardly see it through the tears, a treasure without price.

"This must be at least 22-karat if not more—at least 92% pure gold," I said. "How did she acquire such a thing?"

"It's beyond me. There's a lot we don't know and probably don't need to."

—

I desperately wanted news from Saigon and details about what happened after I'd gone, but it took some time for Steve to tell me. When he first arrived in Bangkok, his mood bordered on depression.

Over the next few days, Steve shared his story as he came to terms with leaving the project and Vietnam behind.

"Chittim bungled the project so badly nobody knew whether to stay or go. When I finally got word to leave, it was at the last minute. I had one day to take care of loose ends. First, Mr. Pho drove me to the docks to check on our crates. A longshoreman assured me they were there, but I wanted to see for myself.

"The guy pointed out three crates. I asked if there was any paint around, and he found some. I wrote my name on each crate and numbered them 1/3, 2/3, and 3/3. Then I cashed the housing allowance check, which left me with a briefcase full of Vietnamese *piasters*. I went back to the dock and paid the shipping fee.

"With the money I had left, I bought two giant bags of rice, one for Muoi and one for Pho. Went to the apartment to get my luggage. I asked Pho to help me take the rice upstairs for Muoi. I told her I was leaving and that she could stay in the apartment as long as she wanted, and . . ."

He couldn't go on. The sadness in his eyes brought tears to mine. I'd never seen Steve in that state. He was always so stoic and in control. Not then.

"And what?" I asked.

"She started to cry . . . it got to me, seeing her that way. I didn't know what to say or do. She knew we weren't coming back and that she was alone. I told her she could stay in the apartment as long as she wanted to, but why didn't I do more for her?"

"We talked about that. You did what you thought was best. What happened at the airport?"

"Bob Taylor and I got to Tan Son Nhut but couldn't find flights to Bangkok. A couple of cargo planes, C-141s, were going to the Philippines. That didn't help us. Finally, Bob tracked down a C-141 coming here. When we landed, the U.S. Overseas Mission rep told us Thailand didn't want us to hang around."

Steve and I left for Istanbul at 1:35 a.m. on April 24, 1975, and just like that, the war was over for us. By sundown six days later, soldiers of the Army of the People's Republic of [North] Vietnam smashed through the gates of Saigon's Presidential Palace in Russian tanks. South Vietnam surrendered. Decades of fighting came to an end, and a struggle for survival began.

Chapter 26

Between the Past and the Future

The future South Vietnam feared arrived at 10 a.m. on April 30, 1975; the past had ended just hours before. South Vietnam's new president, Duong Van Minh, appeared on television to announce the country's unconditional surrender to the Communist invaders.

Throughout April, terrified expats had left in droves. The citizens of South Vietnam realized that they had been abandoned and turned on foreigners still in the country, especially Americans, with a vengeance. Looters targeted vacant buildings in search of anything they could sell or repurpose.

Saigon's citizens, shocked into silence, huddled along the quiet boulevards, almost afraid to breathe, as they watched the Northern army enter the city in Russian tanks and Chinese trucks. The weary soldiers looked surprised at their victory. To the sophisticated Saigonese, the Northern conquerors appeared vulgar.

What would happen now? Would the victors be liberators or conquerors? Would there be a blood bath, or would the Communists embrace the people of the South as family?

An exuberant mob of locals waving flags of Vietnamese Communism—a yellow star in the center of a red field—ran joyously alongside the tanks. These people, called the 30th of Aprils, were the most feared traitors to the South. Once cleaners at the school, fishmongers in the market, or cyclo drivers, they took the opportunity of victory to brutally harass anyone as proof of their loyalty to the new government.

Uneducated, poor rural farmers who had been cajoled and coerced into joining the Viet Cong filled jobs at every level. With the power they now wielded, these new officials tracked down and arrested anyone who had associated with Americans, the South Vietnamese armed forces, or the former government and sent the unfortunate souls to prisons, which masqueraded as re-education camps. Days of hard labor and poor sustenance nearly killed them.

The swift victory caught Hanoi unprepared to administer the large population, creating hellish conditions for the South's people. Life became a daily exercise in survival. Shops closed, banks collapsed, life savings disappeared. New currency replaced the *dong*, which could be exchanged only in small amounts.

To feed their families, resourceful Vietnamese turned their possessions into cash. Clandestine businesses sprang up throughout the city. Homeowners with a bit of sidewalk rented space to entrepreneurs. They improvised and survived.

The new *modus operandi* encouraged neighbors to spy on each other. Capitalist behavior, real or imagined, became a criminal offense punishable by serving time in the reeducation camps. Some chose the camps as the only alternative to death. Others planned their escape.

—

Steve and I lunched at one of Istanbul's cafés overlooking the Bosphorus the last week of April. We'd arrived from Thailand the day before.

"I called my boss at Jorgensen to tell him where we are," Steve said. "He didn't have good news."

"What happened?"

"They don't have another project for me right now. I'm basically out of a job."

"Did they let you go?"

"Not exactly. There aren't enough project slots for the number of us coming out of Vietnam. They'll let me know when they have something."

"Look, we're in Europe now," I said. "Why not stay for a few weeks? Heaven knows we could use a break after what we've been through. Maybe they'll have a project for you by the time we get back."

"What are you thinking?"

"How about Germany, for starters?"

In Frankfurt a few days later, Steve rented a car, and for the next six weeks, we toured Germany, Austria, France, Italy, Switzerland, and England like a couple of footloose college kids. Eventually, though, the novelty wore off. We needed structure, income, and a good old American hamburger. In early June, we decided to return to the States.

Outside Washington, D.C., the airport taxi dropped us off at the Holiday Inn near Jorgensen's office. The motel offered nothing special, just industrial anonymity. Steve checked us in and then paid a visit to his boss.

"The job situation hasn't changed," Steve said afterward.

His clenched jaw, gloomy expression, and the deep furrows between his eyebrows told the tale. The man bordered on depression. He'd lost his identity.

"No home, no job, no money," Steve said. "Don't even have a car."

"We do have a car," I said. "It's stored in a garage in Pennsylvania. Let's go get the Jag."

He brightened.

"We can spend a few weeks with my parents while we figure things out."

I've always believed that action sends despair packing. In Pennsylvania, we had time to consider options surrounded by people who cared about us.

"I knew you'd be back soon," my father said over his morning coffee and cigarette, referring to his comment at Christmas.

"Too soon," I said. "We weren't finished."

"You're home safe. That's all that matters."

Is it? Could we/should we have done more?

Readjusting to American life wasn't easy. Friends and family expected us to pick up where we had left off as if we'd been on a two-year vacation, but Vietnam had changed us. A tornado had turned our lives into trash. We'd lost everything. No one could understand.

"Where did you go?" My mother asked as I stared into nothingness during our conversation. "You look so far away and sad."

"Sorry," I said, snapping back into the moment. "Sometimes I feel guilty about leaving Vietnam the way we did."

"Hmm . . . do you mean you, personally, or the U.S.?"

"Both, really? We got involved in a bad situation and abandoned people who depended on us. Doesn't seem fair."

"Nothing about the situation is fair. All you can do is what you think is right at the time."

"We should have brought Muoi and her daughter out with us."

"Would that have been possible?"

"I don't know, but we should have tried. Steve thought Muoi was too old to adjust to life here, but her daughter is only seven; she'd do fine."

"Maybe Steve didn't want the responsibility."

"We were cowards not to try." I wiped away tears.

The tiny animal footprints on the grimy Jaguar told us that the car had been a playground for field mice. Steve got it on the road again. I stayed out of his way. The friend who'd stored the car knew of a company looking for engineers, and Steve set up an interview.

By the end of the week, Steve received a job offer to work in the company's Washington, D.C. office. We were back in business and rented an apartment in Arlington, Virginia. I found a job in Georgetown. We added graduate school to our schedules. Eventually, we bought a house. As our commitments grew, we lost sight of our marriage and each other. We were coasting. Then one day a phone call changed everything.

"I talked to Jorgensen today," Steve said. "They want to know if I'm interested in a project in Africa."

"Africa? Where in Africa?"

"Addis Ababa, Ethiopia."

"What did you say?"

"I said, 'Hell yes.'"

It sounded like a godsend, a chance for us to reconnect. Unlike Vietnam, I pictured us going to Ethiopia together, figuring out how to live there as a team. I'd find a job, like always. Steve had another idea.

"I think I should go on ahead," Steve said. "Find a place to live, check out the political situation. You keep your job here and take care of the house. I'll let you know when to join me."

Devastated and hurt, I could make no argument that would change his mind. I felt duty-bound to go along with his plan. A week after he arrived in Addis Ababa, I received a letter with a long list of things to send him. The following week . . . another letter, another list.

Infuriated that Steve decided my life with no input from me, I rebelled. My dream of having a new lease on our marriage vanished, and I took a long look at my life. I'd always been dependent on someone else: my father, my husband, but never myself. *What can I accomplish on my own?* I made a decision and called Ethiopia.

"How are you, Steve?"

"Good. The project is taking off. How are you?"

"Fine, but I think our marriage is over," I said, ripping off the bandage.

"I'm coming back."

Within a week, we were in Key West, trying to reconnect. It worked for the short term, and Steve convinced me I should join him as soon as possible. He returned to Ethiopia, and Jorgensen sent me a plane ticket to Addis Ababa. Meanwhile, I prepared to close the house and join him. But something in me knew that joining him would be the wrong move. I was tired of waiting for his permission and doing his bidding. I made another phone call.

"Hello?" Steve said.

"Hi, it's me . . ."

He guessed something was off by the sound of my voice. "You're not coming, are you?"

"No . . . I'm so sorry."

I believe Steve mourned the loss of our marriage, but he moved on soon enough. Wanting to see how far I could go, I became a commercial pilot. In addition to my day job, I flew sightseers over the beautiful Virginia countryside on weekends in a single-engine Cessna. I would not leave Virginia until 2005 when my new husband and I retired.

Don Burgess, Steve's colleague and boat-building friend from Saigon, was also in Addis Ababa on a Jorgensen project when tragedy struck. His Vietnamese wife, Nga, succumbed to carbon monoxide poisoning caused by a faulty bathroom heater. Don and their daughter, Marian, stayed in Ethiopia until the end of the project. Being a good friend, he also introduced Steve to the woman who would eventually become Steve's second wife.

Steve and Don remained lifelong friends but never sailed their boat nor shipped her to the States. However, the boat's sail and fittings that Steve had purchased in Hong Kong arrived with our household goods, most of which had disappeared en route. The lacquer chest Steve had taken such care to entrust to a USAID shipment was never seen again. Its brass, tiger-shaped key, which Steve had kept with him, remained a painful symbol of all we'd lost.

Epilogue

Life Again After Chaos

September 2008

The hustle and bustle of Ho Chi Minh City amazes me. Motorbikes carrying young people roar down the wide boulevards *en masse*. Traffic stops for no one. Gaggles of children wearing red scarves around their necks in honor of Uncle Ho cavort on their way to and from school.

Downtown, the streets are swept clean. Sunlight glances off new skyscrapers that cast long shadows over the crumbling old city. Sophisticated shops and restaurants line a street once known as Tu Do—now Dong Khoi—where American G.I.s had barhopped. Workers labor to restore the old French opera house, the meeting place of the former regime's National Assembly. The city is almost unrecognizable. I'd expected something more austere.

Where is the Saigon I remember?

At my hotel, the Metropole, two women in prim *ao dai* manage the reception desk. Their name tags read "Mai" and "Linh." They are too young to remember Saigon before reunification, and the 1970s-era street map I spread out on the counter fascinates them.

"I'd like to go here and here and here," I say, pointing to various sites on the map.

"Can I see?" Mai asks. I push the map closer to her. "This map is very old," she says. "Many street names are different. Maybe you should hire a guide."

"Can you recommend one?" I know she'll get a kickback, but a guide would help. I agree, and Mai makes a quick phone call. "Mr. Loc will meet you in the lobby tomorrow at 10 a.m."

The young man who greets me the next morning resembles a happy Buddha. A crisp, white shirt stretches across his round body. Being a tour guide provides a good living.

"*Xin chao.* Good morning, Ms. Karen," Loc says, bowing slightly and extending a hand. "Today, I will take you on a walking tour of the downtown."

"Great, but first, I want to exchange some money. Is it better to use the hotel or a bank?"

"You don't have to use either one. You can get cash at an ATM on our walk. Good rates, too."

His voice is triumphant, and I become an instant Vietnamese millionaire when I received two-and-a-half million *dong* for my one hundred U.S. dollars.

ATMs on the streets of Saigon! Who would have guessed?

"You speak English well," I say. "Did you learn in school?"

"Yes, in school. Young people want to learn English, especially for work in the tourist business. Most visitors to Vietnam can speak English. We used to learn French, but only the old people speak French now."

We walk along Le Loi Street, accompanied by the roar of motorbikes zipping in and out of traffic, dancing with danger. The scent of spiced meat wafts to us from the doorway of a bookshop. *That's odd.* I peek inside to see a woman stirring a huge pot in the back—probably her lunch.

I catch glimpses of familiar buildings. The twin spires of the Basilica of Notre Dame, a few blocks over, still stretch skyward. The ornate French Colonial building that served as Saigon's city hall sports a cheerful new yellow exterior. An immaculately landscaped park occupies the entire block in front of the building. At the far end stands a massive statue of Ho Chi Minh, Uncle Ho, reading to a child.

"The gardens are beautiful, nothing like I remember. What is that building used for now?" I asked.

"That is the People's Committee Hall . . . very old, but now restored."

People's Committee Hall, Ho Chi Minh City (Saigon), Vietnam 2008

The climate hasn't changed. Saigon sizzles. I'd forgotten how very oppressive it can be and need a break. "Can we please find some air conditioning?"

"No problem," Mr. Loc assures me. "We can stop at Givral for a coffee. It's there on the corner opposite the Continental Hotel." He motions toward the café.

"I remember this place," I say between sips of dark, rich espresso. "So much happened here."

"Oh yes. In the seventies, politicians and journalists came to discuss the latest rumors and political gossip. Writers, too. It has a long history. Down the street is the Rex Hotel. Do you remember it?"

"Of course, who can forget the Rex? During the war, journalists gathered there daily for the U.S. military's press briefing. They called it the Five O'clock Follies."

"The Rex has a good roof-top restaurant. We will have dinner there."

From the restaurant, we have a stunning view of Le Loi Street, spruced up with new landscaping, a layer of polish on a rusty antique. I have trouble reconciling the scene before me with my memory of the crumbling street.

We listen to a four-piece band playing Western pop music. Young partiers dance the night away. The crowds below celebrate Tet Trung Thu, the Moon Day Festival. A light rain falls, but nobody cares.

Le Loi Street from the roof of the Rex Hotel, Ho Chi Minh City (Saigon), Vietnam, 2008

The next morning, I stand at the window of my room on the seventh floor of the Metropole Hotel and watch two strong-shouldered women wearing conical hats and mismatched outfits carry pole baskets filled with produce, a slice of old Saigon. I grab my camera, capture the image, and hurry to the lobby to meet Mr. Loc for the day's adventure, a visit to the streets where I used to live.

Vendors with pole baskets, Ho Chi Minh City (Saigon), Vietnam, 2008

"This is Nguyen Dinh Chieu Street," Loc says as the taxi turns onto a bustling street. "Can you find your villa?"

"The villa was the first house we rented . . . three stories, but I don't see it. There's too much traffic."

"The authorities changed the city plan a few years ago. Maybe they demolished the villa to make way for a new street."

"I remember the owner was a South Vietnamese Army officer."

"Then the government officials could have reclaimed the land for the good of the people, and the owner would not have been able to stop them."

I accept Loc's explanation but regret not seeing the villa. "Let's go on to Ky Dong Street. We lived in an apartment building in a lane off Ky Dong."

I recognize the lane immediately. "This is it! Stop the car!" I jump out and almost sprint down the lane, Mr. Loc close behind. The apartment building is still occupied. It's shabbier but has changed less than I expected.

Are the curtains still in the windows? How many people live there now? Should I knock on the door of my old apartment?

"You might not want to go in," Loc says as if reading my mind. "Many people are hanging around. They might not understand."

He's right. Besides, I'd rather not have my happy memories dashed.

Lane to the apartment building off Ky Dong Street, Saigon, Vietnam (L. 1975, R. 2008)

Apartment building off Ky Dong Street, Saigon, Vietnam (L. 1975, R. 2008)

The following day, my taxi honks its way through traffic to Tan Son Nhut International Airport. I work hard at letting go of the past and reluctantly say goodbye, doubting I will return.

The flight to Da Nang, in the Central region, offers new adventures in parts of the country that had been out of bounds thirty-three years before.

Mr. Vinh, my hired guide in Da Nang, meets me at the airport with a car and driver. A well-groomed man in his early forties, Vinh remembers the Communist takeover of his country only vaguely. He speaks English well.

We drive along the coast to the ancient trading port of Hoi An. Images of the war replay in my mind on an endless loop—thick jungles, wide open rice paddies, and impenetrable forest-covered mountains. Are villagers friend or foe?

Hoi An, famous for its silk industry, charms me. The entire town, the color of saffron, exists in a time warp. A wooden bridge built by the Japanese in the 1400s spans one of the canals. I'm thankful to be here before tourists take it over.

For the next several days, we work our way north: the Hai Van Pass, the Khe Sanh Battlefield, Hue's Imperial City, and the Quang Tri Citadel, where the sound of a beating heart memorializes the fierce fighting there.

We pass laborers repairing roads and restoring buildings using only manpower and crude tools. There is no sign of modern construction equipment. The ancient, ostentatious mausoleums of Vietnam's emperors cover acres in the countryside. Out here, it is peaceful.

The curvy road follows a muddy stream, not quite wide enough to be called a river. Tin-roofed huts dot the lush green hills on both sides.

"Vinh, who lives here?" I ask.

"Montagnards," he says, "hill tribe people whose ancestors have lived on this land for centuries. We can visit them."

The United States recruited Montagnards as front-line fighters during the war. Afterward, the Communist government targeted them as traitors.

The driver parks the car on the roadside, and we climb a dirt path to one of the huts. Curious children stare at us from the window. Vinh hands some *dong* to a woman who appears to be their mother; she lets me take a photograph.

Montagnard family, Vietnam, 2008

"Now we are going to the Vinh Moc Tunnels," Vinh says as the driver maneuvers the car back onto the road.

The tunnels, begun in 1966 and completed in 1972, cover more than 2,000 miles in Quang Tri Province. They intrigued me from the moment I learned of their existence. We walk along a packed dirt trail bordered by food stalls to one of the sixteen entrances while Vinh fills me in.

"The villagers built the tunnels for protection. This area marks the old border between North and South Vietnam, and there was lots of bombing. The whole village moved into the tunnels when they heard the signal gong. All villagers survived. Do you know seventeen children were born in the tunnels?"

"How deep are they?"

"More than fifty meters . . . and three levels. We will walk in the first level today."

We enter the tunnels down a short flight of stairs. I can stand almost upright. Single bulbs strung at intervals along the wall spread uneven light into the darkness and across the well-worn floor. Stifling air exacerbates my claustrophobia.

Vinh points out the various rooms carved into the limestone off the main corridor: living quarters for each of the sixty families in the area, kitchens, a hospital room, a toilet, a washing room, and even a performance room. The place fascinates me, but exiting the tunnels is a relief, even though the air outside is heavy and hot.

"What kind of car do you have in America?" Vinh asks me out of the blue as we drive to the former DMZ (Demilitarized Zone).

"A Jeep." I won't reveal that my husband and I also have a second car, a Mercedes-Benz. Vinh chuckles. *What has he heard about Americans?*

We arrive at the Ben Hai River. The driver parks the car at the south end of a bridge, and Vinh explains that the river was established as the demarcation line between North and South Vietnam in 1954 after the Communist Viet Minh defeated the French.

"You can walk across if you want to," Vinh says, hanging back.

"Don't you want to come?"

"I'll wait for you here."

A sense of foreboding surprises me as I step onto the bridge and approach what had once been enemy territory. Although the area surrounding the bridge is deserted, it pulses with the lingering force of war as if the spirits of the fallen hadn't yet settled down. Reverence and grief surround me. When Vinh says it's time to go, I'm more than ready to leave.

The next day, I say *tam biet* (goodbye) to Vinh at the airport in Hue and fly to Hanoi, where I meet Mr. Joe, my local guide. Hanoi fascinates me. Tiny shops and restaurants fill the dusty but charming streets of the Old Quarter. Tall willow trees overhang Hoan Kiem Lake in the center of town. A pagoda sits like a crown on a tiny island. Lovers walk hand in hand or sit quietly on stone benches, heads bent close together.

A water puppet show is the first night's entertainment. Long bamboo poles support the wooden puppets. The puppeteers, standing in a waist-deep pool behind a curtain, make the puppets look like they are floating over the water. A small orchestra provides background music, and a vocalist sings songs that tell the story being acted out by the puppets.

Water Puppet Show, Hanoi, Vietnam, 2008
(Photo credit Nancy Wolejsza, used with permission)

Only a portion remains of the infamous Hoa Lo Prison, better known to American prisoners of war as the Hanoi Hilton. The government demolished most of it to make way for a hotel.

At the entrance, I'm surprised to see an umbrella in an umbrella stand. Prison, umbrella stand . . . the two seem incompatible until I realize this is now a museum. Windows set high in bare concrete walls the color of thunderclouds line one long, narrow room.

The exhibit in this room features plaster figures of men seated side by side on a wooden platform, each shackled by one ankle. Its purpose is to portray the harsh treatment given to the Vietnamese prisoners by the French Colonial government.

But wait! Isn't there an exhibit of American prisoners of war captured by the Viet Cong? The world knows what happened to them here.

Then I turn a corner and see it. In a small room tucked out of the way in what remains of the original structure, supposedly happy American POWs smile from black-and-white photographs as they enjoy a sumptuous Thanksgiving meal. Future generations might believe it.

An excursion to Ha Long Bay for an overnight stay on a junk anchored amid the limestone pillars erases some of the repulsion of the prison visit. The following day, Mr. Joe waits for me at the landing.

I introduce him to a Vietnamese-American gentleman whom I met on board. To my surprise, Mr. Joe refuses to interact with the man, whose parents had fled Vietnam in the seventies. Contemporary Vietnamese consider those people cowards and deserters and want nothing to do with them.

Two days later, on a Korean Air flight bound for the United States, I try to reconcile past with present, but it's impossible. I have too much new information, and Saigon, as I knew it, is smoke in the wind.

In the space between sleep and dreams, I stand outside an open gate contemplating the apartment building that had once been my home—time and space contract. I watch as my younger self smiles and waves from the entrance, climbs three flights of stairs, and enters the door Muoi holds open for her. Muoi, my indispensable maid and loyal companion of two years places lunch on the dining room table — half a sandwich and a cola with ice. She goes into my bedroom and turns on the air conditioner. Soon, the sound of bare feet slapping against tile announces her presence. My lunch plate is empty.

"*Madame fini?*" Muoi asks.
"*Oui*, Muoi, *Madame fini*."

Acknowledgments

This book would not exist without the loving support of Robert Byrne, with whom I have shared my life for over three decades. He could usually find me behind my closed office door, gazing at the computer screen, waiting for words to come. The answer to his question "What are you going to do today?" was most often "Write." Sometimes impatient but always on my side, I know he celebrates the completion of this project.

Steve Griffith shared the Saigon experience with me in a special way and was an invaluable source of first-hand information from a different perspective. His reminiscences helped flesh out my memories of events. Without access to Steve's Saigon work diary this memoir would be lacking.

Don Burgess added a unique perspective, for his wife, Nga, was a Vietnamese national. Through him, I met Bang Pham, Nga's brother-in-law, who filled me in on the family and conditions in Saigon after the communist takeover.

A lucky twist of fate delivered me into the Manatee Writers' Group. Thanks to Michele Knudsen, Will Clapper, Sue Brite, Michael Schafer, Bart Huitema, Barb Busenbark, Jim Garrison, Ralf Thompson, Dennis Dunigan, and Mary Bulliner, whose kind critiques and comments helped me see what worked and where I was going wrong.

Discovering the Phoenix Study Group Facebook page catapulted me back to when I worked at one of my favorite library jobs. Thank you to Tony Mariano, who responded to my request for PSG students' stories with a couple of whoppers, and Kat Fitzpatrick, a third grader in 1974-75, who reconnected with me over Zoom and provided resources that I thought no longer existed.

The beta readers of the manuscript — Cele Cannizzaro, Nancy Wolejsza, Mary Weber, Anna Drailios, Max Teplitzky, Tim Fenley, Don Burgess, and Steve Griffith — deserve awards for taking the time to share their impressions, all of which are most appreciated. Thank you everyone.

Finally, thank you to Nan Fornal for her editing work, Maggie McLaughlin for the book design and publishing help, and Caroline Winter for doing the final proofreading. You pulled everything together. I could not have done this without you.

Sources

"1973 in the Vietnam War." *Wikipedia: The Free Encyclopedia,* en.wikipedia.org/wiki/1973 in the Vietnam War.

"1974 in the Vietnam War." *Wikipedia: The Free Encyclopedia,* en.wikipedia.org/wiki/1974 in the Vietnam War.

"1975 in the Vietnam War." *Wikipedia: The Free Encyclopedia,* en.wikipedia.org/wiki/1975 in the Vietnam War.

Adair, Dick. Dick Adair's Saigon: Sketches and words from the artist's journal. New York, NY: Weatherhill, 1971.

Appy, Christian G. Patriots: the Vietnam War remembered from all sides. New York, NY: Penguin Group, 2003.

Butler, David. The fall of Saigon: scenes from the sudden end of a long war. New York, NY: Simon & Schuster, 1985.

Doling, Tim. "Old Saigon Building of the Week – Former Cercle Sportif Saigonnais." Historic Vietnam, 20 July 2014, www.historicvietnam.com/cercle-sportif-saigonnais.

Fitzgerald, Frances. Fire in the lake: the Vietnamese and the Americans in Vietnam. New York, NY: Back Bay Books, Little, Brown and Company, 1972.

Hughes, Ken. "The Paris Peace Accords were a deadly deception." Washington, DC: The George Washington University, Columbia College of Arts & Sciences, History News Network, January 31, 2013.

Hughes, Ken. Fatal politics: the Nixon tapes, the Vietnam War, and the casualties of reelection. Charlottesville, VA: University of Virginia Press, 2015

Larsen, Jerame, et al. The silver thread, video. Salt Lake City, UT: Church of Jesus Christ of Latter-Day Saints, 2007.

Markham, James M. "Vietnam Reds set fuel depot afire." New York, NY: New York Times, December 3, 1973, p. 6.

Nguyen, Ciecie Tuyet. Shock peace: the search for freedom. Mustang, Oklahoma: Tate Publishing, 2016.

Smith, Harvey H., et al., Area Handbook for South Vietnam. Washington, DC: US Government Printing Office, 1967.

Snepp, Frank. Decent interval: an insider's account of Saigon's indecent end told by the CIA's chief strategy analyst in Vietnam. New York, NY: Random House, Vintage Books, 1977.

White, Ralph. Getting out of Saigon: how a 27-year-old American banker saved 113 Vietnamese civilians. New York, NY: Simon & Schuster, 2023.

The Dragon's Mouth, Newsletter for parents of students at the Phoenix Study Group, October – November 1974.

Letters, Karen Kaiser Griffith to Mr. and Mrs. Russell Kaiser, July 1973 – April 1975.

Work Diary of Steven K. Griffith, Roy Jorgensen and Associates, Saigon May 1973 – April 1975.

Photographs, unless otherwise noted, were taken by the author.

About the Author

KAREN KAISER grew up on a small farm south of Syracuse, New York, where she discovered the world through National Geographic magazine. Living in Vietnam at the end of the war, she became a witness to history.

Karen's writing has appeared in the Journal of the Photographic Society of America and Transitions Abroad Travel Magazine. This is her first book. In addition to writing, Karen fills her time with yoga, photography, and books.

Made in the USA
Middletown, DE
27 November 2024